Sports Competitions for Adults Over 40

Sports Competitions for Adults Over 40

A Participant's Guide to 27 Sports

THOMAS A. JONES

McFarland & Company, Inc., Publishers

Jefferson, North Carolina, and London

LIBRARY OF CONGRESS CATALOGUING-IN-PUBLICATION DATA

Jones, Thomas A., 1941–
Sports competitions for adults over 40 :
a participant's guide to 27 sports / Thomas A. Jones.

p.   cm.
Includes bibliographical references and index.

ISBN 978-0-7864-3465-7
softcover : 50# alkaline paper ∞

1. Sports—United States—Directories.
I. Title.
GV583.J54   2009   796.084'4—dc22   2009006115

British Library cataloguing data are available

Cover image ©2009 Shutterstock

Manufactured in the United States of America

McFarland & Company, Inc., Publishers
Box 611, Jefferson, North Carolina 28640
www.mcfarlandpub.com

To my father,
whose sense of fair play in competition
and enthusiasm for sports of all kinds
sparked my desire to write this book.

Acknowledgments

This book has been years in the making and I have been helped by countless individuals along the way. My first debt is owed to the many athletes against whom I have competed. They not only brought out the best in me, but were unfailingly enthusiastic, supportive, and encouraging as I talked to them about Masters Sports. Second, the various organizations that sponsor sports for Masters Athletes have been helpful in providing data and guidance. Third, I should acknowledge Rick Beizer, Gary Temple, and David Carroll, who offered their comments on draft sections of the book. Fourth, my thanks to Sandy Beccia, who helped me format, edit and pull the chapters together with her usual smooth efficiency. Finally, the book would never have come into being without the love and support of my wife, Suzette. Her patience and encouragement have been, as my granddaughter says, AWE-SOME. Of course, none of these people are in any way responsible for the errors or oversights in the book. Those are all my doing.

Table of Contents

Acknowledgments   vii

Preface   1

Introduction   5

Alpine Skiing	9	Rowing	82
Badminton	13	Soccer	87
Baseball	17	Softball	90
Basketball	22	Speedskating	101
Canoeing	26	Squash	104
Cross-Country Skiing	32	Swimming	109
Cycling	36	Table Tennis	116
Diving	43	Tennis	120
Fencing	46	Track and Field	126
Handball	50	Triathlon	132
Ice Hockey	55	Volleyball	138
Orienteering	60	Weightlifting and	
Platform Tennis	65	Powerlifting	144
Racquetball	69	Multi-Sport Events	151
Road Racing	76		

Appendix A: National Champions   159

Appendix B: Websites of Sponsoring Organizations   210

Appendix C: Selected Comparisons   212

Appendix D: Outstanding Masters Performances   213

Appendix E: Studies on Exercise and Longevity   214

Index   217

Preface

This book is a designed to provide men and women over 40 years of age with information on competitive sports. As the U.S. population ages, more and more adults will be seeking healthy, challenging, fulfilling outlets for their time and energy. Many adults are already participating in a wide range of competitive sports. These adults are often referred to as Masters Athletes. Their numbers are likely to grow.

I have been competing in sports since my elementary school days, but my interest in Masters Sports really took hold in 1994 when I participated in the World Masters Games in Brisbane, Australia, where more than 24,000 men and women from 74 countries gathered to compete in 30 sports, from archery to weightlifting. Their enthusiasm, dedication, good will, and energy were infectious. I certainly caught the bug. Since then, I have competed against Masters Athletes in three other World Masters Games, several national championships, and countless other races, meets, and matches.

In this book, I have profiled 27 sports, providing information on the organizations that support and promote each sport, the types of competition available to adults over 40, a summary of the current state of competition in the sport, and suggestions on how to get started. My sources have included the Web sites and publications of the various sponsoring organizations, conversations with many Masters Athletes, and my own experiences as a competitor.

There are a number of fine books written to help Masters Athletes compete in specific sports and many of these titles are cited in this book. However, up to now there has not been a comprehensive guide to the full range of opportunities for competitive sports for adults. I hope this book will fill this gap and encourage more adults to try sports competition.

Organization of the Guide

The guide is organized around the profiles of 27 sports, one chapter for each sport. To present a uniform picture of the sports profiled and to provide baseline data which is both complete and consistent, I have used data from 2007 and 2008, which was the most complete at the time of writing. The specific event information in the text and appendices is provided to give readers an idea of the range of sports opportunities available to them, including the variety, frequency and length of events within individual sports; age groups, ability levels and numbers of participants found in various competitions; and to provide a representative picture of what to expect from future Masters Sports events.

Each chapter is divided into the following sections:

Introduction

This section offers some remarks about the sport and its relevance to Masters Athletes.

National Sponsoring Organization

This section identifies the organization, or organizations, that support and promote competition for Masters Athletes. Contact information for each organization (mailing address, phone and fax number, e-mail address, and Web site) is included. In cases where there is more than one organization, I have given the contact information for each one, as well as the specific area the organization has staked out. In addition, when the National Sponsoring Organization operates through state or regional affiliates, these are identified and contact information for these is given. The cost of joining the organization and some of the key membership benefits are also described.

In addition to the growth of adult sports, there is a technological revolution going on and many organizations are becoming increasingly sophisticated in their use of the Internet and e-mail. Appendix B lists the Web sites of all the organizations cited in the guide.

Competitive Opportunities

This section of each chapter describes the kinds of competitive opportunities available to Masters Athletes. The criteria used to define competitive classes are described as well as the way in which competitions themselves are organized. This section also includes the location and dates of national championships for most sports. Several sports, such as tennis and softball, have more than 80 national championship events and in some of these cases, the reader is referred to the appropriate Web address. While the novice competitors will probably not be ready for national competition, I believe the list of national championships is useful because it is always instructive to attend one of these events to see the skill and enthusiasm at the highest levels of the sport.

Competitive Landscape

This section attempts to give some insights into the size and depth of the competitive field. Wherever possible, I have presented the number of competitors, by gender and age group, who participated in the most recent national championship. In some cases, I have also listed the number of players who are nationally ranked by age group and gender. Of course, novices are more likely to begin by participating in local or regional competitions where the field is likely to be smaller and less competitive.

Appendix A lists the current national champions in the 27 sports profiled in the guide. Appendix C compares the sports in terms of gender and age group participation. In the guide, the term "competitors" refers to those individuals competing in a single event. In sports such as swimming, track and field, and rowing, an individual can compete in more than one event. In these cases, a single man or woman becomes multiple "competitors."

How to Get Started

This section briefly describes the skills needed for the sport, the equipment necessary to participate, the availability of coaching, and access to the venues. This is just a beginning and the readers are urged to pursue their interests through the sponsoring organizations.

Recognition

This section explains how competitors are recognized in individual meets, tournaments, or races. It also indicates if the sponsoring organization ranks competitors and selects national age-group teams.

Resources

This section of each chapter offers some suggestions for books or videos that might help the novice appreciate and understand the sport as well as become familiar with how to get started.

The world of sports competition for adults is changing rapidly, driven by an aging population, new discoveries in health and sports medicine, and a technological revolution that is changing the way we work together and communicate. Consequently, this guide must be a work in progress. The organizations, contact information, and various summary tables are certain to change. I hope the list of sports profiled here can be expanded. Those readers who discover errors, disagree with my conclusions, or feel that sins of omission have been committed are invited to contact me and make their case.

Meanwhile, the organizations that support and promote adult sports are working hard to keep up—which makes it a great time to begin to compete.

Introduction

Sports competition for adults is a vital and growing phenomenon. Driven by a blossoming interest in healthy living by the generation of baby boomers, competitive sports for men and women over 40 has seen impressive growth over the past two decades. More than 12,000 athletes over the age of 50 participated in the 2007 National Senior Games, a five-fold increase since 1987. The first World Masters Games in Toronto, Canada, in 1985 drew 8,305 competitors. By 2002, more than 24,000 senior athletes were competing in the Games in Melbourne, Australia. Demographics suggest this trend will continue.

The purpose of this guide is to exhibit and describe the opportunities for competitive sports in the United States. The guide's intended audience is:

- Adults who get little or no exercise and wish to find the motivation for becoming more active;
- Adults who now exercise for fitness and are interested in going to the next level and competing; and
- Adults who are now competitors in a sport, but are interested in opportunities for cross-training in other sports.

The opportunities for sports competition for adults are broad and deep. That is, there is a wide variety of sports which invite adult competition, from well-known and popular sports such as swimming and tennis to lesser-known ones such as orienteering and fencing. Furthermore, the depth of competitive opportunities means that these sports welcome all comers, from unrefined beginners to experienced competitors.

Who Are Masters Athletes?

For the purposes of this guide, Masters Athletes are men and women over 40 who compete in sports. This age criterion is hardly universal. U.S. Masters Swimming sets the lower age limit for Masters at 18. For U.S. Rowing, the youngest Masters are 23. The National Senior Games sets the lower age limit at 50. Because my purpose is to profile competitive sports for older Americans, I believe 40 is a reasonable compromise and the one I have chosen to use here.

Which Sports?

In selecting the 27 sports which are profiled here, I have used two criteria. First, the sport must be physically demanding. At competitive levels, they elevate the heart rate. No golf, bridge, or shuffleboard. Second, only sports that offer significant opportunities to adults over 40 have been included. You will not find skateboarding, gymnastics, or boxing profiled here. There are some sports which are certainly demanding and in which older adults compete but which do not appear to offer truly broad opportunities to Masters Athletes. These include judo, water polo, and rugby. It may be that these, or other sports, deserve a place in this guide and I hope that proponents of other sports will contact me and make their case. I would be delighted to enlarge the list of sports.

Why Compete?

Most adults recognize that exercise is an important component of healthy living. A significant body of research shows that adults who exercise live longer, healthier lives than those who do not. For those who doubt this or are unfamiliar with this research, Appendix E lists half a dozen of these studies. Of course exercise can take the form of a brisk walk three or more times a week and this is certainly better than no exercise at all. However, as several of the studies in Appendix E indicate, increased benefits result from more vigorous exercise. What benefits does competition offer? Here are the ones most commonly cited by adults who compete:

Camaraderie: Competition builds camaraderie. Athletes have a shared sense of purpose, with their teammates and their competitors. A coach and Masters Athlete for the Boston Running Club notes that even track and field generates an infectious team atmosphere at the club level, despite the fact that most of the events involve individuals. The joy of achieving a personal best is magnified when it is shared with others who understand the hard work that has gone into it.

Even the most popular sport has a relatively small universe of competitors. If you compete regularly, you will meet and compete against many of the same people at each game, meet, or race. For years, I have competed against a group of Masters in kayak racing in New England. At each race, we expect to meet each other and look forward to testing ourselves against each other and the river.

In general, Masters Athletes are mature, not only in chronological age, but in outlook. The kind of trash-talking, whining, and excuses so common in professional sports are virtually unheard of in Masters Sports. The degree of mutual encouragement and support, for teammates and competitors, grows out of two traits of Masters Sports. First, the stakes are on a human scale: no multi-million dollar purses or bowl bids, no shoe contracts or product endorsements, no TV packages or incentive money. It may be that television's hunger for content (the 500 channel maw that must be filled) will move Masters Competition toward the center of commercial sports, but such a move does not appear imminent. The second trait of Masters Sports is the long competitive horizon and its natural by-product, patience. Masters Athletes are in for the long haul. It just doesn't make sense to alienate someone you compete against throughout the year(s).

Goal Setting: Competition provides a consistent and objective measure of performance. Exercise without competition can be measured by the clock or milepost, but it lacks the added challenge of a human opponent. There is something fundamentally human about seeking a sense of progress, a sense of moving forward. Schools have grade levels and degrees; corporations have hierarchies and reward systems. Sports can also provide a sense of progression. In every competition, the athlete establishes a marker against the field of competitors and, in many sports, against the clock. A fifth-place finish, a narrow victory, or a seven-minute mile are examples of markers. Subsequent competitions offer an opportunity to improve on the marker. Of course, steady progress is not inevitable. Hard work and intelligent training play an important part. But the opportunity for progress is always there.

Recognition: Closely related to goal-setting is recognition. If you achieve or surpass a goal, it is nice to be recognized. Even the most humble person appreciates well-deserved acclaim. Competition offers public recognition of your accomplishments. Most Masters Athletes are ambivalent about ribbons, medals, or trophies awarded at competitive events. On the one hand, a trophy is a tangible memento of the event and the hard work that went into competing. On the other hand, a trophy's importance diminishes with time, eventually cluttering up attics or garages. However, I have never been to a competition where a winner has declined an award honestly won.

Physical Benefits: Any exercise is better than none. Moderate exercise, such as a brisk walk for 20 minutes three times per week, expending about 500 calories per week, provides great cardiovascular benefits compared with doing nothing.

Two recent studies support the case for more vigorous exercise. A longitudinal study of more than 17,000 Harvard graduates over 33 years shows that maximum longevity was achieved by those men who expended at least 1,500 calories per week. Those exercising at this rate had a 25 percent lower risk of dying at any age.

The results of the Harvard study were confirmed by a study of 27,500 British civil servants in which vigorous, dynamic aerobic exercise was shown to protect against heart disease and mortality. Those subjects exercising vigorously had a 50 percent reduction in heart disease. See Appendix E for further information. Competition generally requires more vigorous exercise, and serious training for most sports demands this level of calorie burn.

Travel: No one competes in order to travel, but it is one of the incidental benefits of sports competition that is often cited by Masters Athletes. While competitions close to home are the rule for most people, there are many opportunities for athletes to test themselves against others across the United States and beyond. The lists of national championships for the sports profiled in this guide testify to this. Regional and national competitions are well-organized, generally offer travel and accommodations at special rates and are held in cities that have bid for the event. The atmosphere around these events is always festive. Local merchants are particularly welcoming, cognizant that many Masters Athletes are at the height of their earning power.

Competition for Women

Although no statistical evidence is available, there seems to be an unusual enthusiasm and even gratitude among women who compete. Unlike many men, very few women have had an unbroken athletic career from school through college and afterward. In fact, many women over 40 have never had the opportunity to participate in team sports or any sports in school or college. In 1972, Title IX of the Higher Education Act required that institutions receiving federal funds, which included most colleges and universities, provide equal opportunities in athletics for men and women. Before 1972, women's sports in coeducational colleges and high schools were an afterthought to men's sports. Sports for high school girls typically consisted of perfunctory exercise in gym class—an awkward, even humiliating experience—and competing for a few coveted spots on the cheerleading squad. Some schools held field days in which boys and girls competed in footraces, softball throws, and various jumping events. In my elementary school, I recall a girl named Marie Moe who easily outran, outthrew, and outjumped every boy in the school. After the field day, the boys resumed competitive sports on a variety of teams and the girls returned to jumping jacks in gym class.

While the growth in women's participation in high school and college sports has grown exponentially, it is nowhere near equality with men. Between 1971 and 2005, women's participation in high school sports increased 904 percent to almost 3 million. Participation by women in college sports increased 456 percent over the same period.

The Boston Marathon first officially allowed women to compete in 1972 and Nina Kusc-siks won over the other eight other women competitors, representing less than 1 percent of all competitors. In 2007, the 7,974 women who finished the race accounted for 39 percent of all finishers.

For women over 40, many of whom had graduated from college before Title IX took hold, competitive events were a revelation. Several women runners for the Boston Running Club cited the electricity in the air at their first Penn Relays—the crowd, the bright uniforms, and the air of anticipation were riveting. "I was determined to go again," said one.

Alpine Skiing

Introduction

Riding up the lift with icy bits of snow buzzing around your face like angry bees makes you wonder why you keep coming back. Your skis hang heavily from the swinging chair, pulling at your stiff knees. Over the hills to your right, the sun, a bright wafer emerging from gray cloud cover, is just now making an appearance. You'll need a nice long warm-up, but there's plenty of time. Plenty of time. And now you're in the start, staring down the mountain at the gates which disappear below in the cloud of swirling snow. You know the course. Nothing wrong with your memory. You have a good feeling about this run. No ice, just a growing blanket of powder. You lean over the wand and prepare to drop into the course ... 3 ... 2 ... 1.

Skiing dates back at least 5,000 years to a short, fat ski discovered in Sweden. Cave drawings in eastern Russia from 4,000 B.C. show a stick figure balanced precariously on an enormous pair of slabs. But skiing remained simply a mode of transportation until the early 18th century. It was then that the people from the Telemark region in southern Norway are credited with developing skiing into a sport. They solved the tricky problem of how to control speed on downhill descents by inventing the Telemark and Christiana (Christie) turns. By the 19th century, the first organized skiing events were held in Scandinavia and soon spread to other parts of Europe. In 1924, the first Winter Olympic Games were held in Chamonix, France. But they included only ski jumping and cross-country skiing. The 1948 Winter Olympic Games were the first to include downhill and slalom ski racing. The 2006 Winter Games, in Torino, Italy, included five alpine disciplines-downhill, slalom, giant slalom, super–G, and combined. The evolution in equipment and techniques for alpine skiing continues, allowing ever steeper terrain to be skied and older skiers to continue to race.

Over the past several years, the number of alpine ski racers over 40 has held steady, and in 2006 more than 200 competitors over 40 (35 competitors over 70), both men and women, competed in the national championships. Alpine ski racing for Masters Athletes is alive and well.

National Sponsoring Organization

The sponsoring organization for alpine skiing is the United States Ski and Snowboard Association (USSA). The USSA has a Masters Alpine Ski Racing Program.

USSA
Box 100
1500 Kearns Blvd.
Park City, Utah 84060
(435) 649-9090
http://www.ussa.org/magnoliaPublic/ussa/en/events/masters.html
http://ussamasters.org/

Participation in masters alpine competition requires membership in the USSA. Annual membership dues for the USSA are $100 and membership forms are available on the USSA Web site. Benefits include sports accident insurance coverage, participation in USSA-sanctioned events, and a subscription to *Alpine Masters,* a quarterly newsletter.

The USSA operates through ten regional associations, each of which has its own Web site, schedule of local and regional races, and other programs. Table 1–1 lists the USSA masters regions and Web site addresses.

Table 1–1
USSA Masters Regions

Association	Web site
Far West Masters	www.farwestmasters.org/
Intermountain Masters	www.intermountainmasters.org/
Midwest Masters	www.midwestmasters.org/
New England Masters	www.nemasters.org/
New York Masters	www.nymasters.com/
Northern Masters	www.northernmasters.org/
Ottawa Masters	www.ottawamasters.org/
PNSA Masters	www.pnsamasters.org/
Rocky Mountain Masters	www.rmmskiracing.org/
Southern Masters	www.skisara.org/

Each of the regional associations offers short-term (one day) memberships for racers who wish to enter a single race. These memberships are typically in the range of $20 to $30.

The USSA's Masters Alpine Racing Program has recently been expanded to include skiers as young as 18 years old. However, in keeping with purpose of this guide, the focus is on competitors over 40 years of age.

Competitive Opportunities

Masters alpine skiing bases competitive classifications on the following criteria:

- Gender: men and women
- Age: 5- or 10-year increments, depending on entries
- Events: In most cases, competitions include three events. All these events require the skier to negotiate a series of gates (i.e., poles stuck in the snow) down a course of varying lengths. In addition, the difficulties of the courses in these events are modified to account for differences in age and gender.
- Downhill: The skier races on a rhythmic and challenging downhill course with a vertical drop of between 400 meters and 700 meters. The fastest time over one run determines the winner.
- Slalom: The skier must negotiate a course around a series of gates (poles) on a course 130 to 180 meters for women and 180 to 220 meters for men. The winner is the competitor with the best aggregate time for two runs on two different courses.
- Giant Slalom: The skier must negotiate a course around a series of gates on a course 250 to 350 meters for women and 250 to 400 for men. The winner is the competitor with the best aggregate time after two runs.
- Super-G: The skier must negotiate a course around a series of gates on a course 350 to 500 meters long for women and 500 to 650 meters for men. The winner is the competitor with the best time after one run.

Competitors start at 60 second intervals.

Naturally, most of these competitions take place in the northern half of the United States, or in areas with mountains with reliable snowfall.

The ten regional ski associations and the 350 local ski clubs sponsored more than 3,000 local and regional competitions in 2007. Not all of these races are Masters competitions. However, if you live in an area where alpine skiing is available, there are probably many opportunities for you to compete. For information, you can contact the regional association in your area through the Web sites listed above.

Competitive Landscape

The 2007 USSA Masters National Championship was held in Big Sky, Montana, from March 10 to 16. The total number of competitors for the four competitions (downhill, slalom, giant slalom, and super–G) was 608. To show the interest in each of the types of races, Table 1–2 shows the number of competitors for each type of race.

Table 1–2
2007 Alpine Masters Nationals—Competitors by Race Type

Race	Competitors Men	Competitors Women	Total
Downhill	83	19	102
Slalom	119	43	162
Giant Slalom	130	42	172
Super-G	125	47	172
Total	457	151	608

Many individuals competed in multiple races. Women represented 25 percent of the competitors and 43 percent of the competitors were over 60 years old.

To show the size and breadth of age group competitors, Table 1–3 shows the number of competitors in each class for each type of race in the 2007 Alpine Masters Nationals.

Table 1–3
2007 Alpine Masters Nationals
Competitors by Age Group[1]

Age	Downhill	Slalom	Giant Slalom	Super-G
40–44	10	19	21	18
45–49	16	24	31	30
50–54	18	27	29	26
55–59	15	21	22	19
60–64	12	18	20	21
65–69	17	23	25	27
70–74	6	13	13	13
75–79	7	10	11	11
80–84	1	6	5	5

1 As noted above, individuals may enter more than one event and may compete down a class (i.e., a 60-year-old may choose to compete in the 55 to 59 age group, as well as the 60 to 64 age group. A list of the 2007 national champions is presented in Appendix A.

How to Get Started

Skills

Skiing requires strength and flexibility. Competitions are designed for experienced skiers and if you have not skied before, you should take some lessons and get some practice under your belt. The USSA notes that many of the competitions are held on world-class courses— not the place for a novice to pick up some skills. However, every ski area offers schools for beginners and an individual wishing to compete can develop the requisite skills in a season of skiing. If you're an experienced skier who wishes to test yourself on the slopes, these competitions offer an excellent opportunity.

Equipment

An alpine skier will need skis, boots, bindings, poles, goggles and appropriate cold weather clothing. Skis, poles, boots, and bindings can be rented at any ski area. The cost will depend on the area, but shouldn't be more than $100 per day. Purchasing equipment requires a much more significant investment and it makes sense to rent equipment until you are familiar with what fits your style and skills. The USSA requires helmets for all competitors.

Coaching

The ski schools at all ski areas are the places to acquire the skills and knowledge to compete in ski racing.

Venues

The masters competitions are sponsored by many of the major ski areas in the United States and, weather permitting, the conditions of the competition courses are excellent. The USSA masters regional Web sites list ski areas in the region, as well as current conditions.

Recognition

Awards

For individual races, awards are presented to men and women achieving the first three places in each age group for each event.

National Teams

At this time, there is no national Masters alpine ski team. Competitors in world competitions compete as individuals and not as members of a national team.

Rankings

Although the USSA calculates national and regional rankings based on the results of sanctioned competitions, it does not include rankings for the age group categories.

Resources

The USSA Web site includes several areas with information on sports science and sports medicine, including educational materials and seminars on physiology, nutrition, fitness and technology. While most of this information is aimed at elite competitors, there is lots of useful information for the masters skier.

Bookstores are loaded with instructional books, but you really can't learn to ski from a book. The best way is to get some lessons from a professional ski instructor and practice. A current and useful guide to alpine skiing is *Anyone Can Be an Expert Skier: The New Way to Ski for Beginner and Intermediate Skiers*, by Harald Harb (Hatherleigh Press, 2003).

Badminton

Introduction

The service sails across the net, the shuttlecock lazily floating toward the deep corner. Your return is sharp, straight down the line. It comes back hard, grazing the net. You step in, smacking the bird at your opponent's body. A quick jab returns it to your backhand. Drop shot. Lunge. Lift. Smash. Lob. Smash. Point.

The sport of badminton has almost nothing to do with the gentle pushing of a shuttlecock over the net in your backyard. It is an explosive sport that USA Badminton calls the world's fastest racquet sport because the shuttle can leave the racquet at almost 200 miles per hour. Like tennis doubles, matches often involve intense battles for dominance at the net. The game can be played by two (singles) or four (doubles). The singles court is approximately 17 feet by 44 feet. The net in the center of the court is about five feet high with no sag in the middle.

Badminton probably originated in India, Japan, and Siam as a cooperative game called battledore in which players hitting a shuttlecock back and forth with a simple bat as many times as possible. In the 19th century, British civil servants in India added a net and called the game Poona. When it was first brought back to England, it was played at Badminton House, the Duke of Beaufort's home in Gloucestershire, and became known among the guests as the Badminton game. It is the only sport I know that is named for a building. Over the next century, badminton developed into a competitive sport and was included in the Olympic Games in 1992.

The Senior National Badminton Championships, which features age group competition, regularly draws over 100 competitors over 40. There were five men's singles competitors over 80 at the 2007 Senior Nationals.

National Sponsoring Organization

Badminton's governing organization, overseeing all competition in the United States, is USA Badminton:

USA Badminton (USAB)
1 Olympic Plaza
Colorado Springs, Colorado 80909
(719) 866-4808
Executive Director: Dan Cloppas
usab@usabadminton.org
http://www.usabadminton.org/

Annual membership for an individual over 22 years of age is $30.00, and a variety of junior and family memberships are also available. Memberships can be obtained directly from USA Badminton, or through the regional associations (see below). Membership benefits include a quarterly newsletter, *CrossCourt*.

USA Badminton recognizes and works with the five regional associations described in Table 2–1.

Table 2–1
USA Badminton Regional Associations

Region / Association	Regions	Web site
Region 1: Northeast Badminton Association (NBA)	DC, VA, MD, DE, PA, NY, NJ, CT, MA, VT, NH, RI, ME	www.northeastbadminton.net/
Region 2: Midwest Badminton Association (MBA)	IN, IL, IO, KY, KS, MI, MO, MN, NE, OH, ND, SD, WV, WI	www.midwestbadminton.com/
Region 3: Southern Badminton Association (SBA)	TX, OH, AK, LA, MS, TN, AL, GA, FL, SC, NC	www.sbabadminton.org/
Region 4: Northwest Badminton Association (NWBA)	AL, CO, ID, OR, MT, WA, WY	www.northwestbadminton.org/
Region 5: Southwest Badminton Association (SWBA)	CA, HI, AZ, NV, UT, NM	www.swbabadminton.org/

The USA Badminton web site has a handy feature for locating venues in every state where badminton is played, including contact information and fees. Links or information to metropolitan or sub-regional associations and clubs can also be found on the web sites of the regional associations. The web sites also publish tournament schedules and tournament results. If you are looking for badminton lessons, upcoming tournaments, or tournament results, these regional association web sites are a good place to start.

Competitive Opportunities

Most badminton tournaments offer competition in singles and doubles for men and women, as well as mixed doubles. Age group competition is typically based on five-year increments starting at the age of 35. Badminton has terms for each competitive age group, including Master I (50+), Master II (55+), Grand Master I (60+), Golden Master I (70+), and Platinum (80+). The sport does not have as much visibility in the U.S. as many other racquet sports, but it develops excellent cardiovascular fitness and offers many opportunities for masters athletes. Yearly regional and local age group tournaments are listed on the association web sites.

Competitive Landscape

USA Badminton holds a Seniors National Championship for players between 35 and 80+. The 2007 Senior Badminton Championships were held in Manhattan Beach, California, from March 6 through March 11, 2007. A total of 347 entries competed. Table 2–2 shows the number of entrants in singles, doubles, and mixed doubles for each age group.

Table 2–2
2007 National Senior Badminton Championships
Entries by Age Group[1]

Age Group	Men's Singles	Men's Doubles	Women's Singles	Women's Doubles	Mixed Doubles	Total
40+ Senior I	8	6	3	6	10	33
45+ Senior II	16	32	0	0	8	56
50+ Master I	10	10	0	8	10	38
55+ Master II	10	4	3	8	10	35
60+ Grand Master I	3	16	0	6	10	35
65+ Grand Master II	8	10	3	6	32	59
70+ Golden Master I	3	8	0	4	16	31
75+ Golden Master II	4	8	3	6	10	31
80+ Platinum	5	6	4	4	10	29
Total	**67**	**100**	**16**	**48**	**116**	**347**

1 *Individual competitors may enter more than one event and may compete down a class (a 60-year old may compete in the 55+ age group)*

Women's entries (singles, doubles, mixed doubles) represented approximately 35 percent of all entries and fully 33 percent of all entries were in mixed doubles. The 2007 National Champions are listed in Appendix A.

USAB also publishes age group rankings, called senior national rankings, and Table 2–3 shows the number of ranked players in each age group. A total of 348 players are ranked.

Table 2–3
Number of Ranked Players—2007 National Senior
Badminton Rankings

Age Group	Men's Singles	Women's Singles	Men's Doubles	Women's Doubles	Mixed Doubles
40+	7	3	8	6	12
45+	9	0	14	2	10
50+	6	1	16	12	14
55+	6	3	10	10	12
60+	5	0	16	6	10
65+	9	3	14	6	16
70+	3	0	10	4	14
75+	5	3	8	8	14
80+	5	4	6	6	12

Table 2–3 indicates the popularity of mixed doubles in badminton competition.

How to Get Started

Skills

Badminton is a fast game played in a relatively confined area that puts a premium on quickness and excellent hand-to-eye coordination. The transition to badminton from other racquet sports is not difficult, but becoming familiar with the nuances of the flight of the shuttlecock takes some time.

Equipment

The equipment requirements for badminton are relatively modest. Shoes and clothing can be the same as for most other indoor racquet sports. A badminton racquet may cost from $50 to $300 and shuttlecocks run about $5 each.

Coaching

USAB has a relatively elaborate coaching scheme with coaching directors for each of the five regions, a coaching course, and high-performance coaches for elite athletes. There is no coaching directed specifically at age group competitors, but coaching is available at many of the venues.

Venues

As noted above, the USA Badminton site has a search feature called Where to Play for locating public and private venues where badminton is played. For example, the site lists sixteen locations in New York State, five locations in Ohio, four in Nebraska, and fifty-six places in California. It is not difficult to set up a badminton court in a gymnasium and many schools include badminton in their physical education program.

Recognition

USA Badminton recognizes masters competitors in several ways.

Awards

In tournaments, awards are typically given to the top two or three competitors in men's singles, women's singles, men's doubles, women's doubles, and mixed doubles for each age group. For national competitions, five-year increments are used to determine age groups. The 2006 National Senior Badminton Champions are listed in Appendix A.

National Teams

Although USAB selects national teams for international competition, such as the Olympic Games and the Pan American Games, there are no national teams for age group competitors.

Rankings

USA Badminton calculates rankings based on the results of ranking tournaments. Ranking for men's singles, women's singles, men's doubles, women's doubles, and mixed doubles for age groups from 35 to 80+ are published each year. The rankings determine the seedings for the national championship. In 2007, a total of 348 players were ranked in the age groups over 40, as shown in Table 2–3.

Resources

Skills, Drills, and Strategies for Badminton by Paup and Fernhall; Holcomb Hathaway Publishers, 2000.

A number of instructional videos, as well as videos of major national and international tournaments, are available on the USAB web site. The costs range from $10 to $25.

Baseball

Introduction

The musical crack of the fungo echoes across the infield and the ball skips lazily across the grass and into a waiting glove. The aroma of oiled leather, the tang of unwashed socks, and the smell of new mown grass fill the air. Everyone's shoulder aches a little with the first few tosses. The umpire arrives and straps on her pads. The other team, having taken their warm-ups, joke with each other or watch without expression. A ball slips past an infielder's outstretched glove and bounces harmlessly into center field. The shortstop backhands a screamer. The crowd, as usual, is sparse and quiet. A few girlfriends and some kids running under the bleachers.

After a few minutes, it all feels easy again. The momentary sting of the ball in the pocket is hardly noticeable. Throws lengthen easily, arcing in from the outfield or lining smartly from third to first. The rhythm of pitching takes hold. A looping curveball finds the heart of the plate and the catcher pounds his fat mitt in approval. You can feel the first rivulet of sweat find its way down your back.

The mental part of the game warms up as well. You need to scrape away thoughts of your job and contemplate the algorithms of the game—the runners, the count, the score, the inning, infield flies and double plays. It's all coming together again.

For those who once played baseball and dream about trotting out on to a field again, there are three programs that offer competitive leagues and several national championships for adult players. According to these programs, interest in adult baseball is growing rapidly and new leagues are springing up all over the country. There are age group divisions for 65 and older, so there's no reason not to compete.

National Sponsoring Organizations

The largest national baseball organization was founded by Steve Sigler in 1996 with four teams on Long Island, New York. It has grown into the Men's Senior Baseball League/Men's Adult Baseball League (MSBL/MABL), a national organization with the slogan, "Don't go soft. Play hardball." In 2004, it had 325 local affiliates, 3,200 teams, and 45,000 members. MSBL/MABL sponsors 30 regional tournaments and 6 national tournaments.

Men's Senior Baseball League
One Huntington Quadrangle
Suite 3N07
Melville, New York 11747
(631) 753-6725
info@msblnational.com
http://www.msblnational.com/main.aspx?action=doc&doc_id=2

Local leagues can be found using a search tool on the MSBL/MABL web site. If no local leagues exist in your area, contact MSBL/MABL and they will help start a league. Fees are assessed by the local leagues and participation in national tournaments requires a team registration fee. Players who are members of MSBL/MABL receive a copy of *Hardball*, which is published five times per year.

The National Adult Baseball Association (NABA) claims to be the "fastest growing adult baseball organization in America" and reports that it has 50,000 member-players in 99 leagues in 39 states across the U.S. The NABA web site includes links to 76 leagues across the country.

National Adult Baseball Association
3609 S. Wadsworth Blvd.
Suite 135
Lakewood, CO 80235
(800) 621-6479—phone
(303) 639-6605—fax
http://www.dugout.org/
Shane Fugita—president and CEO
NABAPresident@aol.com

The NABA web site also offers a Find a League list on its web site to help those interested locate a league in their area. The NABA allows players to sign up on its web site and be placed in the nationwide player pool. If no local league is available in your area, the NABL will assist you in starting a league. *Baseball Today* is the NABL official online publication and is sent to all member-players.

Somewhat smaller is Roy Hobbs Baseball, founded in 1988 by Ron Monks and named for the protagonist in Bernard Malamud's novel *The Natural*. It is currently run by Tom and Ellen Giffen.

Roy Hobbs Baseball
2048 Akron Peninsula Road
Akron, Ohio 44131
(888) 484-7422
royhobbs@royhobbs.com
http://www.royhobbs.com/

Fees to join Roy Hobbs Baseball are $8 to $20 per player, depending on the number of players and teams. Roy Hobbs Baseball acts as a consulting service to help individuals, teams, and leagues organize themselves. It also provides certain insurance benefits. It hosts an annual World Series in Fort Myers, Florida, each year.

Competitive Opportunities

All three adult baseball organizations organize competitive divisions by age groups. The MSBL/MABL and NABA also divide divisions by skill level. For its national tournaments, the MSBL/MABL has six age group divisions (18+, 28+, 38+, 48+, 58+, 65+, as well as a father-son division). Their five skill levels are based on the number of players with professional players on the team.

- MSBL/MABL National Division—No more than five ex-professionals.
- MSBL/MABL American Division—No more than three ex-professionals.
- MSBL/MABL Continental Division—No more than one ex-professional.
- MSBL/MABL Federal Division—No more than one ex-professional; none for 45+ and 55+ age groups.
- MSBL/MABL Central Division—No ex-professionals.

The NABA offers five age group divisions (18+, 28+, 38+, 48+, and 57+) and three skill levels for adults:

- AAA (Advanced) for players with college or professional experience,

- AA (Intermediate) for "players with college or high school experience, and
- A (Recreational) for players "whose love of the game perhaps exceeds their level of experience."

Roy Hobbs Baseball offers six competitive divisions based on age:

- Open—28+
- Women's Division
- Veterans—38+
- Masters—48+
- Legends—55+
- Classics—60+
- Seniors—65+
- Father/Son.

Although the majority of games that adult baseball teams play will be within their own league, each of the three national sponsoring organizations offers a variety of national tournaments. Table 3–1 lists the major tournaments scheduled for 2008, the sponsoring organization, dates and locations. The 2009 schedule is posted on the sponsoring organization's website.

Table 3–1
Major National and Regional Adult Baseball Tournaments—2008

Tournament	Sponsoring Organization	Dates	Location
Disney Holiday Classic	MSBL/MABL	Jan. 18–21	Orlando, FL
Desert Classic	MSBL/MABL	Jan. 19–21	Palm Springs, CA
Las Vegas Classic	MSBL/MABL	March 8–17	Las Vegas, NV
Las Vegas Open	MSBL/MABL	May 24–26	Las Vegas, NV
World Series	MSBL/MABL	Oct. 12–Nov. 1	Phoenix, AZ
Fall Classic	MSBL/MABL	Oct. 30–Nov. 8	St. Petersburg, FL
California Kickoff	NABA	Jan. 19–21	Los Angeles, CA
Las Vegas Kickoff	NABA	Feb. 16–18	Las Vegas, NV
Boricua Caribbean Classic	NABA	Feb. 22–24	San Juan, PR
Alamo-Riverwalk Classic	NABA	March 15–17	San Antonio, TX
Las Vegas Memorial Day	NABA	May 23–26	Las Vegas, NV
Atlantic City Memorial Day	NABA	May 23–26	Atlantic City, NJ
Hall of Fame Tournament	NABA	July 3–6	Cooperstown, NY
NYC Firecracker Tournament	NABA	July 4–6	New York, NY
Mile High Tournament	NABA	July 4–6	Denver, CO
Blue & Gray Classic	NABA	Aug. 30–Sept. 1	Washington, D.C., and Northern VA
Saturn Labor Day Tournament	NABA	Aug. 30–Sept. 1	San Diego, CA
World Championship Series	NABA	Sept. 25–Oct. 11	Phoenix, AZ
Over 50/60 National Championship	NABA	Oct. 20–25	Las Vegas, NV
Florida World Championship	NABA	Nov. 6–9	Jupiter, FL
World Series	Roy Hobbs	Oct. 25–Nov. 22	Fort Meyers, FL

This list of tournaments is an indication of the broad interest in adult baseball.

Competitive Landscape

One of the ways of measuring the competitive landscape is to look at the number of teams that compete in a given baseball tournament. Table 3–2 lists the number of teams that participated in various divisions of the 2007 MSBL/MABL World Series, which was held in Phoenix, Arizona, from October 16 through 31. Only the teams playing in the 45+ age group and older are shown.

Table 3–2
Number of Teams Competing in the 2007 MSBL/MABL World Series

Age Group	Division	Number of Teams
45+	National	7
45+	Mountain	10
45+	Central	20
45+ (Wood Bat)	National	5
45+ (Wood Bat)	American	8
45+ (Wood Bat)	Central	19
50+ (Wood Bat)	National	7
50+ (Wood Bat)	American	8
55+	National	4
55+	American	6
55+	Central	10
60+ (Wood Bat)	National	7
60+ (Wood Bat)	American	12
65+	—	10

The NABA ranks member teams based on their results in local, regional, and national tournaments, the skill level, and age group. In 2007, 182 teams were ranked by the NABA, meaning that these teams played in at least one of eight tournaments sponsored by the NABA. In the 38+ age group, 32 teams were ranked, in the 48+ age group 14 teams were ranked, and in the 57+ age group seven teams were ranked. Table 3–3 lists the number of teams competing in two NABA World Series: the 2007 World Series, held in Phoenix, AZ, and the 2007 Over 50/60 World Series, held in Las Vegas.

Table 3–3
Number of Teams Competing in the 2007 NABA World Series

Age Group	Division	Number of Teams
38+	Wood Bat	5
38+	A	6
38+	Rookie	12
48+	Wood Bat	5
48+	A	5
57+	Wood Bat	7
50+	AAAA	3
50+	AAA	5
50+	AA	3
50+	A	3
60+	AA	3
60+	A	3

The Roy Hobbs Baseball World Series included all competitive divisions and Table 3–4 lists the number of teams in each division over 38 years old.

Table 3–4
Number of Teams Competing in the 2007 Roy Hobbs Baseball World Series

Age Group	Division	Number of Teams
38+	AAAA	12
38+	AAA	13
38+	AA	12
38+	A	13
48+	AAAA	11
48+	AAA	11
48+	AA	11
48+	A	12
48+	B	11
55+	AAAA	9
55+	AAA	9
55+	AA	9
60+	AAAA	9
60+	AAA	9
65+	—	7

Although women's divisions were included in both the NABA and the Roy Hobbs World Series, there were no age groupings for women. The national champions in all adult divisions (over 38 years) of the three organizations are included in Appendix A.

With hundreds of teams in these three organizations there are ample opportunities to play baseball after 40 years of age. Both the MSBL/MABL and the NABL have nice search features on their web sites to find leagues in your state. If you wish to start your own team or league, you can contact any of these organizations and they will help you.

How to Get Started

Skills

Most of the baseball programs are aimed at athletes who have played baseball before and do not appear focused on teaching people how to play the sport. If you played in your youth and want to play again, these programs look ideal. If you never played baseball before, you should check carefully to see if your local league can accommodate you.

Equipment

Players are expected to provide their own shoes and gloves. League and team fees cover balls, uniforms, bats, umpires, and arrange for venues. The cost of baseball mitts can range from $100 to $400 and a reasonable pair of baseball cleats can cost less than $75.

Coaching

In baseball, coaching may involve teaching basic skills (batting and fielding) and strategy. For Masters Athletes, coaching will help an adult player refine and adjust his or her skills to the realities of aging. For a novice, find a coach with the patience to help acquire the basics.

Venues

Leagues typically arrange for venues, i.e., playing fields for teams, and are compensated through team fees. The MSBL/MABL, NABL, and Roy Hobbs Baseball arrange for fields for their regional and national competitions and are compensated through team fees for the tournaments.

Recognition

Awards

In addition to trophies for winners and runners-up in each of their tournament brackets, MSBL sponsors a hall of fame and has inducted 17 members—players, sponsors, and organizers—since 1997.

Roy Hobbs Baseball provides trophies for winners and runners-up in each of the tournament brackets.

National Teams

The national champions, as determined by the World Series for each of the three organizations, are listed in Appendix A. None of the sponsoring organizations selects an age group all-star team or national team.

Rankings

The NABA ranks teams by age group and, in 2007, 53 teams were ranked in the three divisions over 38 years of age, about 30 percent of the total number of ranked teams.

Resources

Baseball Coaching: Skills and Drills, Bragg Stockton; Coaching Choice Books, 2002.

Play Baseball the Ripken Way: The Complete Illustrated Guide to the Fundamentals, Ripken, Ripken, and Burke; Ballantine Books, 2005.

Each of the three sponsoring organizations publishes a periodical with news, statistics, and other information on its program.

Basketball

Introduction

The magic of good adult basketball is its purposefulness. Everyone seems to know where they're going. Players constantly move without the ball. Individual skills rarely include the gymnastics of 360 degree dunks but often include the well set pick that blocks the defender, the precision pass to a rolling teammate, the measured fast break forcing the opponent to commit first, the extra pass that makes the difference between a 20-footer and a bunny-hop layup. It is the missed opportunity that, having disappeared, is forgotten in the instant as the next opportunity begins to form. At its best, it is seamless, flowing, merging, integrated, blending. Play moves without recrimination, blame, or frustration. It doesn't have time to belittle the other team, mock, or chide. There's only time to keep moving, to keep looking for the opening, finding the chance, creating the opportunity.

Finding a good game may be more difficult than in many other sports because teams, leagues, and tournaments are local or regional. There is no national sponsoring organization, so a competitor must seek opportunities where they can be found. This is easier than it sounds, because opportunities for competition are local.

National Sponsoring Organizations

Masters basketball is one of the most grassroots of adult sports. If you are over 40, the best place to start looking for a basketball team is your local parks department, fitness club, YMCA, or industrial basketball league. Leagues for players over 40, over 50, over 60 and beyond can be found in most metropolitan areas. Some areas, like Chicago and Portland, Oregon, are hotbeds of adult basketball competition. Unlike some other sports which organize competitive classes by skill level, basketball leagues rarely separate the skilled from the unskilled. The players themselves do this. With only five players on the floor, it becomes immediately obvious when a player is well below, or above, the levels of the other players.

There are several major tournaments that are open to any teams that wish to compete. The Men's Masters Basketball National Championships hosts an annual tournament in Coral Gables, Florida. The web site is http://www.mastersbasketball.org/index.html. The only contact information on the web site is a return e-mail form.

There are also several three-on-three basketball competitions that incorporate the age of the players into their competitive brackets. For example, the NBA Hoop It Up competition (http://www.hoopitup.com/) divides players by level of competitiveness, height of the tallest player, and average age of the players on a team. However, Hoop It Up has only two divisions for adults: a 30+ competitive division and a 30+ recreational division.

The Amateur Athletic Union (AAU) has a men's basketball program and an individual responsible for Masters programs, but it is unclear exactly how the AAU promotes, sponsors, or supports adult basketball.

AAU Men's Basketball
Tom Ficara, Masters chairman
1631 Equestrian Drive
Henderson, NV 89002
(702) 567-5277
aausports.org/exec/aau/handbooks/mens_bball/VI_program.pdf.

Competitive Opportunities

As noted above, most competition in adult basketball for players over 40 is organized and sponsored at the local level. For example, Table 4–1 lists a selection of adult leagues found by searching the Internet for "Adult Basketball" and "Masters Basketball."

Table 4–1
Selection of Adult Basketball Leagues in the United States

City	Web site
New York, NY	www.chelseapiers.com/fhAdBaInfo.htm#
Austin, TX	www.ci.austin.tx.us/parks/basketball.htm
Scottsdale, AZ	www.scottsdaleaz.gov/sports/bball.asp
Tacoma, WA	www.metroparkstacoma.org/page.php?id=522
Puget Sound, WA	www.pugetsoundflight.org/new_page_33.htm

City	Web site
Southern Maine	mainejewish.org/page.html?ArticleID=113821
Minneapolis, MN	www.minneapolisparks.org/default.asp?PageID=566

The 2008 Men's Masters Basketball Championship was held in Coral Gables, Florida, on May 11 through 17, 2008. The divisions included six men's divisions, with age groups from 40+ to 70+ and two women's divisions (or more if entries are adequate). Play is very competitive with former college and NBA players participating. For more information, go to http://www.mastersbasketball.org/

The 2008 Buffalo Masters North American Basketball Championship was held March 14 through 16 in Buffalo, New York. The 12 age group divisions included ages from 30+ to 75+. For more information, go to http://www.buffalomasters.com/.

Competitive Landscape

Because there is no organization overseeing all local and regional competition of adult basketball, it is impossible to estimate how many athletes compete nationwide. Based on the number of local leagues in major metropolitan areas, it is reasonable to assume there are thousands of adult basketball players. The winners of leagues in major cities and national tournaments include many former college and NBA players. However, there are plenty of opportunities for the average player to find a team and enjoy the game.

Many teams from local leagues or league all-star teams enter the national and international tournaments. Table 4–2 lists the number of teams in each age group that competed in the 2007 Men's Masters Basketball Championships in Coral Springs, Florida.

Table 4–2
Number of Teams in the Men's Masters
Basketball National Championships

Division	Number of Teams
40+ Men	6
45+ Men	8
50+ Men	10
55+ Men	4
60+ Men	5
65+ Men	6
70+ Men	4

The national champions for each age group in the Men's Masters National Championships and the Buffalo Masters North American Championships are listed in Appendix A.

How to Get Started

Skills

Most age group teams are made up of players who participated in either high school or college basketball teams. Rarely does the team teach individuals how to play basketball, although there is often informal coaching on the team level for offensive plays, various defenses, and presses. Because full-court basketball requires both speed and stamina, a basic level of fitness is needed to participate. The finer skills of basketball—passing, rebounding, dribbling, and defense—are acquired over a long period of time. Shooting a basketball, a key skill, can be practiced on your own, but quite soon you will want to learn the team game. A good way for the novice to begin is to try some pick-up half-court games.

Like most team sports for adults, practices are difficult to arrange because of other personal and business commitments of the players. The exception may occur if the team is in a tournament or preparing for a major competition, such as a national championship. Of course, individuals often shoot and play one-on-one or three-on-three.

Equipment

All you need is a good pair of basketball shoes. Unless you can find a generous sponsor to buy uniforms, the players usually have to chip in to buy their own. Referees, basketballs, and scorers are usually provided by the organization (parks department, fitness club, YMCA) in return for a fee assessed to each team.

Coaching

In addition to informal coaching that occurs in many local leagues, there are a number of adult fantasy basketball camps that are run by college or NBA coaches or starts, including:

Mike Krzyzewski Fantasy Camp	www.coachk.com/camp-k-academy.php
Bill Russell Fantasy Camp	www.friendsofbillrussell.com/
Michael Jordan	www.mjflightschool.com/message.asp

Venues

The United States is blessed with hundreds of excellent basketball courts and most communities have at least three or four in schools, churches, community centers, fitness clubs, and armories. Again, the organization sponsoring the league usually has access to a court.

Recognition

Awards

The Men's Masters Basketball National Championships awards trophies to the winners and runners-up in each age group division and selects an all-tourney team and most valuable player for each division.

The national champions for each age group in the Men's Masters National Championships and the Buffalo Masters North American Championships are listed in Appendix A.

National Teams

The lack of a single national sponsoring organization means that there are no national age group basketball teams

Rankings

Neither of the sponsoring organizations publish national rankings for age group basketball teams.

Resources

There are many instructional books on basketball which will give a novice the basics for playing game, most of which are aimed at young players.

Converse All-Star Basketball: How to Play Like a Pro; (Converse All-Star Sports), Jossey-Bass Publisher, 1996.

Basketball Fundamentals; Jon A. Oliver, Human Kinetics Publishing, 2003.

Pat Conroy's memoir, *My Losing Season*, gives an entertaining account of playing the game by someone who is good, but not a superstar. *My Losing Season*; Pat Conroy, Nan A. Talese, 2002.

Canoeing

Introduction

The best and worst aspect of endurance racing is that you have plenty of time to think. Plenty of opportunity to reflect on that training session you aborted, or your technique slipping into slop, or second-guessing your race strategy. A 20-mile canoe race offers plenty of time to reflect on your aging body, the fatigue creeping into your shoulders and forearms. Don't drop the stroke rate; reach to insert the blade in the water; twist the torso and use the power of your back, not your arms. As the bow cuts through the wake of the paddler just ahead, try to pull up on the tiny wave running toward you. Even that slight advantage will save precious hundredths of a joule. In your peripheral vision, the river bank slides by, spruce and alder falling away. Ahead, a bend in the river unwinds a new vista, a fresh goal.

Canoe and kayak racing is a great outdoor sport in which the line between recreation and competition can be crossed often and easily. Many racers began by cruising rivers, camping on remote lakes, and surfing ocean waves. It's a very inviting sport for Masters Athletes. More than a third of the competitors in the 2007 National Marathon Championships were over 60 years of age and more than 20 percent were women.

National Sponsoring Organizations

The broadest range of competitive opportunities in canoe racing is in marathon events in which paddlers race from five to 30 miles, or more. There are canoe racers over 40 competing in other disciplines, such as whitewater slalom, canoe sailing, and canoe poling, but the number of events in these disciplines is relatively small.

Two organizations oversee marathon canoe racing in the United States. The United States Canoe Association (USCA) supports a wide range of marathon races and sponsors the Marathon National Championships each year. The USCA does not have an office, but its web site is http://www.uscanoe.com/. Its executive director, John Edwards, can be reached at canoechamp@aol.com, and the membership secretary is Paula Thiel, who can be reached at 55 Ross Road, Preston, Connecticut, 06365. Various categories of membership are available. A single adult membership for one year is currently $20 and includes the bi-monthly magazine *Canoe News*.

Regional and local marathon canoes races are sponsored by USCA-affiliated divisions and canoe clubs. Table 5–1 lists the clubs that sponsor marathon races. Their web sites include current race schedules and race results.

Table 5–1
USCA Clubs Sponsoring Marathon Canoe Races

State	Web site
Florida	www.geocities.com/1F6978/index.html
Illinois	www.illinoispaddling.org/
Indiana	www.indianapaddlers.com
Maine	www.mackro.org/
Michigan	www.miracing.com/
Midwest	www.midwestcanoesport.com
Minnesota	www.canoe-kayak.org/pages/racing.html
New England	www.neckra.org
New York	https://www.nymcra.org/
Texas	www.txcanoeracing.org/
Wisconsin	http://wicanoeracing.com

The U.S. Canoe and Kayak Team (USCKT) supports and holds trials for the United States Marathon Racing Team, which includes a Masters class for competitors over 40. However, as the national governing body for Olympic sprint racing and whitewater slalom, its focus is on developing Olympic athletes. The USCKT also oversees several other racing disciplines including rodeo, freestyle, and dragon boat racing.

U.S. Canoe and Kayak Team
David Yarborough, executive director
301 South Tryon St., Suite 1750
Charlotte, NC 28282
(704) 348-4330
info@usack.org
http://www.usacanoekayak.org/MC_About_USACK.aspx

The United State Marathon Canoe and Kayak Team also has its own web site at http://www.geocities.com/txpaddler/.

The largest canoeing organization in the U.S. is the American Canoe Association (http://www.americancanoe.org/) with 50,000 members, but their support and sponsorship of canoeing racing competitions is minimal. However, they do support several other canoeing disciplines, such as canoe sailing and canoe poling.

Competitive Opportunities

With 7.6 million Americans enjoying canoeing and kayaking as a recreational activity, it's no surprise that there is a broad range of competitive opportunities. These opportunities come in an astonishing variety of disciplines. The most popular disciplines in the United States include marathon, slalom, sprints, canoe sailing, outrigger, downriver (wildwater), freestyle, canoe orienteering, and kayak polo. At the present time, the discipline offering the greatest number of opportunities for adult athletes is marathon canoeing and it is the focus of this chapter. Sources of information on participating in the other canoeing disciplines are provided at the end of this chapter.

Marathon canoe and kayak racing involves getting from point A to point B as fast as possible. Races are generally from two to 25 miles long, although some races are considerably longer, including multi-day events that cover more than 200 miles. The races are held on relatively flat water (excluding the effect of wind) or rivers with little or no current. Races often include portages in which the racers must carry their boats and paddles over land around dams or between bodies of water.

Marathon races offer an array of competitive classes. For example, thirty classes were offered for adults at the 2007 Marathon National Championships. These classes were based on four criteria:

- Gender—Classes for men, women, and mixed (men and women)
- Number—Classes for single and double person boats. One- and two-person canoes are referred to as C-1 and C-2; one- and two-person kayaks are designated as K-1 and K-2.
- Boat Types—Classes for standard (heavier) and racing canoes; for sea kayaks, downriver kayaks, and Olympic sprint kayaks. Each of these types of boats is defined by specifications that may include weight, length, and width. For details on boat specifications, go to http://www.uscanoe.com/2002canoespec.html,
- Age Groups—Masters (over-40), Seniors (over-50), Veterans (over 60), and Grand Veterans (over 70).

The result of combining these criteria are classes such as Men's C-1 Grand Veteran, K-1 Sea Kayak, C-2 Mixed Standard, and Women's C-2 Master. Participation in all the classes at the 2008 Marathon Nationals is shown below.

Marathon canoe racing is not evenly spread across the country. The competitive hotbeds are currently Michigan, Wisconsin, Illinois, Indiana, Minnesota, New York, Florida, Texas, and New England, not necessarily in that order. Table 5–2 lists some of the major marathon races in 2008.

Table 5–2
2008 Major Marathon Canoe Races

Race	Location	Date	Length
2008 Marathon Nationals	Bristol, IN	Aug. 5–10	15–20 miles
2008 Aluminum Canoe Nationals	Bastrop, TX	Sept. 27–28	30 miles
General Clinton Canoe Regatta	Bainbridge, NY	May 27–31	70 miles
AuSable River Canoe Marathon	Grayling, MI	July 26–27	120 miles
La Classique Internationale	Quebec, ON	Aug. 29–31	120 miles

Hundreds of local and regional marathon races can be found on the web sites of the USCA divisions and club affiliates.

Competitive Landscape

The 2007 National Marathon Canoe Championships were held in Warren, Pennsylvania, on August 7–12. The results are posted below and can be downloaded from the USCA web site at http://www.uscanoe.com/.

The number, age, and gender of competitors in various classes at the 2007 Nationals provide a snapshot of the breadth and depth of the competition. Of course, each race will present a different profile of competitors. The 2007 Marathon National Championships had more than 800 entries. Many entries were individuals who signed up for more than one event. In the Adult Sprints, there were three classes over 40—Masters (40+), Seniors (50+), and Veterans (60+). In the 15-mile marathon race there were as many six age group classifications—Masters (40+), Senior (50+), Veteran I (60+) Veteran II (65+), Grand Veteran I (70+), and Grand Veteran II (75+). In the over-40 marathon classes, there were approximately 205 male entries and 61 female entries. This estimate is low because some over-40 paddlers competed in open classes and the ages of some paddlers were not published. Table 5–3 shows the number of age group competitors for the 2007 National Championships.

Table 5–3
2007 Marathon Nationals Competitors by Age Group and Event[1]

	C1	C2	K-1	Total
Over 40	24	68	29	121
Over 50	24	18	18	60
Over 60	19	18	18	55
Over 65	10	2	0	12
Over 70	6	6	0	12
Over 75	4	2	0	6
Total	**87**	**114**	**65**	**266**

1 *These figures represent the number of entries in the various age group classes. The ages of some entries were not published.*

The largest classes were the C-2 Mixed Master—40–49 (34) and the Men's C-1 Master—40–49 (18), Men's C-1 Senior—50–59 (22), and Men's C-1 Veteran—60–69 (19). The oldest competitor was Grand Veteran Phil Cole of Contoocook (NH) who is 88. Marathon canoe racing offers plenty of opportunities for men and women over 40 to compete. The list of 2007 National Marathon Canoe and Kayak Champions is presented in Appendix A.

Canoeing's Triple Crown

The premier marathon canoe races in North American are the three competitions known as the Triple Crown of Canoeing. The first of these three races, known as the General Clinton Canoe Regatta, takes place on the Susquehanna River in New York State on Memorial Day. Paddlers race from Cooperstown, NY, to Bainbridge, NY, 70 miles. The fastest time for the 2007 General Clinton was 7 hours, 24 minutes, and 59 seconds.

The Ausable Canoe Marathon is the second jewel in the Triple Crown. The 120-mile race on Michigan's Ausable River takes place in July with $50,000 in prize money, the largest purse in the sport. The winning Ausable Marathon time in 2007 was 14 hours, 48 minutes, and 55 seconds.

The last race in the series is the La Classique International de Canots de la Maurice. This is a 120-mile, three-day, three-stage race on the St. Maurice River in central Quebec with a purse of $40,000. The winning time in this event in 2002 was 13 hours, 1 minute, and 57 seconds.

The team that achieved this winning time was Steve Corlew and a legend in marathon canoe racing: Serge Corbin of St. Boniface, Canada. Corbin has won 98 percent of the marathon races he has entered and won La Classique 25 times with 10 different partners. Still racing in his late 40s, Corbin is proof enough that age is no barrier to success in canoe racing.

How to Get Started

Skills

Marathon canoe racing is an endurance sport. To be successful, you should be able to paddle hard for periods from 1 to 3 hours or more, as well as meet the demands of portaging. Many races are won or lost on the portages. Paddling requires good upper body strength and a strong mid-section.

Marathon canoe racing is also a low-impact sport which allows competitors in their 60s, 70s, 80s, and older to participate. The range of classes and the large number of local races offer an excellent way for beginners to enter the sport. Races are generally held on beautiful rivers and lakes and you can compete with simple equipment at relatively low cost. Many families race together, especially those who enjoy camping and the outdoors.

Equipment

You'll need a canoe or kayak, a couple of paddles, and a personal flotation device (PFD). You can buy a serviceable used canoe, to christen in some local races, for a few hundred dollars. A new racing canoe or kayak, in the latest design, made of Kevlar or carbon fiber can be $2,000 or more.

Paddles should fit the paddler and the boat. Inexpensive wooden or plastic canoe paddles can be purchased for less than $50. Kayak paddles may be slightly more expensive. Top of the line carbon fiber canoe or kayak paddles run in the $200 to $400 range.

PFDs are essential for any boater and many states require that they be worn, or at least carried in the boat at all times. Competitors have been disqualified from races for not having an approved PFD.

You will also need some way to carry all this equipment. You can build a serviceable roof rack with some 2x4s and specialized hardware that may cost around $25. You can also purchase very sturdy roof rack systems for $150 to $250.

Coaching

Canoeing is a skill that must be learned. You can pick up the basic skills—skills enough to allow you to participate in local races—in a matter of a few hours. The American Canoe Association provides instruction in canoe and kayak skills by certified instructors. For more information, including how to find an instructor in your area, see the ACA instructional program at http://www.americancanoe.org/instruction/instruction.lasso.

Venues

Races are held on rivers, lakes, or ponds. Although the water on which marathon races are held usually has little or no current, windy conditions can create waves that make paddling tricky. Check with the local race organizers and keep an eye on the weather. Most venues are beautiful places that are typically underused. Your local paddling club or rental center can direct you to good places to paddle. Remember you'll need access to the water and a safe place to park.

Recognition

Awards

Typically, marathon races award prizes to the first three finishers in each class with the number and types of classes determined by the demographics of the entries. There are also pro races with cash prizes and a few elite paddlers can almost make a living paddling, between prize money and endorsements. However, canoeing is a deeply amateur sport and a welcoming one to novices.

National Teams

Each year a U.S. Marathon Team is selected and includes a Masters division. However, age groups above 40 have not yet been established by the USCKT. The list of 2007 National Marathon Canoe and Kayak Champions is presented in Appendix A.

Rankings

At the present time, there is no ranking system for marathon paddlers.

Canoe and Kayak Disciplines

One of the remarkable aspects of the sport of canoeing and kayaking is the number of disciplines, offering all sorts of new opportunities to compete. Here are the most important disciplines.

- Whitewater Slalom: Canoe and kayak slalom was again an Olympic event in China in 2008. The USCKT sponsors an age group national championship with classes for Senior (30+) and Masters (40+). The 2008 championships were held on June 28 in Wausau, WI. For more information go to http://www.usacanoekayak.org/Slalom.aspx.
- Outrigger: An important competition in Hawaii and other parts of the world which is rapidly growing in the continental U.S. Good places to learn more are the following web sites: http://www.nwcanoe.com/outrigger/outrigger.html and http://www.paddlenut.com/.
- Canoe Orienteering: An interesting and growing discipline that combines paddling and navigation. http://www.geocities.com/canoeo/.
- Sprints Racing: Another Olympic discipline sponsored by the USCKT. Limited opportunities for and participation by paddlers over 40. For more information, go to http://www.usacanoekayak.org/Sprint.aspx.
- Freestyle (Rodeo): A fast-growing discipline with X-Games leanings, this discipline involves doing tricks in a kayak, or playing, in a set of rapids. Try this site: http://www.expertvillage.com/interviews/kayaking-basic-freestyle.htm.
- Canoe Sailing: More recreation than competition, but a new application for a traditional craft. http://www.enter.net/~skimmer/.
- Canoe Poling: Like to go upstream without a paddle? Try this ACA web site: http://www.americancanoe.org/recreation/types_poling.lasso.
- Downriver (Wildwater): Another discipline sponsored by the USCKT. Very limited opportunities and participation by athletes over 40. For more information, go to http://www.usacanoekayak.org/Wildwater.aspx.
- Kayak Polo: A popular canoeing team sport, but with limited opportunities and participation by those over 40. It has its own organization. For more information go to http://www.kayakpolo.com/uscpc/.
- Dragon Boat Racing: An international discipline that is part competition and part festival. For information, go to http://www.dragonboats.net/dragon_boat_races_usa.htm.

The best way to keep up with these is to watch the web sites of the USCKT, USCA, and the ACA. For a more complete list of canoe- and kayak-related web sites, try http://users.bestweb.net/~keech/cc-links.htm. Much of this growth in opportunities is in new types of competition and it will be interesting to see which of the many canoe disciplines become most attractive and popular with competitors over 40. Also the recent growth in sea kayaking has led to the creation of a race class for these boats. There were 22 entries in the K-1 Sea Kayak class at the 2007 Nationals.

Resources

An excellent source of information and instruction on marathon racing is *Canoe Racing: The Competitor's Guide to Marathon and Downriver Canoe Racing* by Peter Heed and Dick Masfield; Acorn Publishers; 2005.

Cross-Country Skiing

Introduction

A mass start of a cross-country ski race is unlike anything in sports. A crowd, which may number twenty or several hundred or more, slips into the start area. Everyone is puffing clouds of steam giving the scene an other-worldly atmosphere. Always, the premier skiers, resplendent in brightly-colored uniforms, gather at the front. They lean on their poles, impatiently scraping their skis over the snow to check their wax. Toward the rear of the pack, the other competitors, in more motley dress, are adjusting their caps and gloves, and looking for a spot to place their skis without standing on someone else's. At the sound of the gun, the racers in front jump out and are out of sight by the time the rest of the pack is moving. Inevitably, skis and poles get tangled and minor pile-ups confuse the already chaotic start. However, within a few minutes, the area is cleared of skiers, leaving only a tangle of ski tracks, and perhaps a discarded water bottle, in the snow.

Cross-country skiing, also called Nordic skiing and X-C skiing, can be a wonderful way to spend an invigorating winter afternoon, or a muscle-wrenching, lung-blasting racing experience. In either case, it is a sport that is enjoyed (however you interpret that verb) by many Masters Athletes.

National Sponsoring Organizations

The organization that promotes and supports Masters cross-country skiing is American Cross County Skiers (AXCS), founded in 1998 to serve adult skiers (over the age of 25 in the U.S. and 30+ internationally). It provides education, promotion, and communication programs.

American Cross-Country Skiers
PO Box 604
Bend, OR 97709
http://www.xcskiworld.com/axcs/axcs.htm
Membership services are provided by Active.com or
(888) 543-7223 ext. 196.

The annual individual membership fee is $35 and a three-year membership is $90. Members receive the *AXCS XC Ski Digest* and *The Master Skier*, as well as discounts on event registrations and information on national and international cross-country skiing competitions for skiers over 25.

AXCS also provides a directory of hundreds of ski areas throughout the United States that offer cross-country skiing to masters skiers.

Competitive Opportunities

The AXCS National Championships and the American Ski Marathon Series are the premier competitions for adult cross-country ski racers. The 2008 AXCS Nationals were held in Bend, Oregon, on March 25–30.

The American Ski Marathon Series consists of 13 races from Vermont to Alaska. Table

6–1 lists the races, locations, dates, and distances for 2008. For more information on the series, go to http://www.xcskiworld.com/events_xc/ASM/ASM_sitepreview.htm.

Table 6–1
2008 American Ski Marathon Series

Event	Date	Location	Distance
Pepsi Challenge	Jan. 19, 2008	Biwabik, MN	70k
Noquemanon Ski Marathon	Jan. 26, 2008	Marquette, MI	51k
Mora Vasaloppet	Feb. 10, 2008	Mora, MN	35k
Craftsbury Marathon	Feb. 2, 2008	Craftsbury Common, VT	50k/25k
Lake Placid Loppet	Feb. 9, 2008	Lake Placid, NY	
Minnesota Finlandia	Feb. 16, 2008	Bemidji, MN	25k/15k
California Gold Rush	March 16, 2008	Soda Springs, CA	42k/21k
Tour of Anchorage	March 2, 2008	Anchorage, AK	50k/25k
American Birkebeiner	Feb. 23, 2008	Hayward, WI	25k
Boulder Mountain Tour	Feb. 2, 2008	Sun Valley, ID	32k
City of Lakes Loppet	Feb. 2–3, 2008	Minneapolis, MN	35k
North American Vasa	Feb. 9, 2008	Traverse City, MI	50k/27k
Yellowstone Rendezvous	Feb, 23, 2008	West Yellowstone, MT	25k

Many other local and regional races are sponsored by the local ski clubs which can be found on the AXCS web site.

Competitive Landscape

Cross-country skiing races typically base competitive classes on:

• Gender (men and women),
• Length of race (e.g., 10 kilometers, 15 kilometers, etc.),
• Competitor's age, in 5-year increments, and
• Skiing style (classic and freestyle). Classic skiing requires the skier to keep skis in parallel tracks, by striding and gliding or double poling. Freestyle allows the skier to push off with each ski, in effect skating on skis.

To indicate the competitiveness of the various classes, Table 6–2 show the number of competitors in the over-40 classes offered at the 2007 AXCS National Masters Championships on March 22 to 25 in Bend, Oregon.

Table 6–2
Number of Competitors in the 2007 National Masters
Cross Country Skiing Championship

Gender/Age	Classic Races	Distance	Freestyle Races	Distance	15k Skiathlon
Men					
40–44	12	15km	20	30km	8
45–49	12	15km	15	30km	4
50–54	17	15km	26	30km	9
55–59	19	10km	24	30km	16
60–64	18	10km	19	20km	15
65–69	13	10km	12	20km	10
70–74	6	10km	7	15km	7
75–79	3	10km	2	15km	2

Gender/Age	Classic Races	Distance	Freestyle Races	Distance	15k Skiathlon
80–84	2	10km	1	15km	3
85–89	1	10km	1	15km	0
Women					
40–44	7	10km	12	20km	8
45–49	6	10km	10	20km	5
50–54	4	10km	7	20km	3
55–59	4	10km	5	20km	3
60–64	5	10km	1	15km	3
65–69	4	10km	5	15km	2
70–74	3	10km	2	15km	1
Total	135		172		99

The total number of competitors over 40, as shown in Table 6–2, is 406: 303 men and 103 women. The most popular type of race was the freestyle, drawing 42 percent of the competitors. The classic races drew a third of the competitors. Women accounted for 25 percent of the competitors and competitors over 60 year of age accounted for 29 percent of the total number of competitors. The national champions for the 2007 AXCS Masters Nationals are listed in Appendix A.

One of the largest races in the American Ski Marathon Series is the American Birkebeiner in Hayward, Wisconsin. This race offers classes by gender, skiing style, distance and age group, a total of more than 60 classes in 2007. Table 6–3 lists the number of male and female entries for the Birkebeiner (51 km) race using both the classic style and freestyle.

Table 6–3
2007 American Birkebeiner Entries

Gender/Age	Classic Entries	Freestyle Entries	Distance
Men			
30–34	21	125	51km
35–39	28	201	51km
40–44	49	265	51km
45–49	78	402	51km
50–54	98	384	51km
55–59	102	248	51km
60–64	51	118	51km
65–69	20	41	51km
70–74	9	5	51km
75–79	—	3	51km
Women			
30–34	6	34	51km
35–39	8	28	51km
40–44	17	40	51km
45–49	20	63	51km
50–54	16	53	51km
55–59	13	27	51km
60–64	7	7	51km
65–69	1	2	51km
70–74	—	1	51km

The classic entries represented approximately 21 percent of the total freestyle and classic entries and the women entries represented 16 percent of the classic entries and 11 percent of the freestyle entries.

How to Get Started

Skills

Cross-country skiing demands fitness, balance, and endurance. The basic techniques can be learned in an afternoon and refined for a lifetime. Regular cross-country skiing is one of the best all-around exercises possible.

Equipment

Nordic skis, the skinny skis, bindings, poles and boots are all essential equipment. A complete package for novice races will cost $250 to $350. High-tech gear will, of course, be more expensive. A good way to determine what you need is to rent equipment at your local ski area and see what works. An excellent summary discussion of ski equipment can be found at http://www.xcskiworld.com/equip/equip_5minute.htm.

Coaching

With a good instructor, the basic Cross-Country skiing technique can be learned in an afternoon and lessons are available at most Nordic ski centers. This will prepare you to ski over relatively easy terrain at a moderate pace. More challenging trails (i.e., steeper uphills and downhills and sharper curves) will require better technique and greater fitness. Improved technique will come with practice and more good coaching.

Venues

Nordic skiing requires snow so venues are located in northern and mountainous states. It is also weather dependent. The southernmost state to list ski clubs is North Carolina. Several hundred cross-country ski centers are listed on the AXCS web site. Keep an eye on the weather.

Recognition

Awards

Prizes are typically awarded to the top three finishers in a class, although some races give awards deeper into the classes.

National Teams

Neither the AXCS or US Ski and Snowboarding select a national masters cross-country team.

Rankings

The AXCS does not rank master cross-country skiers.

Resources

The Essential Cross Country Skier by Lovett and Petersen; Ragged Mountain Press, 1999.
Caldwell on Competitive Cross-Country Skiing by John Caldwell; Stephen Greene Press, 1979.
Long Distance: A Year of Living Strenuously by Bill McKibben; Simon & Shuster, 2000.

Cycling

Introduction

Long training rides are a staple of the bicycle road racing training regimen. On a bright Sunday morning, you might be riding with a group, listening to the hum of tires on macadam, as well as the rhythm of your own heart and lungs. After a few miles the stiffness in your knees and thighs disappears. Your back loosens. The smells of newly cut hay, wet leaves, and, yes, the faint tang of diesel fumes are in the air. This is one of those times when training is a delight.

Bicycle racing offers a variety of opportunities for Masters Athletes. Racing on roads, tracks, and steep mountain trails, on one- or two-person bikes, against the clock or other competitors is possible. Women racers are still in the minority, as are competitors over 60, but those that do race are dedicated and enthusiastic. This chapter addresses four cycling disciplines: road racing, track racing, cyclo-cross, and mountain biking.

National Sponsoring Organizations

The umbrella organization that oversees competitive cycling in the United States is USA Cycling.

USA Cycling
210 USA Cycling Point, Suite 100
Colorado Springs, CO 80919
(719) 434-4200
membership@usacycling.org
http://www.usacycling.org

Within USA Cycling are five associations:

(1) National Off-Road Bicycle Association (NORBA), which oversees mountain biking.

(2) United States Cycling Federation, which oversees track racing, road racing, and cyclo-cross.

(3) United States Professional Racing Organization, which oversees all professional bicycle racing in the United States. Because professional racing is outside the scope of this guide, we have not included a discussion of it here. However, USA Cycling's web site or office can provide more information.

(4) National Collegiate Cycling Association which, as its name indicates, oversees college cycling, and

(5) BMX Association, which oversees BMX racing.

Of these five associations, the two offering the greatest competitive opportunities to Masters Competitors are NORBA and USCF.

A one-year adult membership to either NORBA or USCF is $60. If you wish to join both organizations the annual fee is an additional $30. Membership provides a license, which is required to compete in any sanctioned event, and access to the network of regional organizations and coaching programs. The local associations and their web sites are listed in Table 7–1. USA Cycling, through its regional organizations, sponsors more than 2,000 cycling competitions each year.

Table 7–1
USA Cycling Local Associations and Web sites

Association	Web site
Alabama Cycling Association	www.alcycling.org
Alabama/Georgia Bicycle Racing Association	www.usacycling.org/algabra/
Arizona Bicycle Racing Association	www.azcycling.com/
Arkansas Bicycle Coalition	arkansasbicyclecoalition.org/default.aspx
Carolina Cycling Association	www.ncsccyclingassoc.com/
Colorado Velodrome Association	www.coloradousac.org/road/
Florida Road Cycling Association	www.floridacycling.com/
Illinois Cycling Association	illinoiscycling.org/modules/news/
Iowa Bicycle Racing Association	www.bikeiowa.org/
Kansas Cycling Association	www.kscycling.org/
Louisiana Mississippi Bicycle Racing Association	www.lambra.org/
Michigan Bicycle Racing Association	www.mbra.org/
Mid Atlantic Bicycle Racing Association	www.mabra.org/
Minnesota Cycling Federation	www.mcf.net/
Missouri Bicycle Racing Association	www.mobra.org/
Montana Bicycle Racing Association	www.montanacycling.net/
Nebraska Cycling Association	www.nebraskacycling.org/
New England Bicycle Racing Association	www.ne-bra.org/
New Jersey Bicycling Association	www.njbikeracing.com/
New Mexico Bike Racing Association	www.nmcycling.org/
Northern California/Nevada Cycling Association	www.ncnca.org/
Ohio Cycling Association	ohiocycling.org/
Bicycle Racing Association of Oklahoma	www.braok.org/
Pennsylvania Cycling Association	www.pacycling.org/
Southern California/Nevada Cycling Association	www.scnca.org/
Southwest Idaho Cycling Association	www.idahobikeracing.org/
Tennessee Bicycle Racing Association	www.tbra.org/
Texas Bicycle Racing Association	www.txbra.org/home/index.asp
Utah Cycling Association	utahcycling.com/Default.aspx
Virginia Cycling Association, Inc.	www.vacycling.org/
Washington State Bicycle Association	www.wsbaracing.com/
Wisconsin Cycling Association	www.wicycling.org/

Those who are not served by one of these local organizations should contact USA Cycling directly.

Competitive Opportunities

Masters competition in cycling is based on classes using four criteria:

• Gender—Classes for both men and women are offered and, in some disciplines, men's, women's and mixed tandem (bicycles built for two) classes are also offered.
• Disciplines—These include road racing, track racing, cyclo-cross, and mountain biking.
• Events—Each of these disciplines includes individual events which are described below.
• Age Group—Masters competition is open to cyclists from the ages of 30 to 80+. Typically broad age group categories are offered, such as 30+ or 35+, but larger races usually have a greater number of age group categories, depending on the demographics of the entrants.

Road racing includes several events including the three that were included in the 2007 National Road Cycling Championships:

- Time trials, in which riders are sent off at one-minute intervals to race against the clock as well as each other. The time trials in the 2007 Road Racing Nationals ranged in length from 20 kilometers to 40 kilometers.
- A criterium, which is a multi-lap race on a closed course with a lap being less than one mile. The criterium races in the 2007 Nationals ranged in length from 30 kilometers to 60 kilometers. A 30-kilometer criterium race would consist of approximately 19 one-mile laps.
- Road races, in which all riders are sent off together, to get from Point A to Point B in the fastest possible time. The road races ranged in length from 54 kilometers to 100 kilometers.

There were divisions for men and women in each event, and tandem events in the time trials and road races.

Track racing events are held in a specially-built facility called a velodrome. The track racing events that were part of the 2007 National Track Cycling Championships included:

- Time trials that ranged in length from 500 meters to 3,000 meters.
- A points race in which a group of riders begin together and sprint against each other on specified laps, accumulating points depending on the position at the end of the laps.
- A sprint in which a group of riders (three or four) begin on one side of the track and a group of riders start on the other side of the track. The lead rider in each group pulls off the track at the end of the first lap, the second rider pulls off the track at the end of the second lap, and the last rider finishes the race. The fastest total time wins the race.
- The Madison, a track race in which teams races for an allotted period of time. Only one member of the team rides at a time, racing around the track as fast as possible. After two or three laps, the rider pulls off and a teammate continues. Changeovers can involve the retiring rider slinging the new rider onto the track. The winner is the team covering the most laps in the time allotted. Although most Madisons are held over several hours, races in the 1920s—the heyday of bicycle racing in the United States—lasted as long as six days. This race is named for Madison Square Garden, where this type of race originated.

Track racing can also involve hybrid events, such as Keirins and Motorpace, in which cyclists race draft behind motorcycles to achieve speeds not possible when bicycles alone are used.

Cyclo-Cross involves racing around short (1.5 to 2 mile) laps through steep terrain or obstacles that often requires the rider to dismount periodically and carry the bike.

Mountain Bike racing generally takes place on steep terrain and events include:

- Cross country, in which, after a mass start, riders on a course which may be 3.5 to 5.0 miles in length,
- Downhill, in which riders begin at intervals (often 30 seconds) and negotiate a steep, rough downhill section,
- Super D, which is a combination of cross-country and downhill,
- Dual Slalom, in which two riders race against another down an identical course, and
- Marathon, in which a rider must race over 80 or more kilometers of cross-country terrain.

Many local and regional cycling races have a broad category for adults, such as 30+ or 35+. In some cases, more age groups may be added depending on the demographics of the entries. The national championship events sponsored by USA Cycling have more age group events (see Table 7–3). Table 7–2 presents the national championship events for Masters Athletes that are sponsored by USA Cycling.

Table 7–2
2008 National Championship Cycling Races

Race	Date	Location
National Masters Road Racing Championship	June 30–July 6	Louisville, KY
National Masters Track Championships	Sept. 11–13	San Jose, CA
Cyclo-Cross Junior/Masters Nationals	Dec. 11–14	Kansas City, MO
Mountain Bike National Championship	July 16–20	Mount Snow, VT

For local and regional races, see the web sites of the local associations in Table 7–1.

Competitive Landscape

One gauge of the competitive landscape is the number of entries in the various classes at the national championships. Tables 7–3 and 7–4 show the number of competitors in each of the classes for the 2007 USA Cycling National Festival in time trial, criterium, and road racing.

Table 7–3
Numbers of Competitors in the 2007 National Cycling Festival

Age Group	Time Trial[1]	Criterium	Road Race[2]
Gender—Men			
40–44	62	71	70
45–49	63	74	84
50–54	48	47	58
55–59	31	31	31
60–64	23	32	23
65–69	20	16	14
70–74	8	7	9
75–79	4	2	3
80–84	2	1	0
Gender—Women			
40–44	17	15	15
45–49	13	18	13
50–54	13	13	12
55–59	10	7	6
60–64	2	2	2
65–69	5	3	3
70+	2	2	0

1 *Does not include tandem racers. There were 10 women, 18 men, and 28 mixed racers in the time trial tandem events.*

2 *Does not include tandem racers. There were 4 women, 16 men, and 16 mixed racers in the road race tandem events.*

There were approximately 1,095 over-40 competitors in the 2007 Cycling Nationals Championships, including racers that did not start or did not finish. Women represented approximately 19 percent of the competitors. Although all three events had approximately the same number of entrants, there were a few more entries in road racing. About 21 percent of the entrants were 60 or older.

Table 7–4
Entries in the 2007 National Masters Track Cycling Championships

Age Group	Time Trials[1]	Track Points[2]	Track Sprints	Track Madison
Gender—Men				
40–44	83	34	8	0
45–49	55	27	8	12
50–54	69	13	8	0
55–59	34	0	8	0
60–64	35	15	8	0
65–69	18	13	7	0
70+	11	4	0	0
Gender—Women				
40–44	13	0	8	0
45–49	17	4	8	0
50–54	16	9	0	0
55–59	7	0	0	0
60+	4	0	0	0

1 Includes 500 meter, 2,000 meter, 3,000 meter, and team springs.

2 Includes 10 kilometer and 25 kilometer point races.

There were a total of 556 entries in the 2007 Track Cycling Championships, including racers that did not start or did not finish. Women represented approximately 15 percent of the entries. The most popular event was time trials. About 16 percent of the entrants were 60 or older—2 percent of the over 60 entrants were women and 14 percent were men.

Track cycling takes place in specially designed facilities called velodromes. There are 21 velodromes in the United States and they are listed in Table 7–5. If you are interested in track cycling, you might visit one of these facilities and get a feel for what it's all about.

Table 7–5
Track Cycling Velodromes in the United States

Velodrome Name	Location
ADT Event Center	Carson City, CA
Alkek Velodrome	Houston, TX
Alpenrose Velodrome	Portland, OR
Baton Rouge Velodrome	Baton Rouge, LA
Brian Piccolo Park Velodrome	Cooper City, FL
Dick Lane Velodrome	East Point, GA
Ed Rudolph Velodrome	Northbrook, IL
Encino Velodrome	Encino, CA
Group Health Velodrome	Redmond, WA
Hellyer Park Velodrome	San Jose, CA
Kissena Park Velodrome	Queens, NY
Valley Preferred Cycling Center	Trexlertown, PA
Major Taylor Velodrome	Indianapolis, IN
Mellowdrome	Ashville, NC
Mike Walden Velodrome	Rochester Hills, MI
National Sports Center Velodrome	Blaine, MN
San Diego Velodrome	San Diego, CA
7-Eleven United States Olympic Training Center Velodrome	Colorado Springs, CO
Superdome	Frisco, TX
Washington Park Velodrome	Kenosha, WI
Penrose Park Velodrome	St. Louis, MO

The 2007 Cyclo-Cross National Championships were held in Kansas City, MO, from December 13 to 15. There were eight over-40 age group categories for men and five for women. Table 7–6 summarizes the competitors in the 2007 Cyclo-Cross National Championships.

Table 7–6
Number of Competitors at the 2007
Cyclo-Cross National Championships

Age Group	Gender	Competitors
40+ and 40–44	Men	281
45–49	Men	120
50–54	Men	71
55–59	Men	45
60–64	Men	12
65–69	Men	11
70+	Men	2
40–44	Women	19
45–49	Women	24
50–54	Women	11
55–59	Women	7
60+	Women	2

As Table 7–6 shows, of the 605 competitors, women accounted for about 10 percent of the competitors in the over-40 age groups and riders over 60 accounted for 4 percent of these competitors.

The 2007 Mountain Bike Nationals were held in West Dover, Vermont, from July 20 to 24. In the over-40 age groups, there were six events for men and six for women. Table 7–7 summarizes the number of competitors in the 2007 Mountain Bike National Championship.

Table 7–7
Number of Competitors at the
2007 Mountain Bike National Championships

Age Group	Gender	Competitors
40+	Men	150
50+	Men	65
60+	Men	14
40+	Women	31
50+	Women	2
60+	Women	0

As Table 7–7 shows, of the 262 competitors, women accounted for about 13 percent of the competitors in the over-40 age groups and riders over 60 accounted for 5 percent of these competitors.

The list of National Champion cyclists can be found in Appendix A.

How to Get Started

Skills

Riding a bicycle is a skill most people learned as a child and those that did not can pick it up fairly quickly. Cycling is a low-impact sport that is relatively kind to human joints. The fitness required to race can be developed over time. Obviously, there is a considerable gap between the skill and fitness required to ride a two-wheeler and that required for bicycle racing. But gaining the necessary skill and fitness can be a rewarding, even at times, a pleasant experience. Many clubs offer beginner races and clinics to help new riders get started.

Equipment

Most people are familiar with thin-wheel road bikes which can be purchased new for $300 to $500 and up. Custom-made bicycles with state-of-the-art components can cost many thousands of dollars. These bikes may have 15, 20, or more gears and handbrakes. Helmets, which are required by law in many states and are mandatory in bike races, cost $30 to $40. It pays to buy the best bike you can afford, since racing a lousy bike is both discouraging and uncomfortable.

Track bikes are different from conventional bicycles and track riders regard them as the purest form of the machine. The pedals are connected directly to the wheels, so there is no coasting or free-wheeling. They have no gears or brakes. The speed is controlled solely by the pedals. The cost of a track bike is comparable to a high-end road bike. Many velodromes offer rental bikes. Track bikes are very simple, but specialized, machines and new riders should try one out before even thinking of purchasing one.

Coaching

If you decide to try competitive cycling, you may want to get some coaching and USA Cycling provides a nice feature on its web site for locating certified coaches. Your local club or bike shop should be able to give you information on good coaches in your area.

Venues

Typically, road races are held on public roads. In some cases, these are closed for the race, but often not. Track races are held on specially designed facilities called velodromes. These are oval tracks made of wood, concrete, dirt, or asphalt, usually 333.3 meters in length. There are twenty-one velodromes in the United States listed in Table 7–5.

Recognition

Awards

Awards in individual races, including the National Championships, are typically given to the first three finishers in each event.

National Teams

There are no national teams for bike racers over the age of 40.

Rankings

There are no rankings for bike racers over the age of 40.

Resources

Bike Racing 101, Wenzel and Wenzel, Human Kinetics Publishers, 2003.
Bicycle Road Racing: The Complete Book for Training and Competition, Edward Borysewicz, Vitesse Press, 2005.

Major Taylor: The Extraordinary Career of a Champion Bicycle Racer, Andrew Ritchie, Bicycle Books, Inc. 1996.

No Brakes! Bicycle Track Racing in the United States, Sandra W. Sutherland, Iris Press, January, 1996.

Diving

Introduction

It might be argued that competitive diving started in Great Britain as plunging which the competitor springs from poolside and tries to travel as far as possible underwater. Britain's National Plunging Championships were held from 1883 to 1937. However, it more likely that diving evolved from gymnastics, rather than plunging or swimming. In the late 19th century, Swedish and German gymnasts preferred to land in water, rather than a hard floor and, in the summer, moved their equipment to beaches so they could land in the sea. Early diving competitions separated plain dives, including the Swedish Swallow (aka the Swan Dive) and the English Header, and fancy diving. Diving became an official sport at the 1904 St. Louis Olympics. But its beginnings were cautious. A report following the 1908 Olympiad recommended elimination of the double somersault because it was believed it could not be executed without risk of injury to the diver. But in the 1920s, fancy diving began to evolve, with dives getting more complex. Today, dives with 2½ somersaults or more are commonly performed.

Most Masters divers have competed in high school or college and want to keep fit and close to the sport. At the present time, the group of Masters competitors is relatively small— 65 men and women competed in the 2007 National Championships. But the energy and enthusiasm of the group appears strong.

National Sponsoring Organization

The governing body of the sport of diving is United States Diving (USA Diving) which oversees all diving, from junior programs to Olympic diving, and includes Masters diving.

USA Diving
132 E. Washington St., Suite 850
Indianapolis, IN 46204
(317) 237-5252
www.usadiving.org

The sport of diving also has an organization for veteran competitors, U.S. Masters Diving, that includes among its dozen objectives:

• To enhance fellowship among participants in Masters programs.
• To promote United States diving throughout age group, senior, and masters programs.
• To propose proper diving training for older age groups.

A Masters diver, according to U.S. Masters Diving, is anyone over 21 years of age, although the international diving organization, FINA, requires masters divers to be 25 before they can compete in sanctioned meets.

For 2008, there are three levels of athlete membership to USA Diving:

• Competitive Gold membership, allowing entry into all meets, for $75;
• Competitive Blue Membership, allowing entry into association and invitational meets, for $20; and
• Limited Athlete Members, for entry into camps and clinics, for $12.

An annual U.S. subscription to *Inside Diving* is an additional $12. USA Diving's Masters secretary is Alex Lapidus. U.S. Masters Diving has its own web site at www.mastersdiving.com, which includes a newsletter at no cost.

The adult diving program for the U.S. Amateur Athletic Union (AAU) divides divers into three categories:

1. Open, for divers that want to compete at the elite level; no age restrictions
2. Masters, for divers that no longer wish to compete in open meets; elite divers must compete within their natural age groups.
3. Masters-B, for divers who are not ready to compete with the full list of dives but still wish to compete.

For more information on the AAU program, see http://aausports.org/sprt_Aquatics.asp ?a=sprt_Diving_AdultMasters.html.

Competitive Opportunities

Diving organizes competitive classes using the following criteria:

• Gender: men, women, and, in some events, mixed.
• Events, including 1-meter, 3-meter, platform, and synchronized diving. A number of different dives, of varying difficulties, are required for each event.
• Age groups, which may be in five- or 10-year increments depending on the demographics of the entries.

USA Diving has a find-a-club locator on its web site to enable interested parties to locate a club in their state. According to USA Diving, there are 42 Local Diving Associations (LDAs) and more than 300 local diving clubs offering coaching and sponsoring competitions. Table 8–1 lists the major Masters diving meets of 2008.

Table 8–1
2008 Major Masters Diving Meets

Meet	Location	Date
Masters Spring Nationals	U. of Tennessee; Knoxville, TN	May 17–19
Masters Summer Nationals	Woodlands; Houston, TX	Aug. 22–24
Dare To Dream Invitational	Waipahu, HI	Jan. 5–6
Huntsville Winter Invitational	Huntsville, AL	Jan. 19
David Nielsen Invitational	Fort Lauderdale, FL	Feb. 16
Tara Tarpon Winter Invitational	Jonesboro, GA	March 8

For more information on scheduled meets consult the USA Diving web site.

Competitive Landscape

To provide one example of the level of participation in masters diving meets, see the results of the 2007 Masters Summer Nationals, held at the Nassau County Aquatic Center in Long Island, New York, from September 15 to 17. Four events were offered: 1-meter, 3-meter, platform, and synchronized diving. The number of entries for each event and age group are presented in Table 8–2.

Table 8–2
2007 Summer Masters National Diving Championship

Age Groups	1-Meter	3-Meter	Platform[1]	Synchronized[2]
40–44—Women	2	3	0	0
45–49—Women	7	5	4	0
50–54—Women	3	2	0	4
55–59—Women	3	2	2	0
60–64—Women	1	1	0	0
65–69—Women	1	1	1	2
70–74—Women	1	0	0	0
75–79—Women	3	1	2	0
Subtotal Women	**21**	**15**	**9**	**6**
40–44—Men	5	4	0	0
45–49—Men	6	4	5	0
50–54—Men	2	2	0	4
55–59—Men	1	1	2	0
60–64—Men	2	2	0	0
65–69—Men	3	2	3	6
70–74—Men	1	1	0	0
75–79—Men	3	3	2	0
80–84—Men	1	2	1	0
Subtotal Men	**24**	**21**	**20**	**10**
Total	**45**	**36**	**29**	**16**

1 *The age group categories for the platform event were in 10-year increments and the number of entries for platform is shown in the age groups ending in "9."*

2 *The age group categories for the synchronized diving event were in 15-year increments and the number of entries for synchronized diving is shown in the age groups ending in "0." For example, the number of competitors in the 50–64 age group is shown at 50. Also, the 10 competitors shown under "Men" were actually in the mixed synchronized diving.*

There were a total of 118 competitors (each competitor could enter multiple events). Of the 118 entries, 47 percent were women and 53 percent were men, and 38 percent of the entries were competitors over 60.

How to Get Started

Skills

Competitive diving requires balance, strength, and great body control. It is not a skill that is learned quickly. If you did not dive or do gymnastics in high school or college, it will be very challenging to become a competitive diver in your adult years. There are surely a few exceptions to this statement, but not many. For those athletes that did dive in high school or college and want to return, many local associations provide training and coaching.

Equipment

A bathing suit.

Coaching

USA Diving has a national coaching scheme, but most coaches are focused on youth or aspiring Olympic divers. However, coaches might be willing to help a Masters diver get back in shape and learn a few new tricks.

Venues

USA Diving's Find-a-Club tool can be used to find pools where diving is taught and practiced.

Recognition

Awards

Typically, awards are given to the first three places in a diving meet. In addition, grand masters awards are given at the national meets to men and women based on total scores on multiple events. The list of winners at the 2007 Summer Masters Nationals is presented in Appendix A.

National Teams

USA Masters Diving does not sponsor a national masters team, nor do they select Masters All-Americans.

Rankings

USA Masters Diving does not rank age group divers.

Resources

In addition to the USA diving and U.S. Masters Diving web sites, you might try an instructional manual:

Springboard & Platform Diving; Ronald F. O'Brien, Human Kinetics Publishing, 2002.

And an account by the greatest U.S. male diver in history, *Breaking the Surface*; Greg Louganis; Plume Books, 1996.

Fencing

Introduction

Fencing is a fast-twitch muscle sport with a rich history that runs from the Egyptians and Romans, through Spanish, Italian, and French fencing masters, to the modern Olympics. Today's competitive fencing requires that a fencer touch his opponent as many as 15 times in a bout, earning a point each time, to eventually win the bout. The bouts involve one of three weapons:

- The *foil*, the lightest of the weapons (17 ounces), began as a training tool for duelists. Points can be scored with the tip of the foil and only on the torso (no cutting or slashing, no touches on the arms, legs, or head).
- The *epee*, French for sword, is heaviest of the three (27 ounces). Points can be scored only with the tip of the epee, but touches may be scored on any part of the body.
- The *saber*, evolved from the scimitar and cutlass, weighs slightly more than the foil. Points can be scored by the edge, as well as the tip of the weapon.

Because only the tip of the foil and epee can score points, these bouts favor a patient, defensive strategy. On the other hand, the saber favors an aggressive, attacking strategy in which bouts may last only a few seconds. Although the weapons are obviously essential to fencing, La Boessiere, a late 18th century French fencing master, hastened the transition from fencing as combat to fencing as sport with his invention of the fencing mask.

How would an Olympic fencer fare in a duel to the death with a 16th century fencing master of comparable skill? Although the Olympian might be at a psychological disadvantage, having fought only for touches and points, rather than blood and life, the skills required would be comparable and the bout might be quite even.

For the modern Masters Athlete, modern fencing offers an unusual, but demanding opportunity to compete.

National Sponsoring Organization

The national governing body of fencing in the United States is USA Fencing.
The United States Fencing Association (USFA)
One Olympic Plaza
Colorado Springs, CO 80909
(719) 866-4511
mailto:info@USFencing.org
http://www.usfencing.org/

A veteran membership in USFA is $60 per year and the USFA publishes an online magazine, *American Fencing Magazine*.

The USFA operates through ten sections and many divisions within these sections. The sections, and the states they cover, are listed in Table 9–1. Many of the USFA divisions have their own web sites as well.

Table 9–1
USFA Sections

Section/Web site	States
Great Lakes Section www.columbusfencing.org/gls/about.html	IN, OH, MI, KY
Midwest Section www.mws-usfa.org/	IL, IA, MN, WI, MO
Rocky Mountain Section www.rockymountainfencing.org/rms/	AZ, CO, KS, TX, WY, NM, NE
Mid-Atlantic Section www.midatlanticfencing.com	PA, NJ, MD, DC
Pacific Coast Section http://pcsfencing.wordpress.com	CA, HI, NV

Section/Web site	States
Southwest Section	
www.southwestfencing.org/	TX, LA, MS, AR, OK
North Atlantic Section	
www.nas-usfa.org/	CT, MA, RI, VT, NH, ME, NY
Southeast Section	
www.nas-usfa.org/	AL, FL, VA, SC, NC, GA, TN
Pacific Northwest Section	OR, AK, UT, ID, WA, MT
pnwsection.com/	
Metropolitan Section	New York City
www.metrodivision.com/	

The USFA web site also has a Find-A-Club locator on its web site at http://www.usfencing.org/usfa/content/category/7/325/80/. Clubs are listed by state.

The Veterans Committee of USA Fencing (USA Veterans Fencing) oversees programs and competitions for athletes over 40. Their slogan—"We have fun—but we keep score!" suggests the balance between enjoyment and serious competition that the Veterans Committee is seeking. The e-mail address for USA Veterans Fencing is www.usaveteransfencing.org.

Competitive Opportunities

The criteria used to determine fencing's competitive divisions include:

- The type of weapon. The foil, epee, and saber are described more fully on the USFA web site at http://www.usfencing.org/usfa/content/view/1569/108/.
- Gender: Men and women
- Age: Veteran divisions are 40+, 50+, and 60+ for both men and women. A proposal to add a 70+ division is under review by the Veterans Committee.
- Classification: Fencing classifications reflect the skill level of the fencer from A (the highest) to E (the novice). They are determined by the results of USFA-sanctioned events in which the fencer competes and may be valid for up to four years.

Regional and local fencing competitions for veterans which can be found on the section and division web sites.

Competitive Landscape

There are several hundred veteran fencers in the United States that compete regularly in local, regional, and national competitions. Table 9–2 summarizes the number of competitors at the 2007 Summer Nationals held in Miami, Florida, from June 29 to July 8. As is often the case, competitors may enter more than one discipline and may also compete down, so that a 60 year old could enter events in the 50 to 59 age group classes.

Table 9–2
Number of Competitors in the 2007 Summer Fencing Nationals

Event	Age Group Class	Male Competitors	Female Competitors
Epee	40–49	60	24
Epee	50–59	55	26

Event	Age Group Class	Male Competitors	Female Competitors
Epee	60–69	26	6
Foil	40–49	45	33
Foil	50–59	39	26
Foil	60–69	24	6
Saber	40–49	15	14
Saber	50–59	24	17
Saber	60–69	16	5

As these results indicate, women represent 34 percent of the 461 competitors, and men and women over 60 years of age represent 18 percent of the total.

USA Veterans Fencing also calculates and publishes age group rankings. Table 9–3 shows the number of ranked fencers for each discipline in each age group.

Table 9–3
Number of Competitors in the 2007 Summer Fencing Nationals[1]

Event	Age Group Class	Ranked Men	Ranked Women
Epee	40–49	79	54
Epee	50–59	90	44
Epee	60–69	55	12
Foil	40–49	71	51
Foil	50–59	65	43
Foil	60–69	38	10
Saber	40–49	35	32
Saber	50–59	57	23
Saber	60–69	26	9
Total		**516**	**278**

1 *As of March 11, 2008.*

Women represent 35 percent of the 794 ranked fencers, and fencers over 60 represent 19 percent of all ranked veterans.

How to Get Started

Skills

Fencing calls for quickness and laser-like focus. Originally, there was no time limit for fencing bouts, until a Masters championship bout in New York in 1930 lasted for seven hours. Today, matches are limited to three minutes for five-touch bouts, and nine minutes for 15-touch bouts. However, the action is intense and unrelenting.

Equipment

A novice may be able to borrow equipment (weapon, mask, jacket, gloves, etc.) from a club where fencing is taught. Purchased new, the cost of this equipment is significant. A beginner's equipment (jacket, gloves, mask, weapon) may cost $300 to $400. More sophisticated advanced equipment will cost thousands of dollars.

Coaching

Given the intricate rules of fencing, as well as the strategy and tactics needed to compete successfully, coaching is even more critical than in many sports. The United States Fencing Coaches Association (USFCA) sponsors a three-level coaching certification program and a list of certified coaches can be found on the USFCA web site http://www.usfca.org/usfca/.

Venues

Fencing clubs are the appropriate places to find the equipment, coaching, and other facilities necessary to compete. Clubs can be located by state on the USFA web site at http://www.usfencing.org/usfa/content/category/7/325/80/.

Recognition

Awards

In major competitions, the top three fencers in each division receive awards—gold, silver, and bronze.

National Teams

Although the USFA does select a national team, there are no national veteran teams or age group teams.

Rankings

The USFA does rank veteran fencers and the number of veterans ranked in 2007 is shown in Table 9–3. The names of all ranked fencers can be found on the USFA web site and in Appendix A.

Resources

Fencing: Techniques for Foil, Epee and Saber, Brian Pitman, Crowood Press, 1988.
Fencing: The Skills of the Game, Henry de Silva, Crowood Press, 1997.
The required and recommended reading for USFCA coaching certification can be found at http://www.usfca.org/usfca/misc/USFCAreadinglist.doc.

Handball

Introduction

Handball is basic, elemental, gladiatorial. No racquets or paddles; no net or out-of-bounds. Just two competitors in a 20' by 40' room with a small black ball and their wits. Like most sports, after a measure of skill is attained, the competition becomes psychological. That's why the strongest or fastest or quickest players don't always win. In handball, because of its elemental nature, the psychological element quickly becomes prominent. It is an ideal sport for those who wish to cultivate their will to win. The sport calls itself "The Perfect Game."

The national sponsoring organization of handball in the United States is working hard to broaden competitive opportunities, particularly among younger players and, as one of the most male-dominated sports considered here, it is also seeking ways to promote handball for women.

National Sponsoring Organization

The United States Handball Association (USHA) is the governing body for the sport of handball in the United States.

United States Handball Association
2333 N. Tucson Blvd.
Tucson, AZ 85716
(520) 795-0434
Vern Roberts—executive director
handball@ushandball.org
http://ushandball.org/

USHA's mission is to "organize, promote, and spread the joy of Handball—The Perfect Game." The 2008 membership fee is $40, which allows discounts on all USHA merchandise, discounted fees for sanctioned tournaments, and a subscription to *Handball Magazine*. The USHA sanctions more than 100 handball tournaments each year. The USHA operates through regional associations which are listed in Table 10–1.

Table 10–1
USHA Regional Associations

Regional Association	States	Members
Central Region	IL, IA, KS, MN, MO, NB, ND	1,209
Mid-American	IN, KY, OH, PA	490
Mid-Atlantic	MD/DC, DE, VA	233
Northeast	CT, ME, MA, NH, NJ, NY, RI	1,137
NorCal/SoCal	CA, NV, HI	1,531
Northwest	AK, ID, MT, OR, WA	779
Rocky Mountain	AZ, CO, NM, UT, WY	684
Southeast	AL, FL, GA, MS, NC, SC, TN	642
Southwest	AR, LA, OK, TX	561

The states with the greatest number of USHA members are California (1,218), New York (944), and Texas (399). Contact information, regional tournaments, a court and player locator, and news are available for each region on the USHA web site, under Regional Info.

Competitive Opportunities

Handball can be played as a one-wall, three-wall, or four-wall game. Adult player classifications may be based on any of the following criteria:

• Game—one-wall, three-wall, four-wall
• Gender—Men, women. Handball doesn't include a mixed doubles class. However, there were no competitors in over–40 age groups for women in any of the 2007 national championships.
• Number of Competitors—Singles or doubles
• Skill Level—Open and B. There is also a professional circuit

• Age Groups—from 35 to 80 in five-year increments, although not all age groups are represented in every tournament.

Like many sports offering age group categories, handball uses its own nomenclature for distinguishing among the categories. Here are the terms for its age groups used in the 2007 National Three-Wall Championships:

Seniors	35+
Masters	40+
Veteran Masters	45+
Golden	50+
Veteran Golden	55+
Super	60+
Veteran Super	65+
Diamond	70+

There are more than 100 handball tournaments sanctioned by the USHA, including two national championships specifically for Masters (35+). Table 10–2 lists these tournaments.

Table 10–2
2008 Major Handball Tournaments

Tournament	Location	Date
USHA Women's Classic	Syosset, NY	Jan. 24–27
USHA Masters National Doubles	San Diego, CA	March 6–9
USHA Masters National Singles	Houston, TX	April 18–20
Canadian 4-Wall Nationals	Calgary, Alberta	May 14–17
USHA National 4-Wall Championship	Overland Park, KS	June 16–22
USHA National 1-Wall Championship	Brooklyn, NY	July 30–Aug. 3
USHA National 3-Wall Championship	Maumee, OH	Aug. 30–Sept. 1

Competitive Landscape

Competitive handball in the United States is currently a male-dominated sport. For example, there were no competitive classes for women over 40 in any of the 2007 Handball National Championships. However, the USHA does have a women's commissioner, Lea Ann Martin, who is working to promote women's handball. There are many women under 40 who are playing handball, Clearly, the field is wide open for good adult women handball players.

Four national championships have been used here to assess the competitive landscape of handball:

• The 2007 National Masters Singles Championship in Dallas, Texas
• The 2007 National Masters Doubles Championship in Overland Park, Kansas
• The 2007 National Three-Wall Championships in Maumee, Ohio
• The 2007 National Four Wall Championships in Minneapolis, Minnesota

These four tournaments attracted approximately 740 entries in the over–40 classes. The number of entries in these tournaments for each class is shown in Table 10–3. None of these tournaments included over–40 age group classes for women.

Table 10–3
Competitors in 2007 National Handball Championships

Age Group Classes[1]	Masters Singles	Masters Doubles	National Three-Wall	National Four-Wall
40+	4	14	48	30
45+	7	12	13	29
50+	15	22	70	48
55+	0	32	15	45
60+	10	28	36	46
65+	12	14	12	51
70+	9	16	23	31
75+	6	12	5	19
80+	0	0	0	4

1 Age group totals include singles, doubles, and "B" classes.

Of the total of 740 entries, 45 percent of these entries were competitors over 60 years of age. For competitors over 40, the largest of the four tournaments was the National Four-Wall with 305 entries and the smallest was the Masters Singles with 62 entries.

The key to finding local and regional tournaments is to locate a facility near you with handball courts where players congregate. Clubs, particularly in metropolitan areas, will often sponsor tournaments. Table 10–4 lists a selection of regional and state handball associations.

Table 10–4
Selected Local, Regional, and State Handball Associations

Association	Web site
New York City Handball	www.nychandball.com/
InnerCity Handball Association	www.icha.org/
Illinois Handball Association	www.illinoishandball.org/
Greater Cincinnati Handball Association	www.gcha.org/
Northern California Handball Association	norcalhandball.org/
Southern California Handball Association	www.handball.org/
Minnesota Handball Association	home.comcast.net/~mnhandball/
Colorado Handball Association	www.cohandball.com/
Pacific Northwest Handball Association	http://pnwhandball.org

For assistance in finding clubs, courts and players, use the locator on the USHA web site at http://www.ushandball.org/component/option.com_mtree_/task.listcats/cat_id.42/Itemid.219/.

How to Get Started

Skills

Although the rudiments of handball are not difficult to pick up, mastering the game takes a lifetime. Hand-eye coordination is critical. Although a handball is hit with less force than the ball in racquet sports, players are required to get closer to the ball in order to hit it. As a result, the players must be fit in order to play the game well. One of the greatest challenges in handball is learning to use your weak hand. Since a good handball player must be ambidextrous, players who cannot play the ball on both sides will find their opponents exploiting this weakness. Good coaching and lots of practice are essential.

Equipment

- Protective eyewear, gloves, and a ball are all that this sport requires.
- Handball—$11 per ball for the USHA ball; $8 for USHA members
- Gloves—$20 to $25 a pair
- Eye Guards—$15 to $20

Coaching

Information on teaching and coaching handball can be found on the USHA web site at http://www.ushandball.org/content/view/364/250/.

Venues

Inquire at your local YMCA or fitness club about the availability of handball courts.

There are 137 clubs with handball courts listed on the USHA web site. Forty-one states have at least one club listed and the states with the most clubs are California, New York, and New Mexico.

Recognition

Awards

Typically, awards are given to the winners and runners-up in each competitive classification. Some tournaments offer consolation brackets for players that lose in the first round and the winners of these brackets also receive awards.

National Teams

The USHA does not name a national age group handball team.

Rankings

Although the USHA publishes rankings in the professional circuit, age group players are not ranked.

Resources

Handball Handbook: Strategies and Techniques; Lance Lowy; American Press, 1991 (Available on the USHA web site or amazon.com).

The USHA sells instructional videos and videos of recent tournament play on its web site at http://www.ushandball.org/Merchant2/merchant.mvc?Screen=CTGY&Category_Code =V.

Ice Hockey

Introduction

Rushing up ice with the puck inches off your stick, a defenseman feints and pokes his stick to throw you off stride. As you cross the blue line, your right winger enters your peripheral vision and you move left; the defenseman slides toward you and the goalie slides right to narrow your angle. A slick pass to your right leaves just enough of the goal open for your winger to lift the puck past the goalie's outstretched glove. Delightful!

Because most adult ice hockey forbids checking, the game is fast, flowing, and safe. The growth of the sport has been fueled by two organizations dedicated to promoting and supporting adult hockey. It appears that participation in competitive ice hockey, especially among girls and women, is growing rapidly across the country.

National Sponsoring Organization

There are two major sponsoring organizations for men's adult hockey in the United States. Hockey North America (HNA) was established in 1980. It is a full service association, sponsoring multi-team leagues in both the fall and winter and spring and summer in the U.S. and Canada and its league championships draws 1,500 competitors. In addition, it sponsors tournaments in North America and Europe. During the 2007 to 2008 season, HNA members played over 5,000 hockey games.

Hockey North America (HNA)
P.O. Box 78
Sterling, VA 20167
Phone: (703) 430-8100
Fax: (703) 421-9205
Player Registration: (800) 446-2539
HNASUPPORT@aol.com
www.hna.com

HNA does not offer individual memberships, but registers teams in one of its leagues.

The other national organization is the adult hockey program with USA Hockey, the governing body for hockey in the United States. Although USA Hockey does not run leagues, the benefits to members and affiliated leagues include:

- Access to USA Hockey-sponsored tournaments (see below)
- Coaching manuals and certification for coaches
- Various educational videos and materials
- Official rulebook; and
- A growing competitive hockey program for women

Adults may register for an annual fee of $30. There are currently 103,533 adult players registered with USA Hockey.

USA Hockey
1775 Bob Johnson Drive
Colorado Springs, CO 80906
Coordinator of Adult Hockey: Ashley Bevan

(719) 576-8724
ashleyb@usahockey.org
www.usahockey.com/adult/main

USA Hockey is divided into 12 districts with 34 affiliate hockey organizations, mostly state or regional associations. Each district registers teams and officials, organizes clinics and educational programs for coaches, and a risk manager to oversee insurance and safety. Table 11–5 presents the districts, the number of registered adult players in each district, and the district web site.

Women's ice hockey may be the fastest growing segment of this sport. In addition to the women's program offered through USA Hockey, there are a number of other organizations sponsoring and supporting women's hockey. Table 11–1 lists some of the most active women's ice hockey organizations. Some of these leagues are affiliated with USA Hockey.

Table 11–1
Women's Ice Hockey Organizations

Organization	States	Web site
United Women's Hockey League	PA, DE, NJ	www.uwhl.org/
Mid-Atlantic Women's Hockey League	PA, DC, DE	www.mawhl.org/
Michigan Senior Women Hockey League	MI	www.mswhl.com
Northern California Women's Hockey League	CA	www.ncwhl.com

One of the best ways to locate local ice hockey leagues and tournaments is by contacting your nearest ice arena. A Web site called www.arenamaps.com/ locates and provides maps for ice arenas throughout North America. The web site allows searches by state or province, city, or arena name. For example, requesting arenas in Massachusetts results in 146 ice arenas with maps, directions, and contact information. The same site also has a tournament directory for the U.S. and Canada.

Competitive Opportunities

The HNA sponsors leagues in 14 cities and offers competition at range of skill levels, including a beginner league in many cities. Divisions are divided by skill level and players may move up or down as their skills improve or deteriorate. The number of divisions and teams indicate the depth of the HNA league in that area. Table 11–2 presents the number of arenas, divisions, and teams for the 2007 to 2008 HNA season.

Table 11–2
2007–2008 HNA Cities and Teams[1]

City	Arenas	Divisions	Teams
Boston, MA (w/sm)	4	7	26
Calgary, AB (w)	7	12	62
Chicago, IL (w/sm)	4	7	36
Cleveland, OH (w/sm)	6	5	20
Detroit, MI (w/sm)	3	4	25
Minneapolis (w/sm)	4	1	7
New Jersey (w/sm)	5	4	28
New York-Westchester (w/sm)	6	5	22
Philadelphia, PA (w/sm)	4	2	10
Rockville, MD (w)	1	2	9
St. Louis, MO (w/sm)	4	6	30

City	Arenas	Divisions	Teams
Vancouver, BC (w)	2	3	17
Washington, DC (w/sp/sm)	5	9	55

1 The seasons in which the leagues are active are noted in parentheses— "w" is winter, "sp" is spring, and "sm" is summer. The arenas, divisions, and teams shown in the table are for the winter leagues.

The HNA web site includes a link to the league in each city, the location and maps of arenas, league statistics, and a link to each team.

The HNA also sponsors a number of hockey tournaments throughout the year, including the league championships. Table 11–3 lists the 2008 HNA tournaments with the location and dates.

Table 11–3
2008 HNA Ice Hockey Tournaments

Tournament	Location	Date
Winter League Finals (Upper Tiers)	Las Vegas, NV	June 13–15
Winter League Finals (Lower Tiers)	Toronto, Ontario	May 30–June 1
Calgary Slush Cup	Calgary, Alberta	May
European Tournament	Amsterdam, Holland	March 21–23
Chicago Tournament	Chicago, IL	May
Atlantic City I	Atlantic City, NJ	April 4–6
Atlantic City II	Atlantic City, NJ	April 11–13

USA Hockey does not run leagues, but it does support them by providing a standard set of rules, league operations software, by running hockey skills clinics, and by certifying coaches. It also sponsors a series of adult hockey tournaments, national championships and adult classics which are listed in Table 11–4.

Table 11–4
USA Hockey 2008 Adult National Championship Tournaments

Tournament	Location	Date
Labatt Blue U.S. Adult Nationals Elite, Full Check	Fond du Lac, WI	April 3–6
Labatt Blue U.S. Adult Nationals U.S. Full Check	Fond du Lac, WI	April 3–6
Labatt Blue U.S. Adult Nationals Elite, No Check	Denver, CO	April 17–20
Labatt Blue U.S. Adult Nationals 40 & Over	Naples, FL	April 10–13
Labatt Blue U.S. Adult Nationals 50 & Over	Brandon, FL	April 24–27
Labatt Blue U.S. Adult Nationals 60 & Over	Ellenton, FL	April 24–27
Labatt Blue U.S. Adult Nationals Recreational	Minneapolis, MN	May 15–18
U.S. Adult Classic, Summer Suburban	Lansing, MI	Feb. 22–24
U.S. Adult Classic, Incredible Ice	Ft. Lauderdale, FL	March 28–30
U.S. Adult Classic, IWSA	Indianapolis, IN	March 28–30
U.S. Adult Classic, Dr. Pepper Star Center	Dallas, TX	April 11–13
U.S. Adult Classic, Regency Sports Rink	Lancaster, PA	April 18–20
U.S. Adult Classic, Subway/Dempsey	Anchorage, AK	April 24–27
U.S. Adult Classic, Chiller Rinks	Columbus, OH	May 2–4
U.S. Adult Classic, Ice Vault	Wayne, NJ	May 2–4
U.S. Adult Classic, Wings Stadium	Kalamazoo, MI	May 16–18
U.S. Adult Classic, Gardens Ice House	Laurel, MD	May 16–18
U.S. Adult Classic, Edge/Family Sports	Denver, CO	May 30–June 1

All classic tournaments include multiple divisions, including women's divisions. A minimum of four teams are necessary to form a division.

USA Hockey also sponsored the Labatt Blue three-on-three adult hockey championship at the Great Lakes Sports City Arena in Detroit, MI, from June 13 to 15. The Labatt Blue USA Hockey Pond Hockey Championship were held from February 15 to 17 on Dollar Lake in Eagle River, WI. It was sold out, with nine divisions and 142 teams.

The HNA and USA Hockey national champions are listed in Appendix A.

Competitive Landscape

The number of adult hockey teams and leagues operating in the U.S. means that, at the highest levels, adult hockey is highly competitive. At the same time, both HNA and USA Hockey have structured their adult hockey programs to accommodate less skilled players and novices, as well as providing clinics to teach hockey skills to novices. Table 11–5 lists the 12 USA Hockey districts and the number of players in each district.

Table 11–5
USA Hockey Districts with Number of Registered Adult Players[1]
(2006/2007)

District	Registered Adult Players	Web sites[2]
Atlantic	7,186	www.usahockey.com/atlantic_1/default.aspx
Central	8,646	www.usahockey.com/central_district/default.aspx
Massachusetts	2,224	www.masshockey.com
Michigan	15,200	www.maha.org/
Mid-America	5,567	www.midamhockey.com/
Minnesota	5,514	www.minnesotahockey.org/
New England	3,528	www.usahockey.com/new_england/default.aspx
New York	7,869	www.usahockey.com/new_york/default/aspx
Northern Plains	NA	www.usahockey.com/northerplains/
Pacific	18,734	www.usahockey.com/pacific_distr2/default.aspx
Rocky Mountain	14,527	www.usahockey.com/rocky_mountain_distr/
Southeastern	14,556	www.usahockey.com/southeast48/

1 Adult players are those over 20 years of age.

2 Some of these web sites were under construction as of 12/2008.

A total of 457,038 players are registered with USA Hockey and 57,549 of these are girls and women. Five years ago, adult players represented approximately 17 percent of all registered players. In 2006 and 2007 adult players represented 23 percent of all registered players. Adult hockey programs are growing.

The 2007 National over–40 age group champions for Hockey North America and USA Hockey are listed in Appendix A. The number of teams that competed in the various divisions of these championships was not available.

How to Get Started

Skills

Ice hockey requires considerable skill and a high degree of team play. Previous experience ice skating is, of course, very valuable. For adults who have never played before, even if they have ice skated, beginner's schools and clinics like those offered by HNA and USA Hockey are highly recommended (see Coaching).

Equipment

Ice hockey is an equipment-intensive sport. Skates, pads, sticks, helmets, gloves and accessories can cost more than $1,000 if purchased new. There are many hockey exchange sales and second-hand sports equipment stores in most cities.

Coaching

HNA and USA Hockey offer beginners' schools and clinics. Two USA Hockey skills clinics were held in 2008, and the NHA offers beginners hockey schools—for information, contact them at 1-800-4-Hockey. Most adult teams are self-coached with the more experienced players acting as player-coaches.

Venues

Hockey leagues charge a fee which includes both referees and ice time at a rink. Because ice time is limited, adult leagues in areas where hockey or skating is popular may play very late at night.

Recognition

Awards

Leagues offer championship tournaments and there are a variety of regional and national tournaments (see above) available to teams who wish to compete against teams from other areas. HNA and USA Hockey recognize national champions in their various divisions. These are listed in Appendix A.

USA Hockey presents an annual award, USAdult Ironman of the Year for outstanding performance by an American-born player during the season.

National Teams

Neither the HNA nor USA Hockey selects adult national teams.

Rankings

Neither the HNA nor USA Hockey calculate and publish national rankings for hockey teams.

Resources

Basic Hockey and Skating Skills, Jeremy Rose, Polestar Calendars, 1994.

Hockey Drills for Passing and Receiving, Gwozdecky and Stenlund, Human Kinetics Publishing, 1999.

Complete Conditioning for Ice Hockey, Peter Twist, Human Kinetics Publishing, 1996.

USA Hockey offers tapes and books on hockey skills and strategy at http://www.usa-hockey.com//Template_Usahockey.aspx?NAV=AU_10&ID=29002.

Orienteering

Introduction

Orienteering is a sport in which getting lost is an option. No one really gets lost for good, but competitors, and not always beginners, may be asking themselves, "Where in the woods am I?" In fact, that is the essence of this underappreciated sport. Setting off into unfamiliar territory, often alone, with only a map and a compass (no GPS, please), locating a series of orange and white cloth controls, and doing it as quickly as possible is the challenge. Learning to find your way, to navigate around swamps, through forests and over mountains can be very rewarding.

By the end of the 19th century, with maps and compasses in common use, most armies commonly set navigation tasks for their soldiers. This was serious business, not a sport. Then, in 1918, a Swedish scout leader and retired army major named Ernst Killander became concerned about the declining interest in track and field and developed a series of running projects for his charges. He created a series of competitions in the Swedish countryside in which each boy was given a map and compass and asked to negotiate a specific course. The mental challenge of finding the various points on the course and the physical challenge of doing it at a run proved immensely popular. The sport grew first in Scandinavia and then spread through Europe. Bjorn Kjellstrom introduced orienteering to the U.S. in 1946, but it was not until 1964 that there was an international organization consisting of eleven European countries. The United States Orienteering Federation was founded in 1971. Kjellstrom also founded the Silva Company, one of the leading compass manufacturers in the world.

It is paradoxical that a sport that presents such fascinating technical and mental challenges is one of the most primitive in terms of equipment and venues. I'm jogging through a pine forest, hoping I'm headed in the right direction. I check the map and the landscape for collecting features—a stone wall, a pond, a hill—that might confirm my hunch.

Recognizing the landscape features is essential. The compass should be used only to orient the map. Bob Putnam, a veteran competitor, says, "Orienteering is a map game. It teaches, instills, and requires the development of map literacy. It is not a compass game." Of course to me, every hummock looks like a hill and stone walls seem to be everywhere. But then, through the underbrush, I see the flash of orange and white; it's the control I'm seeking. This moment of triumph and satisfaction, repeated a dozen or more times in a typical orienteering course, is my reward. But these are the thoughts of a rank beginner. Elite competitors are thinking several marks ahead and figuring out how to shave a few seconds off their time. In both cases, the mental and physical challenges are why orienteering calls itself "The Thinking Sport."

National Sponsoring Organization

The national governing body for this sport is the US Orienteering Federation (USOF) with approximately 1,400 family and individual members.

US Orienteering Federation
PO Box 1444
Forest Park, GA 30298
rshannonhouse@mindspring.com
http://www.us.orienteering.org/

USOF has 55 member clubs in eight geographic regions that are shown in Table 12–1. The best way to contact your local club is through the Internet (most have web sites or e-mail addresses, or both). You can also contact the representatives listed below and many of the clubs are listed on the USOF web site.

Table 12–1
USOF Regions

Region	States with Local Clubs	Contact/E-mail
Heartland	CO, IL, KS, MN, MO, WI, WY	Ian Harding iriharding@aol.com
Mid-Atlantic	DE, NJ, PA, VA, DC, MD	Jim Eagleton eagleton@alum.mit.edu
Midwest	IN, KY, MI, OH	Eric Tullis indyjeneric@yahoo.com
Northeast	CT, ME, NH, VT, RI, MA, ME, NY	Joanne Sankus jsankus@aol.com
Northwest	AK, ID, OR, WA	Scott Drumm sdrumm@pacifier.com
Pacific	AZ, CA, NV	David Irving daveirving@earthlink.net
Southeast	AL, FL, GA, NC	Jim Hall tsugaspur@hughes.ne
Southwest	LA, NM, TX	Ralph Courtney courtneyrj@cableone.net

Annual individual membership fee in the USOF is $30. Membership benefits include reduced fees at meets and a one-year subscription to *Orienteering North America*, a monthly magazine. Many of the member clubs have their own newsletters as well.

Orienteering has been adapted to many other forms of locomotion and a list of these other O events and the relevant web site are shown in Table 12–2.

Table 12–2
Alternative Orienteering Events

Event	Web site
Canoe Orienteering	www.geocities.com/canoeo/
Mountain Biking Orienteering	www.comtecil.demon.co.uk/index/trailque/index.htm
Trail Orienteering	www.trailo.org/
Ski Orienteering	www.xcski.org/
Horseback Orienteering	www.nacmo.org/

Competitive Opportunities

Hundreds of local orienteering meets are held each year. Three factors are used to design competitive classes and each factor has several variables:

- Gender—There are classes for men, women, and teams
- Age Group—Classes in five-year increments are used in most meets
- Course Difficulty—Courses can be offered at levels of difficulty. Each level is given a different color.

Table 12–3 shows the seven levels of difficulty, including typical course length, and the age groups that usually compete at each level.

Table 12–3
Orienteering Courses

Course	Difficulty	Length (km)	Age Group
White	Beginner	2 to 3	F/M—10, F/M—12
Yellow	Advanced Beginner	3 to 5	F/M—14
Orange	Intermediate	4.5 to 7	F/M—16
Brown	Advanced	3 to 4	F—18, 50+, 55+, 60+, 65+, 70+ M—65+, 70+
Green	Advanced	3.5 to 7	F—20, 35+, 40+, 45+ M—18, 50+, 55+, 60+
Red	Advanced	6 to 10	F—21+; M—20+, 35+, 40+, 45+
Blue	Advanced	8—14	M—21+

Because each orienteering course takes place in different terrain, it is impossible to describe the precise difference between, for example, a Green course and a Red course. However, the challenges of more difficult courses involve course length, placing controls in less obvious locations and using terrain to create navigational problems ("Do I run directly through this swamp or take the longer, drier way around it?").

Orienteering is a very beginner-friendly sport. Almost every meet offers instruction to novices. Maps are included in the modest entry fee, and compasses are usually available to borrow or rent. You just have to show up.

Orienteering began as a shoes-on-the-turf activity and most meets continue to involve running through the woods (Foot-O). However, the sport has broadened its appeal by developing competitions using other modes of travel including skis (Ski-O), mountain bikes (Bike-O), canoes (Canoe-O), and even horses. It is not difficult to imagine that these hybrids have been a source of one of the fastest growing pursuits in the country—adventure racing.

Another variation on the orienteering theme is the rogaine, an acronym for "rugged outdoor group activity involving navigation and endurance." As the name implies, rogaining is a team activity in which groups of two to five visit as many controls as possible in a period of 12 to 24 hours. A rogaine course, set over a large area, has a starting point, a finish, and enough controls to keep teams from getting to all of them in the allotted time. The team visiting the most controls, thereby amassing the most points, in the allotted time wins. Rogaining demands orienteering skills of a very high order and is not the place for beginners to enter the sport.

The USOF sponsored a series of A meets and national championship events in 2008 and they are listed in Table 12–4.

Table 12–4
2008 National Orienteering Championships

Tournament	Location	Date
Flying Pig XII A Meet	Amelia, OH	April 4–6
West Point A Meet	West Point, NY	May 3–4
U.S. Rogaining Championships	Salamanca, NY	June 14–15
Tahoe 3-Day A Meet	Truckee, CA	June 20–22
Northwest Forest Frenzy A Meet	Elum, WA	Aug. 2–3
Laramie Daze A Meet	Laramie, WY	Aug. 4–10
North American Championships	Onondaga and Oswego Counties, NY	Sept. 26–28

In addition to these A meets, there are hundreds of local and regional Foot-O meets from early summer to late fall. These can be found on the local orienteering club web sites which are posted on the USOF web site.

Competitive Landscape

The 2007 USOF National Championships in Orienteering were held near Triangle, Virginia, on November 2–4. In the over–40 age groups, there were a total of 311 competitors in the sprint and individual events. Women represented approximately 25 percent of the competitors. Table 12–5 shows the distribution of gender and age groups for entries over the age of 40.

Table 12–5
Number of Competitors in the 2007
National Orienteering Championships

Gender	Age Group	Course	Sprint Competitors	Individual Competitors
Women	40+	Brown	2	10
Women	45+	Brown	8	12
Women	50+	Brown	8	12
Women	55+	Orange	6	6
Women	60+	Orange	2	8
Women	65+	Orange	2	7
Women	70+	Orange	1	4
Women	75+	Orange	1	1
Subtotal Women			30	60
Men	40+	Green	19	15
Men	45+	Green	18	29
Men	50+	Green	23	37
Men	55+	Green	13	23
Men	60+	Green	17	31
Men	65+	Brown	7	16
Men	70+	Brown	5	9
Men	75+	Brown	0	3
Men	80+	Brown	1	2
Subtotal Men			103	165
Total Entries			133	225

Of the 358 competitors in the 2007 Orienteering National Championship, 25 percent were women and 32 percent of the competitors over 40 were over the age of 60. The list of national champions in both the sprint and individual events is presented in Appendix A.

A second way to assess competitive depth is to look at the age group rankings that the USOF publishes each year. Rankings are calculated by course type (Brown, Red, Green, etc.). Table 12–6 presents the national age group rankings for the past three years.

Table 12–6
National Age Group Rankings—2000 to 2002
(Age Group Rankings for 40+ and over)

Gender/Course/ Age Group	Ranked in 2005	Ranked in 2006	Ranked in 2007
Women/Green/40+	9	12	9
Women/Green/45+	12	15	16
Women/Green/50+	15	14	12
Women/Brown/55+	12	15	14
Women/Brown/60+	9	7	12
Women/Brown/65+	8	11	15
Women/Brown/70+	2	7	4

Gender/Course/ Age Group	Ranked in 2005	Ranked in 2006	Ranked in 2007
Women/Brown/75+	0	0	2
Subtotal—Women	67	81	84
Men/Red/40+	20	29	35
Men/Red/45+	43	49	63
Men/Green/50+	33	33	31
Men/Green/55+	23	26	28
Men/Green/60+	23	36	24
Men/Brown/65+	12	7	24
Men/Brown/70+	7	5	10
Men/Brown/75+	0	0	5
Men/Brown/80+	0	0	2
Men/Brown/85+	0	0	1
Subtotal—Men	138	185	223
Total Ranked	205	266	307

As Table 12–6 shows, women represent approximately 30 of the ranked age group competitors over 40. It is interesting to note that competitors in the 75+ and over age groups were added to the rankings in 2007.

How to Get Started

Skills

Orienteering requires endurance, good overall fitness and clear thinking. Once you have grasped the basics—how to orient and read a map and how to select an efficient course—the best way to improve is to enter as many meets as you can. As soon as you feel comfortable completing a Yellow Course, choose an Orange Course your next time out. In this way, you can measure your progress not only by your times, but by the color of the course.

Equipment

Orienteering requires very little equipment. A compass for beginners can cost as little as $10 and more advanced models for serious competitors can cost $75 or more. You'll need sturdy clothing and many seasoned competitors wear gaiters to keep their pants or legs from getting torn up by brambles. A good pair of running shoes or cross-training shoes works quite well. Dress for the weather and remember that you'll be moving all the time.

Coaching

Every local meet I've ever attended offers instruction for beginners. One of the best ways to learn the sport is to tag along with an experienced competitor. Finding someone willing to help you may take a little planning, but at local meets, it is often possible to do this. The courses are graded according to difficulty from short, simple courses set on trails to longer, more difficult courses requiring cross country jaunts. It is quite common to see families with toddlers negotiating string courses. Participants can move from easy courses to more difficult courses as their skills and confidence improve. Many clubs also offer workshops for beginning and intermediate competitors.

Venues

Orienteering meets are held in forests, parks, and public open spaces. Arrangements to use the area are made by the club that is organizing the event. It is a wonderful way to see natural landscapes in a whole new way.

Recognition

Awards

Typically, meets award prizes for the first three places in each class and the number of classes depends on the demographics of the entries.

The 2007 national age group champions are listed in Appendix A.

National Teams

Annually, the USOF names a national team, although no age group categories are included in this team.

Rankings

As shown in Table 12–6, the USOF publishes national rankings for age groups annually. The IOF also publishes world rankings.

Resources

There are many books, videos, and other teaching aids to help competitors become more proficient. Here are some good ones.

Be an Expert with Map and Compass, Bjorn Kjellstrom, Hungry Minds, Inc; 1999.

Orienteering, Steve Broga, Stackpole Books, 1997.

Rogaining, Cross-Country Navigation, Phillips and Phillips, Outdoor Recreation in Australia.

Platform Tennis

Introduction

Platform tennis is a sport played in a cage, most often as doubles. A platform tennis court is a raised 44' by 20' wooden platform with a wire screen 12 feet high surrounding the playing surface. The ball can be played at any height and can be played off the screen which surrounds the court. In the cage, players use a paddle 18" long and about 9.5" wide, and a pressurized rubber ball with specifications approved by the national sponsoring organization. Traditional tennis scoring (15, 30, 40, game) is used. Based on the location of members and the venues for tournaments, platform tennis is a well-established East Coast game with pockets of interest in other parts of the country.

In addition to platform tennis, there are several other tennis-like sports. Because platform tennis appears, at this writing, to have the largest and most active organization, it is the subject of this chapter. However, there are four other sports that have enthusiastic followings and offer competitive opportunities for participants over 40 years of age. These sports include paddle tennis, one-wall paddleball, four-wall paddleball, and pickleball. Table 13-1 provides a summary of some of the important differences among these sports.

Table 13–1
Summary of Tennis-Like Sports

	Paddle Tennis	Paddleball (One-Wall)	Paddleball (Four-Wall)	Pickleball
Court size	20' x 50'	20' x 40'	20' x 37'	20' x 44'
Object	Net game	Wall game	Wall game	Net game
Venue	Outdoor	Outdoor	Indoor	Outdoor
Paddle	Solid Wood	Solid Wood	Solid Wood	Solid Wood
Ball	Special ball	Deadened tennis ball	Special ball	Wiffle ball
Service	Underhand	Bounce First	Bounce First	Underhand
Scoring	Like tennis	Games to 21	Games to 21	Games to 21
Sponsor	PaddleTennis.biz	USPA	NPA	USAPA
Address	—	7642 Kingsdon Portage, MI 49002	12021 SW 131 Ave Miami, FL 33186	PO Box 7354 Surprise, AZ 85374
Phone	—	(718) 233-3520	—	—

The web sites for these sports are:

- Paddle Tennis: http://www.paddletennis.biz/
- One-Wall Paddle Ball: http://uspaddleballassociation.org/
- Four-Wall Paddle Ball: http://paddleball.org/
- Pickleball: http://www.usapa.org/

National Sponsoring Organization

The national governing body of platform tennis is the American Platform Tennis Association (APTA):

American Platform Tennis Association
109 Westport Drive
Pittsburgh, PA 15238
(888) 744-9490
Executive Director: Ann Sheedy
annsheedy@platformtennis.org
http://www.platformtennis.org/about/

The APTA has approximately 8,000 members. An individual annual membership in the APTA is $40.00 and includes a subscription to *Platform Tennis Magazine.*

The organization is divided into seven regions, each with a regional director who oversees the development of platform tennis in his area. Table 13-2 is a list of the APTA regions, contact persons, and telephone numbers.

Table 13–2
Platform Tennis Regions

Region	States	Contact and Phone
Region I	NJ, NYC, CT (Fairfield Co.)	Michael Cochrane (914) 722-4600
Region II	ME, NH, VT, RI, MA, CT, NY (East)	Rob Coster (203) 915-7828

Region	States	Contact and Phone
Region III	MD, WV, DE, PA (East), DC, VA (North)	Fred Gumbinner (703) 577-6696
Region IV	OH, PA (West), NY (West), Ontario	Nancy Budde (937) 304-4439
Region V	SD, ND, NE, KS, OK, TX, MS, MO, LA, AR, IA, IL, IN, WI, MN, MI, KY, TN, AL	Bill O'Brien (630) 325-6827
Region VI	WA, OR, CA, UT, MT, ID, NV, NM, AZ, WY, CO	Beach Kuhl (415) 781-7900
Region VII	VA (South), NC, SC, GA, FL	Peter Lauer (202) 256-1170

A separate organization, the Professional Platform Tennis Association, certifies teaching professionals. For more information, see http://www.platformtennis.org/ppta/.

Competitive Opportunities

Platform tennis competition classes are based on gender (men, women, mixed) and age groups. A specific national championship for husbands and wives mixed doubles is sponsored by the APTA. The APTA, through its seven regions, sponsors more than 100 platform tennis tournaments each year. The national championships are contested in a series of eight tournaments. Table 13–3 shows the location and dates for the 2008 national championship tournaments.

Table 13–3
2008 APTA National Championship Tournaments

Tournament	Location	Date
Men's and Women's Nationals	Rochester, NY	March 13–16
Women 40+/60+ Nationals	Summit, NJ	Feb. 6–7
Women 50+/70+ Nationals	Scarsdale, NY	Jan. 16–17
Men 50+, 60+, 70+ Nationals	Scarsdale, NY	Feb. 22–24
Men 145+ Nationals[1]	Sleepy Hollow, NY	Feb. 21–22
Mixed Nationals (Husband/Wife)	Fairfield, CT	Feb. 29—Mar. 2
Men 45+, 55+, 65+ Nationals	Chicago, IL	Mar. 7–9
Senior Mixed Nationals	Nassau, NY	Mar. 29–30

1 Total age of the doubles team must be over 145 years

Regional and local platform tennis tournaments for adults are listed on the APTA web site.

Competitive Landscape

Competitive platform tennis is primarily a doubles game. Teams are ranked and compete for national championships. In 2007, 64 teams competed for the Women's National Championship and 128 teams competed for the Men's National Championship in Pelham, New York. Table 13–4 shows the number of nationally ranked teams in each APTA class at the end of 2007.

Table 13–4
2007 Year-End APTA National Rankings

Class	Ranked Teams
Men	34
Women	18
Mixed	16
Husband-Wife	5
Mixed Masters 50+	2
Women 40+	16
Women 60+	6
Women 70+	8
Men 45+	8
Men 50+	10
Men 55+	8
Men 60+	10
Men 65+	8
Men 70+	10

How to Get Started

Skills

In addition to good hand-to-eye coordination and fitness, platform tennis requires team play, since most matches are doubles. Also, the relatively confined space of the game rewards economy of movement. Playing the ball off the screen will also take some getting used to. A few lessons and some practice with experienced players are always useful.

Equipment

A platform tennis paddle can cost from $100.00 to $150.00 and balls, in colors such as neon pink and optic yellow, cost about $15.00 for three. These items, as well as tennis shoes, gloves, and other apparel, can be found online at the APTA web site or your local sporting goods store.

Coaching

The coaching certification program for platform tennis is carried out by the Professional Platform Tennis Association (PPTA). There are more than 70 certified professionals in the United States.

Venues

There are approximately 4,000 platform tennis courts in the U.S., most in the Northeast and Midwest. The majority of the courts are located at country clubs and other private facilities, but APTA is currently promoting the construction of public facilities to help spread the game.

Recognition

Awards

Prizes are typically awarded to the winners and runners-up for each class in tournament play.

National Teams

The APTA does not designate a national platform tennis team.

Rankings

The APTA ranks platform tennis teams based on their best finish in three tournaments, one of which must be out of region. Rankings also factor in the weight of each tournament, based on the size and strength of the draw. In 2007, the APTA ranked teams in fourteen categories and the number of teams ranked in each category is shown in Table 13–4.

Resources

How to Play Platform Tennis *by Dick Squires; Squirrel Publishing Company, 1993.*

Racquetball

Introduction

Hitting a racquetball is especially satisfying because every place on the court is in bounds. There is no tin as there is in squash, and the lively ball puts a premium on hard shots. You stand in the middle of the court with the ball ricocheting around you, as if you were in the middle of a three-dimensional pinball game. It's the only racquet sport that I know of that keeps track of dives, the number of times a player leaves her feet to play a point. The slogan of the sport is "Fast Furious Fitness."

Joe Sobek, a tennis, squash, and handball player from Connecticut, invented racquetball in 1949. Using a handball court, a racquet patterned after a platform tennis racquet, and a child's rubber ball, Sobek developed a new indoor racquet sport which he called paddle racquets. In 1968, he teamed with Robert Kendler, then head of the United States Handball Association, to help promote the sport. Kendler re-named it racquetball. It surged in popularity in the late 1970s and by the late 1990s there were an estimated several million players in the U.S.

National Sponsoring Organization

The national governing body of racquetball is the USA Racquetball (USAR), also known as the US Racquetball Association (USRA):

USA Racquetball
1685 Uintah
Colorado Springs, Colorado 80904
(719) 635-5396
Executive Director: James Hiser
jhiser@usra.org
http://usra.org/Home.aspx

According to the USAR, there are 4.5 million racquetball players worldwide. The USAR, founded in 1969, has more than 13,000 members, about 17 percent of whom are female.

An individual annual membership in the USAR is $35.00 and includes a subscription to the bi-monthly *Racquetball Magazine*. Membership applications and renewals are processed online on the USAR web site. The USAR has 50 state organizations. Table 14–1 is a list of the state web sites and e-mail contacts.

Table 14–1
USAR State Organizations

State and Web site	E-Mail Contact
Alabama	
www.ntcsites.com/bamarball/	rac432@aol.com
Alaska	
alaskaracquetball.com/phpnuke2/index.php	pinch@alaska.com
Arizona	
www.azracquetball.com/	azra@azracquetball.com
Arkansas	
www.arkansasracquetball.org/	arpackerbacker@cox.net
California	
www.californiaracquetball.org/	peggine@pacbell.net
Colorado	
coloradoracquetball.com/	lamacoach@msn.com
Connecticut	
connecticutrballassoc.com/	julescra99@cs.com
Delaware	
www.dara.org/	jeffrey.m.zegna@citigroup.com
Florida	
www.floridaracquetball.com/	andypaw@attglobal.net
Georgia	
www.georgiaracquetball.com/	ggwilsonrball@gmail.com
Hawaii	
www.hawaiiracquetball.org/	prbigedhara@hawaii.rr.com
Idaho	
www.idahoracquetball.org/	renwylie@aol.com
Illinois	
www.illinoisracquetball.com/	auntlollyd@aol.com
Indiana	
www.insra.org/	drolland@midwestmetal.com
Iowa	
www.geocities.com/iowarball/	whitemichaelj.@johndeere.com
Kansas	
www.ksracquetball.com/	dchecots@KPTS.org
Kentucky	
www.kyracquetball.com/	rmarr47@comcast.net
Louisiana	
www.laracquetball.org/	lraprez@yahoo.com
Maine	
www.racquetballmaine.com/	igmatats@aol.com
Maryland/DC	
mwraweb.com/	val@teamektelon.com
Massachusetts	
www.massracquetball.com/	racquetballchamp@hotmail.com
Michigan	
www.michiganracquetball.net/	Not Available
Minnesota	
www.mnracquetball.org/	mike327@earthlink.net
Mississippi	
www.msracquetball.com/	chrisb@mscourthouse.com
Missouri	
www.missouriracquetball.org/	dwhitley@vettasports.com

State and Web site	E-Mail Contact
Montana	
www.montanaracquetball.org/	LanceReithmeier@financial.wellsfargo.com
Nebraska	
nebraskaracquetball.com/	lmoore@ncfcomm.com
Nevada	
www.usaracquetballevents.com/nevada/	
racquetball-events.asp	neeserball@aol.com
New Hampshire	
www.nhracquetball.com/	kbeane6@aol.com
New Jersey	
njracquetball.com/	jonathan_m_clay@hotmail.com
New Mexico	
nmracquetball.com/	gmampro@aol.com
New York	
www.nyracquetball.com/joomla/	pat@racquetworld.com
North Carolina	
www.ncracquetball.com/	lstephens@ncracquetball.com
North Dakota	
www.ndracquetball.com	kross@ideaone.net
Ohio	
www.ohioracquetball.com	ganim@earthlink.net
Oklahoma	
www.oklahomaracquetball.com/	racqpro@aol.com
Oregon	
www.oregonracquetball.org/	Connie.Martin@CascadeAthleticClubs.com
Pennsylvania	
www.pa-racquetball.com/	johnbarrett.psra@adelphia.net
Rhode Island	
www.neracquetball.com/	jpatalano@cox.net
South Carolina	
www.scracquetball.org/	tuckeriii5@aol.com
South Dakota	
Not Available	rackitdoug@hotmail.com
Tennessee	
www.tennesseeracquetball.com/	ultimateracquetball@comcast.net
Texas	
www.txra.net/	lance@gilliamcpapc.com
Utah	
utahracquetball.org	randymg@networld.com
Vermont	
tggweb.com/gmra/	jdvallieres@hotmail.com
Virginia	
www.cvra.org/	driveserve@email.com
Washington	
www.washrball.org/	NHEGGEN@YAHOO.COM
West Virginia	
Not Available	pkincaid@hntb.com
Wisconsin	
wiracquetball.org/	tkctgriffith@charter.net
Wyoming	
wyra.net/	bhall@wyoming.com

A second sister organization, the National Masters Racquetball Association (NMRA), was founded in 1971 specifically to support round-robin racquetball competition for players over the age of 45. It emphasizes the opportunity to compete through its motto, "Where players are guaranteed matches ... no more one round and out."

National Masters Racquetball Association
959 Matadero Ave.
Palo Alto, CA 94306
(650) 856-2292
http://www.nmra.info/
mkelley959@aol.com
Membership in the NMRA is $45.00 for three years and applications are available online on the NMRA web site.

The Women's Senior/Masters Racquetball Association promotes competitive racquetball for women over 35 and more information on this organization can be found at http://my.execpc.com/~tutsch/_WSMRA/main.html.

Competitive Opportunities

Both the USAR and the NMRA sponsor national championship tournaments. In addition, each year hundreds of local and regional racquetball tournaments are sponsored by the USAR state associations and are listed on their web sites, as well as on the USAR web site. The USAR sponsors three national championships. Table 14–2 shows the locations and dates of the 2008 USAR National Championship tournaments.

Table 14–2
2008 USAR National Championship Tournaments

Tournament	Location	Date
USAR Women's Senior Masters Championship	Overland Park, KS	Jan. 25–27, 2008
USAR National Doubles Championships	Tempe, AZ	Feb. 13–17, 2008
USAR National Singles Championships	Houston, TX	May 21–26, 2008

The NMRA hosts two national championships and the locations and dates are shown in Table 14–3.

Table 14–3
2008 NMRA National Championship Tournaments

Tournament	Location	Date
NMRA National Championships	Orem, UT	March 5–8, 2008
NMRA International Championships	West Allis, WI	July 16–19, 2008

The 2008 NMRA national champions are shown in Appendix A.

Competitive Landscape

The large number of racquetball players provides both a high level of competition and plenty of opportunities for players at all levels to find competition suited to their skill level. The USRA not only offers age group competition and skill-level competition for both men and women, but also a combined category for players at each skill level of different ages. For example, at the national level, players at the novice or beginner skill levels, C and D, can compete within their own age groups. The classes offered in local and regional tournaments will depend on the size and demographic composition of the field.

For example, there were 530 players in 69 divisions entered in the USAR Singles championship held in Houston, Texas, from May 23 to 28, 2007. The divisions included:

(1) Open
(2) Age group (age 24 and five-year increments from 25+ to 85+)
(3) Skill level (Elite, A, B, C, and D). Skill levels are determined through an allocation made by the USAR of the national rankings
(4) Combined skill and age (e.g., 40+A, 40+B, 40+C, etc.).

All competitors were required to have competed—in any division—in a recognized regional-state qualifying tournament. Table 14–4 shows the number of entrants in the 2007 National Singles Championship age group divisions for competitors over 40 years of age.

Table 14–4
Number of Competitors in Age Group Divisions
Over 40 in the 2007 USAR National Singles Championships

Age Group	Male Competitors	Female Competitors
40+	21	9
40+A	20	0
40+B	15	0
40+C	8	0
45+	22	6
45+A	16	0
45+B	17	9
45+C	13	0
50+	21	5
50+A	20	0
50+B	15	0
50+C	11	0
55+	19	6
55+A	17	0
55+B	10	0
55+C	11	0
60+	18	6
65+	9	0
70+	12	0
75+	0	0
40A/45A	0	5
40B/50B/55B	0	5
40C/45C/50C/60C/65C	0	3
50A/55A	0	6
65/75	0	5
60A/65A	6	0
60B/65B	6	0
60C/65C	8	0
80/85/90	3	0
Total Competitors	**324**	**64**

As Table 14–4 indicates, 16 percent of the entrants in these divisions were women and approximately 21 percent of the competitors were in age groups over 60. The USAR national racquetball singles and doubles champions are listed in Appendix A.

The 2007 USRA National Doubles Championships were held at Arizona State University in Tempe, Arizona, from September 26 to 30. Divisions were similar to those in the

National Singles Championships; however, no regional qualifiers were required for participants.

The 2008 NMRA National Championships were held in Orem, Utah, from March 3 to
8, attracting 396 competitors in five divisions—men singles, men's doubles, women's singles, women's doubles, and mixed doubles. No regional qualifiers were required to participate. Table 14–5 lists the entries for the 2007 NMRA National Championships.

Table 14–5
Number of Competitors in the 2008 NMRA Championship

Event	Age Group Class	Male Competitors	Female Competitors
Singles	45+	5	4
Singles	50+	16	6
Singles	55+	13	2
Singles	60+	11	4
Singles	65+	11	6
Singles	70+	13	0
Singles	75+	6	0
Singles	80+	8	0
Singles	85+	2	0
Singles	90+	1	0
Doubles	45+	16	8
Doubles	50+	24	6
Doubles	55+	52	0
Doubles	60+	48	4
Doubles	65+	28	4
Doubles	70+	24	0
Doubles	75+	24	0
Doubles	80+	10	0
Mixed Doubles	45+	3	3
Mixed Doubles	50+	7	7
Mixed Doubles	55+	4	4
Mixed Doubles	60+	3	3
Mixed Doubles	65+	4	4
Mixed Doubles	70+	1	1
Total Competitors		334	62

Women represented approximately 16 percent of the total competitors and the number
of competitors over 60 years of age represented about 55 percent of all competitors. The 2008
NMRA national racquetball champions are listed in Appendix A.

How to Get Started

Skills

Like all racquet sports, racquetball requires good hand-to-eye coordination, quick feet,
and excellent fitness. Because of the short racquet and lively ball, racquetball is an easier
game to learn than either tennis or squash for most people. Playing at a high competitive
level requires the same kind of dedication and practice as any sport.

Equipment

Because of the speed of the game, you should have and use protective eyewear. Goggles
or eyeglasses will cost about $20.00. You will also need a racquet, which can cost from $100.00

to $300.00 or more. Many clubs and YMCAs have racquets you can borrow while learning. The balls generally cost less than $4.00 for a can of two balls. You can acquire specialty shoes and other clothing as you get more proficient.

Coaching

Coaching is usually available at most places where there are racquetball courts and it is a good idea to begin with a lesson or two.

Venues

Racquetball courts can be found at most athletic clubs and YMCAs. Some of the state association web sites have a tool for locating racquetball courts.

Recognition

Awards

Tournaments typically give awards for the winner and runner-up in each division. Occasionally, the awards go deeper into finalists. The USAR names a male and female age group athlete of the year.

National Teams

There are no national age group or masters racquetball teams chosen by either the USAR or the NMRA.

Rankings

The USAR uses a skill-based ranking system in which a player can move up in the rankings by defeating a higher ranked played in a USAR-sanctioned tournament. The USAR publishes both national rankings and state rankings. A total of 7,984 men are ranked and 1,402 women. To provide a glimpse of how the top age group players compare with all ranked players, Table 14–6 shows the national ranking of the men and women ranked #1 in their age group. For example, Cliff Swain is the highest ranked player in the 40+ age group and is the 8th ranked player nationally. Ruben Gonzales is the highest ranked player in three age groups (45+, 50+, and 55+) and is the 9th ranked player nationally.

Table 14–6
2007 National Racquetball Rankings (as of November 28, 2007)

Age Group	Men's Age Group Ranking	Men's National Ranking	Women's Age Group Ranking	Women's National Ranking
40+	1	8	1	3
45+	1	9	1	7
50+	1	9	1	31
55+	1	9	1	32
60+	1	385	1	45
65+	1	588	1	169
70+	1	735	1	343
75+	1	1403	1	343
80+	1	104	1	402
85+	1	104	1	402
90+	1	104	1	402

It is very impressive that 55 men and 13 women have rankings in the 90+ age group.

Resources

Racquetball Fundamentals *by Jim Winterton, Human Kinetics, 2004.*

Winning Racquetball: Skills, Drills, and Strategies *by Ed Turner and Woody Clouse; Human Kinetics, 1995.*

The USAR sells CDs of the U.S. Open for various years on its web site, as well as the rule book for racquetball and instructional videos.

Road Racing

Introduction

The difference between running and racing can be the difference between singing in the shower and soloing on stage. But road racing is not only an individual test, it can also be a social encounter as well as an athletic event. Pre–race conversations among competitors, jangly with the adrenaline rush, hum with carbo-loaded jargon. Because long-distance running demands so little equipment, hydration and the weight of your singlet assumes great significance because the milliliters and grams are multiplied over miles. For an ordinary runner, the start can be frustrating as the elite runners bolt out and, slowly, so slowly, the rest of the competitors unpack toward the starting line and, at last, set out to actually race. For the individual racer, a race with thousands of competitors soon becomes a neighborhood affair. A few dozen runners of equal ability and fitness become companions over the race course. The neighborhood reflects the democracy of running, a wonderful mix of genders, ages, ethnicity, and shoe brands, including that intriguing pair of bright red Chuck Taylor All-Stars. Serious competitors are grim, the fittest clowns gambol, the rest move in and out of their heads—one second critiquing their pace or technique, the next second checking out that attractive redhead just ahead. At the finish, the sweat, relief, lactic acid, joy, Gatorade, fatigue, times and splits, excitement, and smiles spill over the crowd. Regret is a stranger.

For the dedicated runner, there is a wide range of distance running events, from three kilometer cross-country races to 100mile trail running events. For this reason, this is perhaps the most accessible competitive opportunity for Masters Athletes in the United States.

National Sponsoring Organizations

There are several organizations that sponsor and support long distance running. The USA Track and Field (USATF) is the national governing organization for long distance running. USATF estimates that there are more than 50 million adult runners in the United States. It sanctions more than 4,000 events each year and has more than 100,000 members. However, all of these members are not long distance runners.

USATF provides a Road Running Information Center on its web site which includes a database of road races, a database of running clubs, a database of running courses (with maps) and other features.

USA Track & Field

132 East Washington Street, Suite 800

Indianapolis, IN 46204
Bill Roe, president
Phone—(317) 261-0500
Fax—(317) 261-0513
membership@usatf.org
http://www.usatf.org/

The USATF is organized through 57 associations that cover the entire United States. Membership applications and fees for the USATF go to the local association. The annual individual membership fee for 2008 is $29.95. Member benefits include a subscription to the quarterly magazine, *Fast Forward*.

Table 15–1 lists the associations, their web sites and the number of current member clubs. To contact the local clubs, the association web site has contact information including phone numbers and a link to the member clubs' web sites. It also indicates those clubs that welcome Masters Athletes. Some local clubs have a specific focus, such as field events, race walking, or long distance running, and these foci are explained on the club web site.

Table 15–1
USATF Member Associations

Association	Web site	Current Member Clubs[1]
Maine—USATF	www.meusatf.org/	10 (7)
New England—USATF	www.usatfne.org/	75 (44)
Adirondack—USATF	www.usatfadir.org/	2 (1)
Niagara—USATF	www.usatf-niagara.org/	29 (23)
Connecticut	www.usatf-ct.org/	5 (2)
Metropolitan (NY)—USATF	www.mactrack.org/	23 (15)
New Jersey—USATF	www.usatfnj.org/	52 (26)
Mid-Atlantic—USATF	www.mausatf.org/	24 (16)
Alabama	www.eteamz.com/alabamausatf/	10 (5)
Potomac Valley—USATF	www.usatf.org/assoc/pva/	23 (8)
Three Rivers—USATF	www.usatf.org/assoc/threerivers/	4 (3)
Virginia—USATF	virginia.usatf.org/	7 (3)
North Carolina—USATF	www.ncusatf.org/	20 (6)
Florida—USATF	florida.usatf.org/	46 (24)
Tennessee—USATF	startuck@earthlink.net (e-mail)	6 (4)
Indiana—USATF	www.inusatf.org/	13 (8)
Ohio—USATF	www.usatf.org/assoc/oh/	14 (10)
Lake Erie—USATF	www.lakeerie.org/	12 (9)
Michigan—USATF	michigan.usatf.org/	10 (3)
Wisconsin—USATF	www.wiusatf.org/	13 (11)
Illinois—USATF	www.usatfillinois.org/	32 (14)
Ozark—USATF	www.usatf.org/assoc/ozark/	14 (5)
Arkansas—USATF	www.arkansasrunner.com/usatf-ar.htm	5 (5)
Southern—USATF	www.usatf.org/	11 (6)
Gulf—USATF	htosports.com/?USATFGULF	7 (3)
Southwestern—USATF	www.swusatf.org/	20 (8)
Oklahoma–USATF	www.usatf.org/assoc/ok/	10 (4)
Missouri Valley—USATF	www.usatf.org/assoc/mv/	15 (3)
Nebraska—USATF	www.nebraskausatf.org/	4 (2)
Minnesota—USATF	www.usatfmn.org/	16 (10)
Montana—USATF	www.mtusatf.org/	8 (5)
Colorado—USATF	www.usatf-co.org/	62 (31)
Southern California—USATF	www.scausatf.org/	63 (24)
Utah—USATF	utah.usatf.org/	3 (2)
Inland Northwest—USATF	http://sites.google.com/site/inlandnwtrackandfield/	9 (7)
Pacific Northwest—USATF	www.pntf.org/	10 (6)

Association	Web site	Current Member Clubs[1]
Oregon—USATF	www.usatf-oregon.org	26 (16)
Pacific—USATF	www.pausatf.org/	70 (44)
Hawaii—USATF	www.usatf-hi.org/	2 (1)
Iowa—USATF	www.usatf-iowa.org/	5 (3)
Kentucky—USATF	kentucky.usatf.org/	3 (2)
New Mexico—USATF	www.usatfnm.org	3 (2)
South Texas—USATF	www.usatfsouthtexas.org/	6 (4)
San Diego—Imperial	www.sdusatf.org/	22 (7)
Georgia—USATF	www.usatfga.org	35 (8)
Central California—USATF	central-california.usatf.org/	4 (2)
West Texas—USATF	west-texas.usatf.org/	1 (0)
Arizona—USATF	www.usatf.org/assoc/az/	43 (25)
Nevada—USATF	www.usatfn.org/	6 (2)
Wyoming—USATF	www.usatf.org/	1 (1)
West Virginia—USATF	http://leaguelineup.com/welcome.asp?url=wvusatf	3 (3)
Dakotas—USATF	dakotas.usatf.org/	5 (2)
Border—USATF	www.usatf.org/assoc/border/	13 (4)
Snake River—USATF	www.usatf.org/assoc/sr/	2 (1)
South Carolina—USATF	www.scusatf.org	12 (4)
Alaska—USATF	www.usatf.org/assoc/ak/	2 (2)
Long Island—USATF	long-island.usatf.org/	35 (26)

1 As of 2/08. Typically a large number of non-renewed clubs are also listed. The numbers in parentheses indicate the number of clubs that welcome Masters Athletes.

The Road Runners Club of America (RRCA) is an association of running clubs, running events, and individual runners dedicated to promoting running as a competitive sport and as a healthful exercise. It has 700 member clubs with a total of approximately 180,000 individual members.

Road Runners Club of America
Executive Director: Jean Knaack
1501 Lee Highway Suite 140
Alexandria, VA 22209
(703) 525-3890
office@rrca.org
http://www.rrca.org/

Membership in the RRCA may be by club, by event, or by individual member. Member benefits include a subscription to the quarterly newsletter, *Inside Track*, and discounts on RRCA sponsors' products. Individual memberships are $25.00 per year. Fees for running clubs depend on the number of members and the type of membership. See the web site for details. The RRCA's web site has a database of member clubs and events. It sends all members of RRCA clubs a copy of *Footloose*, its quarterly running publication.

The American Trail Running Association (ATRA) was formed in 1996 as a Colorado not-for-profit corporation to serve the trail and mountain running community. Its mission is "to represent and promote trail and mountain running."

ATRA
Executive Director: Nancy Hobbs
PO Box 9454
Colorado Springs, CO 80932
(719) 573-4133
trlrunner@aol.com
www.trailrunner.com

It seeks to be a clearinghouse for the sport and it works with race organizers, the media, and the athletic industry to support long distance running events. The calendar on its web site includes hundreds of races, from 5Ks to 100 miles, as well as a number of snowshoe races, cross-country ski races, and multi-sport events. Individual memberships are $25.00 per year and include subscriptions to *TrailRunner* and *Running Times* magazines. Memberships are also available for clubs and events.

Competitive Opportunities

Competition in distance running is available throughout the United States, an obvious outgrowth of the popularity of recreational running. In all but the most rural areas, racers can participate in a race or two every weekend throughout the year. Distance races, ranging from two miles to 100 miles or more, typically offer competitive classes based on:

• Gender—men and women
• Age Groups—five- or 10-year increments
• Terrain—paved road to mountain trails

With thousands of competitive runners in the country, the competition at the top is serious. However, the number of local and regional races makes it easy to begin competing.

The USAFT and RRCA national championship events in 2008 are shown in Table 15-2.

Table 15–2
2008 National Championships

Event	Date	Location
USA Half-Marathon	1/13/08	Houston, TX
USA 50 Kilometer	3/2/08	Lloyd Harbor, NY
USA 15 Kilometer	3/8/08	Jacksonville, FL
USA Men's 8 Kilometer	3/15/08	New York, NY
USA 100 Kilometer	4/12/08	Madison, WI
USA 25 Kilometer	5/10/08	Grand Rapids, MI
USA 20 Kilometer	9/1/08	New Haven, CT
USA 5 Kilometer	9/21/08	Providence, RI
USA Women's 8 Kilometer	9/28/08	Akron, OH
USA Men's Masters Marathon	10/5/08	Minneapolis, MN
USA Women's 10 Mile	10/5/08	Minneapolis, MN
Masters 5k Cross Country	10/12/08	Greensboro, NC
USA 50 Mile	10/11/08	Boalsburg, PA
USA Women's 10 Kilometer	10/13/08	Boston, MA
RRCA Marathon	3/2/08	Napa Valley, CA
RRCA 10 Mile	4/6/08	Washington, DC
RRCA 5 Kilometer	5/3/08	Cincinnati, OH
RRCA Ultra Runs	7/19/08	Lake Tahoe, CA
RRCA Half Marathon	8/16/08	Parkersburg, WV
RRCA 10 Kilometer	11/1/08	Birmingham, AL

The calendar sections of the USATF and RRCA web sites also lists hundreds of masters road races, masters cross-country races, trail-off-road races, and mountain trail races. The RRCA web site also lists eight state and regional championships. The AATRA has a full calendar of local and regional events on its web site.

For an adult who seeks competition in long distance running, there is no shortage of opportunities.

Competitive Landscape

The sport of running has beaten Father Time, in a sense. It has produced a compendium of age-graded tables which provides data on how to rate one's performance as a runner at any age. The tables have been assembled by the World Association of Veteran Athletes (WAVA) and the World Masters Athletics (WMA) and are based on thousands of actual results. However, the research and compilation of the data is not without controversy (see http://masterstrack.com/blog/001357.html).

Basically, this is how age-grading works. The tables include an age factor and a standard for every distance and age. These two pieces of data allow a competitor to compute an age-graded time and a performance level percentage (PLP). For example, a fifty-year-old woman runs a 10k in 42:37. The age graded tables tell us that the 10k age factor at 53 is .8545. Multiplying her time by the age factor (42:37 x .8545) gives an age-graded time of 36:25. Based on the tables, her performance is superior to a 25-year old who has run a 36:26. The second computation, the PLP, uses the 10k standard, which is 35.01. Dividing the standard by the actual time (35.01/42:37) yields a PLP of 82 percent. While age grading is the best way to the compare times of competitors of different ages, prizes based on age grading are controversial. Critics of age grading believe that true winners are those runners with the fastest times. Period. For a discussion of age grading, see Jonathan Beverly's essay "Ageless Results" on the RRCA's web site.

USA Track and Field maintains records for 13 age groups from 40–44 to 100–104 and 23 road running events from one mile to 144 hours. Table 15–3 shows the current records for selected distances and age groups.

Table 15–3
Selected Age Group Distance Running American Records

Distance	Gender	Age Group	Performance	Record holder
5 kilometers	Men	40–44	14:13	Eddy Hellebuyck
5 kilometers	Women	40–44	15:48	Colleen DeReuck
5 kilometers	Men	55–59	16:07	Vic Heckler
5 kilometers	Women	55–59	18:32	Shirley Matson
5 kilometers	Men	70–74	18:01	Warren Utes
5 kilometers	Women	70–74	24:36	Toshiko d'Elia
5 kilometers	Men	90–94	40:32	Lloyd Walters
5 kilometers	Women	85–89	45:41	Edith Allen
10 kilometers	Men	40–44	29:05	Eddy Hellebuyck
10 kilometers	Women	40–44	32:50	Colleen DeReuck
10 kilometers	Men	55–59	32:27	Jim O'Neil
10 kilometers	Women	55–59	38:55	Shirley Matson
10 kilometers	Men	70–74	41:09	Alfred Funk
10 kilometers	Women	70–74	49:13	Myra Rhodes
10 kilometers	Men	90–94	1:14.49	Paul Spangler
10 kilometers	Women	90–94	3:29.08	Ruth Rothfarb
Marathon	Men	40–44	2:17.02	Kenneth Judson
Marathon	Women	40–44	2:28.40	Colleen DeReuck
Marathon	Men	55–59	2:33.09	Norm Green
Marathon	Women	55–59	2:52.14	S. Rae Baymiller
Marathon	Men	70–74	3:00.58	John Keston
Marathon	Women	70–74	3:46.18	Ginette Bedard
Marathon	Men	90–94	6:54.25	Ernest Van Leeuwen
Marathon	Women	90–94	8:53.08	Mavis Lindgren
24-Hour	Men	40–44	254200m	John Geesler
24-Hour	Women	40–44	222556m	Randi Bromka

Distance	Gender	Age Group	Performance	Record holder
24-Hour	Men	55–59	221604m	Roy Pirrung
24-Hour	Women	55–59	203050m	Sue Ellen Trapp
24-Hour	Men	70–74	151728m	Howard Henry
24-Hour	Women	70–74	165343m	Helen Klein
24-Hour	Men	80–84	117787m	Howard Henry

A full list of the American distance running age group records can be found on the USATF web site. A list of national champions at selected distances is presented in Appendix A.

How to Get Started

Skills

Recent studies have suggested that running is one of the activities that separates us from other primates. Although running seems quite natural, coaching can help make a runner more efficient and less prone to injury. Most running clubs have formal or informal coaching available.

Equipment

Shoes are the name of this game and a good pair of running shoes can be purchased for $60.00 to $150.00 or more. However, be sure to try lots of styles and brands before purchasing. You'll be spending a lot of time with your shoes, so a proper fit and appropriate structure are important.

Coaching

As noted above, most running clubs have coaches or experienced runners who can help the novice get started. An article by Hal Higdon titled "How to Find a Running Coach" is posted on the RRCA web site at http://www.rrca.org/coaches/howfind.php.

Venues

The USATF certifies road racing courses for distance and a course must be certified to have results on that course accepted for records or rankings. All good road races should provide safe, challenging courses. Longer races include water and aid stations. Urban races have spectators lining the course encouraging runners. Rural and trail races usually take place on lovely, if not spectacular, country.

Recognition

Awards

Awards in distance races are given to the first three finishers in each age group. In many races age-graded awards are also presented. The USATF keeps careful records and those competitors achieving certain threshold times are awarded All-American honors. Bengay also sponsors the selection of a Master Athlete of the year for long distance running.

Each year the RRCA names the male and female Masters runners of the year. The AATRP has four annual awards—men's and women's Masters mountain runner and men's and women's ultrarunner.

The USATF national champions at selected distances are listed in Appendix A.

National Teams

No organization names a Masters or age group national team for road racing or long-distance running.

Rankings

Although no organization ranks Masters or age group runners, the USATF keeps meticulous records by distance and age group.

Resources

The authoritative periodical on long distance running for Masters Athletes is the *National Masters News*, published monthly for an annual subscription price of $28.00. It also covers Masters track and field and race walking. In addition to a calendar of coming events and the results of recent races, it has columns on health, fitness, and the political machinations of running organizations.

Ever since the 1970s when the enthusiasm for running began to capture the American imagination, many books on running and training have been published.

Running and Being: The Total Experience, George Sheehan, Second Wind II, September, 1998.

The Runner's Handbook, Bob Glover, Penguin, May 1996.

The Complete Book on Running for Women, Claire Kowalchik, Pocket, March 1999.

Rowing

Introduction

One thousand meters, a typical distance for a rowing race, can be covered in less than four minutes by a good eight-oared shell. The time of the winning eight in the 2007 Masters National Championships for a men's heavyweight crew 60–64 was 3:11.84. Pretty quick. Three or four minutes is not a long time—unless you are pulling a carbon-fiber oar through the water with all your strength *and* keeping in sync with your seven crewmates. The pain of all-out exertion combined with the exhilarating swing of a crew in unison is actually thrilling. That is why people row.

Rowing is one of the most supportive and beneficial sports for Masters Athletes. In addition to a strong national governing body, the sport has an organization, Masters Rowing Association, specifically to promote, encourage, and support the sport for older competitors. The growth of women rowers in the past few years also makes it one of the most gender-equal sports around.

National Sponsoring Organizations

The national governing body of rowing, and the oldest governing body for a sport in the United States, is USRowing.

USRowing
2 Wall Street
Princeton, NJ 08540
Glenn Merry, executive director
Phone—(800) 314-4769
member@usrowing.org
http://www.usrowing.org/index.aspx

According to USRowing, there are more than 1,000 rowing sites in the United States and the USRowing web site has a club locator using zip codes to identify member clubs. More than 14,500 individual members participate in hundreds of regattas each year. Current annual membership in USRowing costs $65.00 for individuals over 27 years of age. Member benefits include a subscription to a monthly electronic newsletter, as well discounts on USRowing merchandise, and insurance coverage. USRowing has a nine member Masters Committee to promote masters rowing.

One interesting facet of rowing is the growth in use of the Concept2 Indoor Rower, more commonly called the "Erg." Originally developed as an indoor training device for rowers, the "Erg" has become the centerpiece of hundreds of indoor rowing competitions around the world. The current schedule for these competitions can be found on the Concept2 website www.concept2.com/us/racing/default.asp

The World Indoor Rowing Championship is held annually in Boston, Massachusetts. Known as the CRASH-B Sprints, it includes age-group competition for a simulated 2000 meter race. In 2008, the oldest male competitor was in the 85–89 age group and the oldest females were in the 80–84 age group. With hundreds of competitors of all ages, many from abroad, the CRASH-B Sprints is an exhausting and exciting event. For more information, go to www.crash-b.org/index.htm.

Competitive Opportunities

Rowing competitions, called regattas, offer classes defined as a combination of:

- Gender (men, women, mixed)
- Weight (heavyweight and lightweight)
- Age groups from 21 to 80+. Masters classes begin at the age of 27.
- Competitive Level (club and open)
- Events (see Table 16–1)

There are nine possible events, determined by the number of rowers, the type of oar, and the presence or absence of a coxswain. Table 16–1 shows the key differences among rowing events.

Table 16–1
Rowing Events

Number Rowers	Oar Type [1]	Coxswain	Name	Abbreviation
1	Scull	Without	Single Scull	1x
2	Scull	Without	Double Scull	2x

Number Rowers	Oar Type [1]	Coxswain	Name	Abbreviation
2	Sweep	Without	Coxless Pair	2-
2	Sweep	With	Coxed Pair	2+
4	Sweep	Without	Coxless Four	4-
4	Scull	With	Coxed Four	4+
4	Scull	Without	Coxless Four Scull	4x
4	Scull	With	Coxed Four Scull	4x+
8	Sweep	With	Rowing Eight	8+

1 A scull refers to a boat in which each rower controls two oars; a sweep refers to a boat in which each rower controls one oar.

The Nationals also offer a special Club category to encourage local clubs to develop teams. The result of these four criteria is many different classes in a single regatta. As noted above, hundreds of regattas are offered by USRowing each year and a calendar of events can be found on their web site at http://www.usrowing.org/Events_Regattas/RegattaCalendar/index.aspx.

Age group classes are included in many regattas and USRowing sponsors a National Masters Championship as well. Table 16–2 shows the location and dates of the 2008 National Championship and other regattas that offer age group competition.

Table 16–2
2008 Masters Rowing Regattas

Event	Location	Date
2008 National Masters Championships	Long Beach, CA	Aug. 14–17
NW Masters Regional Championship	Vancouver, WA	June 20
Midwest Masters Regional Championship	Indianapolis, IN	July 12
King's Head XXII Regatta	Philadelphia, PA	Sept. 28
Head of the Charles	Boston, MA	Oct. 18–19

Competitive Landscape

One way to gauge the competitive landscape is to look at the profile of competitors at the national championship. The number of competitors, the participation in various disciplines, and the mix of men and women taking part are all part of this profile. The 2007 Masters National Championship Regatta was held in Oak Ridge, Tennessee, from August 9 to 12. During the four-day event, more than 250 separate races were held involving 3,175 competitors in the over–40 age groups. A summary of the entries by discipline and weight class is shown in Table 16–3 and a summary by age group and gender in Table 16–4.

Table 16–3
Competitors in 2007 National Masters Rowing Championships[1]
Discipline and Weight Class

Class	Heavyweight	Lightweight	Total
Singles	130	79	209
Pairs/Doubles	384	96	480
Quads/4+Cox	1,376	102	1,478
Eights	1,008	0	1,008
Total	2,898	277	3,175

1 The figures in Table 16–3 are not exact due to the mixing of classes and age groups in certain events.

A lightweight men's crew must average no more than 154 lbs with no member more than 159 lbs. A lightweight women's crew must average no more than 125 lbs with no member more than 130 lbs. Lightweight competitors represented about 9 percent of all competitors in the 2007 National Masters Championships. Although the National Masters Rowing age groups begin at age 27, only age groups that included rowers over 40 have been included here.

Table 16–4
Competitors in 2007 National Masters Rowing Championships[1]
Age Group and Gender

Age Group	Men	Women	Mixed	Total
36–42	214	333	122	669
43–49	302	414	127	843
50–54	334	300	104	738
55–59	249	165	70	484
60–64	138	73	27	238
65–69	102	13	16	131
70–74	36	0	4	40
75–79	21	1	0	22
80+	10	0	0	10
Total	1,406	1,299	470	3,175

1 The figures in Table 16–4 are not exact due to the mixing of classes and age groups in certain events.

Approximately 48 percent of the competitors over 40 were women and competitors over 60 years of age accounted for 14 percent of all competitors.

How to Get Started

Skills

Rowing requires strength, endurance, and balance. Although it appears to require great upper body strength, strong legs are critical to successful rowing. The sport involves all the body's major muscle groups. In pairs, fours, and eights, teamwork is essential. Rowing can be learned at any age.

Equipment

The equipment for rowing—boats (called shells or sculls) and oars—is expensive and seems to be continually evolving. For this reason, it is necessary to row with a club that owns and maintains this equipment. The USRowing web site lists clubs by state and region at http://www.usrowing.org/NewToRowing/RowingClubsByState_USRowingRegion/index.aspx.

Coaching

Although rowing may look easy, it involves a very complex series of coordinated movements. Good coaching is essential. Self-coached rowers are rare indeed. Most clubs provide coaching for novice crews and there are a number of rowing camps where beginners can learn the basics and more experienced rowers can refine their technique. Table 16–5 lists some rowing camps offered in 2008.

Table 16–5
Rowing Camps

Center	Location	Contact Information
Florida Rowing Center	Wellington, FL	(800) 996–0021
Northeast Rowing Center	Raymond, ME	(781) 934–6192
Craftsbury Sculling Center	Craftsbury, VT	(800) 586–7767
Calm Waters Rowing	Lancaster, VA	(800) 238–5578
Lake Union Crew	Seattle, WA	(206) 860–4199
San Diego Rowing Club	San Diego, CA	(619) 792–6834

A good web site for looking up camps and coaching is http://www.rowinglinks.com/usa/camps/. USRowing designated June 7, 2008, as Learning to Row Day and encouraged member clubs to teach people the joys of rowing.

Venues

Rowing takes place on rivers, lakes, estuaries, and other bodies of water. The clubs and camps noted above are all located on suitable venues.

Recognition

Awards

At most regattas, winners and runners-up in various classes are given awards.

National Teams

USRowing does not select national age group rowing teams.

Rankings

The USRowing does rank Masters rowers.

Resources

USRowing offers coaching DVDs and other instructional material for sale on its web site at https://www.usrowing.org/rowingstore/merchandise/_products.aspx?ctg_1Key=30.

Rowing has produced some excellent books, including:

The Red Rose Crew: A True Story of Women, Winning, and the Water, *Boyne and Halberstam, The Lyons Press, 2005.*

Mind Over Water: Lessons on Life from the Art of Rowing, *Craig Lambert, Mariner Books, 1999.*

Rowing Against the Current: On Learning to Scull at Forty, *Barry Strauss, Scribner, 2001.*

Soccer

Introduction

The world's most popular sport, soccer crosses artistic boundaries as easily as a winger lofts the ball on a corner kick. Amazon.com lists 59 music CDs under the keyword "soccer music," including *Football Fever* by the Delta Soccer Lads, *Volvo Driving Soccer Mom* by Everclear, and *Music of the World Cup—Allez! Ole! Ola!* by various artists. Tunes like "Hot Legs" from Denmark, "I Love Football" from Cameroon, and Ricky Martin's World Cup song, "The Cup of Life" capture some of the energy and universality of this sport, and The Uruguayan poet Eduardo Galeano celebrates soccer's "carnal delight of embracing the forbidden adventure of freedom."

In the United States, adult soccer has evolved from a grassroots game played primarily by recently arrived immigrants to a broader, more organized sport. The growth of soccer in youth leagues, high schools, and colleges, for both men and women, over the past several decades has resulted in an expanding group of players who wish to continue to compete as adults. To play soccer is to participate in a truly global love affair with sport.

National Sponsoring Organization

The United States Soccer Federation (USSF) is the governing body of soccer in the United States and is organized into four councils, one of which is the Adult Council. The United States Adult Soccer Association (USASA) is the only member of the USSF Adult Council. It oversees adult soccer in the United States and, among other activities, stages a national competition for soccer players over 40 years of age.

United States Adult Soccer Association
9152 Kent Ave., Suite C-50
Lawrence, IN 46216
Phone: (317) 541-8564
Fax: (317) 541-8568
info@usasa.com
www.usasa.com

The United Soccer League (USL) provides opportunities for elite level soccer leagues, but not for older players (http://www.uslsoccer.com/).

The USASA is divided into four regions and operates through 55 national state associations which stage local and regional leagues and tournaments. The USASA sponsors an annual tournament for club teams, veterans teams, and coed teams.

More than 240,000 players in 49 states registered with the USASA for 2006 and 2007. The four USASA regions, the states within each region, and the number of players registered for 2006 and 2007 are shown in Table 17–1.

Table 17–1
USASA Regions and Affiliates

Region	States within the Region and Web site	Registered Players
I	CT, DE, NY, ME, MD, VA, MA, NJ, NH, PA, RI, VT, WV www.usasa.com/directory/northeast/index_e.html	56,446

Region	States within the Region and Web site	Registered Players
II	IL, IN, IA, KS, KY, MI, MN, MO, NE, OH, SD, WI www.usasa.com/directory/midwest/index_e.html	33,746
III	AL, AR, FL, GA, LA, MS, NC, TX, OK, SC, TN_ www.usasa.com/directory/south/index_e.html	83,147
IV	AK, AZ, CA, CO, HI, ID, MT, NV, NM, OR, UT, WA, WY www.usasa.com/directory/west/index_e.html	68,390

The states with the greatest number of registered players for 2006 and 2007 were Texas (41,597), California (30,186), Metropolitan DC/VA (14,884), and Massachusetts (12,321). Most of the associations and leagues have their own web sites and links to these web sites can be found on the USASA web site. As an affiliation of adult soccer leagues and associations, the USASA does not offer membership to individual players. Players become members through their affiliated league or association.

Competitive Opportunities

Like any team sport, soccer requires a relatively large organization to assemble teams, provide venues and referees, and organize leagues and tournaments. Men's, women's and co-ed adult soccer leagues, both indoor and outdoor, are sponsored locally. The following programs are examples of local soccer leagues that are currently available around the country.

- The Palo Alto Adult Soccer League Palo Alto, CA, offers competition for men and women over 25; plays two seasons (spring and summer) with two men's divisions, based on skill level, and one women's division. No standings are kept. See http://www.paasl.org/cgi-bin/build.pl?root=template.htm&Content=main.htm.
- Southern Ohio Adult Soccer Association supports non-professional adult soccer for players over 18 in Columbus, Dayton, and Cincinnati. Leagues for men, women, and co-ed teams. See http://www.osysa.com/Amateur.html.
- Central Virginia Soccer Association in Richmond, VA, has been operating for 32 years and has 114 teams and more than 7,100 players with six divisions, including a Masters division. See http://www.cvsasoccer.org/.
- Florida State Soccer Association in Tampa, FL, is an affiliation of soccer leagues in Florida and the representative of U.S. Soccer in Florida. To find a league in Florida, see http://www.fssa.org/default.htm.
- Huntsville Adult Soccer League in Huntsville, AL, has 22 teams registered and is starting an over–40 league. See http://www.hasl.org/.

The best way to find a team and league in your area is to search the Internet, check with your local parks and recreation department, or inquire at the USASA.

The 2008 USASA Veterans Cup was held in Bellingham, WA, from July 8 to 13. It offered competition in fourteen age group divisions—eight men's divisions and six women's divisions. The team fee was $400. An application could be downloaded from http://www.veteranscup.us/2008%20Application.pdf.

Competitive Landscape

With more than 250,000 players, hundreds of teams and leagues, adult soccer is highly competitive at its highest levels. However, most leagues provide opportunities for inexperienced or less skilled players to compete.

In addition to the league play and tournaments sponsored by individual associations and leagues, the USASA sponsors the annual Veterans Cup for adult players. The 2007 USASA Veterans Cup Tournament was held in Bellingham, WA, from July 21 to 26 and had 82 teams participating in twelve divisions. Table 17–2 lists the divisions and the number of teams competing in each division for the 2007 USASA Veterans Cup.

Table 17–2
Divisions and Number of Teams in the 2007 USASA Veterans Cup

Division[1]	Number of Teams
Women Over 40 (Premier)	5
Women Over 40 (1st Division)	6
Women Over 45 (Premier)	4
Women Over 50	11
Women Over 55	4
Women Over 60	5
Men Over 40 (Premier)	6
Men Over 40 (1st Division)	6
Men Over 50	10
Men Over 55	12
Men Over 60	9

1 *Players on a Premier team cannot also play on a 1st Division team.*

The winners of the 2007 Veterans Cup in the over–40 age groups are listed in Appendix A. It is interesting to note that divisions for men and women and for older age groups have been added during the past five years, suggesting that there is growing interest in competitive soccer among these players. In 2008, this tournament offered 13 divisions.

• Men over 30, 35, 40 Premier and 1st Division, 45, 50, 55, and 60
• Women over 30, 40, 45, 50, and 55

However, the final number of divisions depended on the demographics of the entries.

How to Get Started

Skills

Soccer demands both fitness and skill; it is a challenging game to learn as an adult. If you do plan to play soccer for the first time, be sure to sign up with a team and league that can accommodate your skill, or lack of skill. While the object of the game and the rules are relatively simple, the coordination needed to control the ball with your feet and head, and the nuances of team play, are demanding. Fitness can compensate for some lack of skill, but the sport really demands both. The USASA has a national coaching scheme, so coaching may be available in your area.

Equipment

A pair of good soccer shoes is essential and may cost from $100 to $200. The rest of the equipment—ball and goals—should be provided by the team or league. However, you may want your own ball to refine your ball-handling skills; the typical cost is $25. The team fee, to cover uniforms, referees and field rental, will vary according to geographic area, length of season, and other considerations. The team fee for the 2008 Veterans Cup was $400.

Coaching

Although the USASA has a coaching committee and two national coaches (one for the men's team and one for the women's team, as well as a men's and women's coach for each of the four regions), these coaches are not responsible for coaching veteran teams. Most veteran teams rely on experienced players or recruit others to provide coaching expertise.

Venues

The quality of the playing field, or indoor venue, makes a tremendous difference in the enjoyment of the game. Leagues typically negotiate for venues. This is not a responsibility for individual players.

Recognition

Awards

In general, winners and runners-up of leagues and tournaments are given trophies or medals. Local or regional tournaments may name all-star teams or MVPs.

National Teams

The USASA does not select any national age group teams.

Rankings

The USASA does not rank teams nationally or name an All-American Team. It does, however, have a Hall of Fame.

Resources

Soccer Skills and Drills, Lennox, Steffen, and Rayfield, Human Kinetics Publishers, 2006.
Soccer Fundamentals, Danny Mielke, Human Kinetics, 2003.
A wonderful book with short pieces on the history, legends, and game of soccer is *Soccer in Sun and Shadow* by Eduardo Galeano (Verso, 2003). Galeano, a well-known Uruguayan poet and writer, presents an idiosyncratic account of the game (translated by Mark Fried).

Softball

Introduction

Softball began in a moment of good-natured horseplay between Harvard and Yale alumni at the Farragut Boat Club in Chicago in 1897. The group had gathered to hear the result of the Harvard-Yale football game. When it was announced that Yale had won 17–8, a Yale alumnus enthusiastically picked up a boxing glove and threw it at a Harvard alumnus who tried to hit it back with a stick. From this simple exchange a game was born. It began as an indoor game but soon moved outdoors, first as a way to keep firemen fit. In its early forms, it was known variously as kitten ball, diamond ball, mush ball, and pumpkin ball. Today, millions of people play organized softball in the United States and throughout the world. Softball was accepted as an Olympic sport in 1991, but it has recently been dropped for the 2012 Olympics.

No sport offers as many world championships and world series for adults in competitive classes that are based on a variety of criteria, including the players' ages, religion, profession, or ethnicity.

National Sponsoring Organizations

Unlike swimming and tennis, which are governed by a single national organization, national softball has a very decentralized administration. There are at least ten organizations that support and sponsor adult softball in the United States. To coordinate the activities of these organizations, a National Senior Softball Summit was created in 1999. More information on the summit can be found at http://www.softballrating.com/ratings.hp?division=50.

These sponsoring organizations include the following associations:

Amateur Softball Association/USA Softball

The largest softball association in the United States and the sport's governing body is the Amateur Softball Association of America (ASA). Founded in 1933, its organization is administered through 84 local associations that register teams and organize leagues throughout the country. The list of state affiliates is shown in Table 18–1. The list of metro affiliates can be found on the ASA web site. The ASA claims to have more than 250,000 adult softball teams bringing together more than four million players each year. All ASA teams are registered through the state or metro affiliates. The contact information for the national office is:

Amateur Softball Association of America
2801 NE 50th St
Oklahoma City, OK 73111
www.asasoftball.com

Table 18–1
State Affiliates of the Amateur Softball Association of America

State	Contact	Phone	E-mail / Web site
Alabama	Al Murray	(256) 413-0719	almurray@bellsouth.net www.alabamaasa.com
Alaska	Rod Hill	(907) 274-3585	rodhill13@gci.net www.alaskaasasoftball.com
Arizona	Don Fishel	(928) 777-1553	don.fishel@cityof prescott.net www.azasa.com
Arkansas	Don McGee	(501) 753-3698	j.d.mcgee@sbcglobal.net www.arasa.com
California-Central	Tom Dowd	(559) 299-3313	tom.dowd@centralcalasa.com www.ccmsasa.org
California-North	Mike Blondino	(650) 533-0864	mblondino@norcalasa.org www.norcalasa.org
California-South	Phil Gutierrez	(760) 945-1981	philgurierrezasa.cox,net www.socal-asa.com
Colorado	Loree Swope	(303) 365-9600	coloasa@comcast.com www.coloradoasa.org
Connecticut	Ed Austin	(203) 874-4036	edwardaustin@optonline.net www.connecticutasa.com
Deleware	Jack Lazartic	(302) 218-7502	Acesb14@aol.com www.dasasoftball.com

State	Contact	Phone	E-mail / Web site
Florida-Central	Tony Galloway	(407) 915-4325	centralfloridaasa@yahoo.com www.asacentralflorida.org
Florida-North	Randy Trousdell	(850) 385-8679	trousden@embarqmail.com www.northfloridaasa.com
Florida-South	Moris Uhler	(954) 600-7891	Baddadmoe1@aol.com www.southfloridaasa.com
Georgia	Al Dattolo	(678) 449-6054	GEORGIAASA@ATT.NET www.Georgiaasa.com
Hawaii	Don Meinel	(808) 523-4757	tamco@hawaiiantel.net www.asahawaii.com
Idaho	Steve Anthony	(208) 667-0827	sranthony1288@aol.com www/idahosoftball.com
Iliinois	Don Brewer	(618) 684-4890	dbrewer@roe30.k12.il.us www.illinoisasa.org
Indiana	Wayne Meyers	(812) 234-0339	inasacomm@aol.com www.indiana-asa.org
Iowa	Tom Topping	(641) 236-5766	tltopping@earthlink.net www.asasoftball.com/iowa/
Kansas	Joe Sproul	(785) 622-4241	jsproul@ruraltel.net www.kasasoftball.org
Kentucky	Bill Bollinger	(270) 683-9307	philly@owensboro.net www.kyasa.org
Louisiana	Bill Skinner	(985) 507-0092	bskinner2@charter.net www.louisianaASA.com
Maine	Bill Cary	(207) 767-7650	wcary@southportland.org www.maineasa.org
Maryland - DC	Jack Mowatt	(301) 621-7152	commissioner@mddcasa.org www.mddcasa.org
Massachusetts	Edward Ladley	(413) 684-1330	eladley@cbrsd.org www.massasa.com
Michigan	Jerry Hanson	(989) 835-5821	jerryhanson@masasoftball.org www.masasoftball.org
Minnesota	Perry Coonce	(763) 488-9995	perry@msf1.org www.msf1.org
Mississippi	E.T. Colvin	(662) 328-3180	et@ayrix.net www.missasa.com
Missouri	Joey Rich	(417) 869-2120	zsportsguy@centurytel.net http://missouriasasoftball. clubspaces.com
Montana	Bob Rowling	(406) 497-6408	browling@bsb.mt.gpv www.montanaasasoftball.com
Nebraska	Joe Patterson	(402) 462-7100	japtterson@cityofhastings.org www.nebraskasoftball.org
Nevada	Tony Pehle	(775) 353-7836	tpehle@cityofsparks.us www.nvasa.com
New Hampshipre	Bob hopley	(603) 610-7111	nhasarep@aol.com www.asa-nh.org
New Jersey	Leo Spirito	(973) 467-4034	lis@njasa.org www.njasa.org
New Mexico	Alice Cox	(505) 523-4336	alicecox09@comcast.net www.zianet.com/nmasa
New York	Robert Farrell	(315) 343-6096	nysasa@twcny.rr.com www.newyorkasa.org
North Carolina	Tony Laws	(336) 222-5030	tlaws@ci.burlington.nc.us www.northcarolinasa.com
North Dakota	Jim Hanley	(701) 772-2709	jimhanley@gra.midco.net www.ndasa.org
Ohio	Warren Jones	(419) 651-3335	warrenjones@zoominternet.net www.ohioasasoftball.org

State	Contact	Phone	E-mail / Web site
Oklahoma	Virgil Ackerson	(580) 628-2475	okcommissioner@hotmail.com www.oasa.org
Oregon	Mike Wells	(503) 445-2420	mwells@mywinsurance.com www.oregon-asa.com
Pennsylvania	Andrew Loechner	(717) 761-4508	asaofpaoff@verizon.net www.paasa.org
Rhode Island	Beverly Wiley	(401) 354-2973	beviwiley@aol.com www.rijoasa.org
South Carolina	Gerald McDonald	(864) 271-6200	geriagmc@bellsouth.net www.southcarolinasa.com
South Dakota	Bill Haher	(605) 642-3576	sdasacomm@yahoo.com www.sdasasoftball.com
Tennessee	James Ellis	(423) 747-8272	ellisJMHA@charter.net www.tennesseeasa.com
Texas	Glenn Morrison	(254) 501-7760	gmorrison@ci.killeen.tx.us www.txasa.org
Utah	Starleen Orullian	(801) 262-2856	UtahASA@hotmail.com www.utahasa.com
Vermont	Lynn Robolini	(802) 229-0969	ribs@verizon.net www.vermontasa.com
Virginia	Henry Pollard	(804) 569-0532	henryandjuliepollard@msn.com www.centralvaasa.com
Washington	Carol English-Hawley	(360) 847-7081	carol.english@ci.vancouver.wa.us www.washingtonasa.com
West Virginia	Andy Dooley	(540) 384-7172	piedmontasa@verizon.net www.wvasa.com
Wisconsin	Tom Raimer	(245) 685-7984	raimertm@msn.com www.wisconsin-asa.org
Wyoming	Ron Merritt	(307) 886-5755	rmerritt@silverstar.com www.wyosoftball.com

Because the organization of the ASA is decentralized, the best way to get involved is to contact your local affiliate. The ASA offer Balls and Strikes Online Magazine at no cost on their web site at http://www.asasoftball.com/about/magazine.asp.

National Softball Association

The National Softball Association (NSA) was founded in 1982 and is specifically designed to help parks and recreation departments and private sports complex operators to organize softball leagues. It organizes and sponsors softball leagues and post-season tournaments. To reach the NSA:

National Softball Association
Box 7
Nicholasville, KY 40340
(859) 887-4114
nashdqtrs@aol.com
www.playnsa.com

The NSA divides its competitive offerings into divisions (men, women, and coed), classes (18 separate classes of skill levels), and programs (23 types including age groups). The NSA lists 117 area, state, or regional directors. A contact for each of the states having an NSA director is shown in Table 18–2. Sanction-registration fees are $20 per year per adult. Online registration is available on the NSA's web site or through the state and regional directors.

Table 18–2
State Affiliates of the National Softball Association

State	Contact	Phone	E-mail / Web site
Alabama	Joe Cothan	(256) 492-3020	jjcothran@bellsouth.net
			www.alabamansa.com
Alaska	Patrick McCabe	(902) 272-4200	pmccabe@gci.net
Arizona	Chris Franciscus	(412) 874-4074	chris@playnsaaz.com
			www.playnsaaz.com
Arkansas	Rick Stocker	(479) 631-0336	rstocker@rogersark.org
California-North	Brian Gregoire	(209) 481-9405	brian@nsacal.com
			www.nsacal.com
California-South	Kristy Nactweh	(619) 593-1484	halkristy03@cox.net
Colorado	Ernie Perez	(303) 619-5648	eperez@nsacolorado.com
			www.nsacolorado.com
Connecticut	David Reno	(203) 415-4642	dtreno33@aol.com
Deleware	John Floyd	(609) 790-0055	njnsasd@comcast.ne
			www.njnsayouth.com
Florida	John Lynch	(609) 790-0055	johnlucicomcast.net
Georgia	Carlos Butler	(678) 793-9583	cbutler9901@yahoo.com
Hawaii	Bruce Sugawa	(808) 677-0049	bruce21@hawaii.rr.com
Idaho	Marty Lalley	(702) 896-3053	mlalley3@cox.net
Iliinois	Gerry Gund	(815) 932-4336	illinoisnsa@comcast.net
			www.illinoisnsa.com
Indiana	Richard Foltz	(312) 293-1776	Rbfoltz@cs.com
			www.indianansa.com
Iowa	Rob Humphrey	(319) 750-0917	hump008@yahoo.com
			www.nsanorth.com
Kansas	Mark Balven	(636) 475-3720	nsamissouri@hotmail.com
			www.nsamissouri.com
Kentucky	Jack Roney	(606) 423-4026	NSAKY@windstream.net
			www.KentuckyNSA.com
Louisiana	J.D. Jones	(318) 791-5999	jdjlsu@hotmail.com
Maine	Steve Collins	(978) 937-5515	Steve@northeastnsa.com
			www.northeastnsa.com
Maryland	Adrian Burns	(301) 633-7573	ab_msua@comcast.com
Massachusetts	Steve Collins	(978) 937-5515	Steve@northeastnsa.com
			www.northeastnsa.com
Michigan	Bill Horton	(810) 629-9551	NSAReg5@aol.com
Minnesota	Jim Valentine	(262) 862-7165	wisconsinNSA@gmail.com
			www.wisconsinnsa.com
Mississippi	Clemon Terrell	(601) 545-4623	cterrell@harriesburgms.com
None			
Missouri	Mark Balven	(636) 475-3720	nsamissouri@hotmail.com
			www.nsamissouri.com
Montana	Marty Lalley	(702) 896-3053	mlalley3@cox.net
Nebraska	Bill Horton	(810) 629-9551	NSAReg5@aol.com
			www.nsanorth.com
Nevada	Marty Lalley	(702) 896-3053	mlalley3@cox.net
New Hampshipre	Steve Collins	(978) 937-5515	Steve@northeastnsa.com
			www.northeastnsa.com
New Jersey	Andy Dill	(609) 978-2548	spankie15@comcast.com
New Mexico	Shelly Gonzales	(505) 294-5405	getdirtysports@aol.com
New York	Chuck Birch	(607) 642-5230	Cebiii@prodigy.net
North Carolina	Michael Poe	(919) 625-6545	mike@carolinansa.com
			www.carolinansa.com
North Dakota	Bill Horton	(810) 629-9551	NSAReg5@aol.com
			www.nsanorth.com
Ohio	John DeLuca	(216) 661-7408	ohionsachief347@roadrunner.com

State	Contact	Phone	E-mail / Web site
Oklahoma	Brad Gordon	(918) 286-0514	bdgordon11@cox.net www.oklahomansa.com
Oregon	Marty Lalley	(702) 896-3053	mlalley3@cox.net
Pennsylvania	Andy Dill	(609) 978-2548	spankie15@comcast.com
Rhode Island	Greg Fleury	(401) 623-0343	GFLEURYRINSA@aol.com
South Carolina	Jeff Williams	(803) 329-9877	jwilliams@lesco.net www.scslowpitch.com
South Dakota	Bill Horton	(810) 629-9551	NSAReg5@aol.com www.nsanorth.com
Tennessee	Connie Jennette	(615) 501-0260	CJUMP4U@aol.com
Texas	Sonja Ritchie	(859) 983-4169	sdr229@aol.com
Utah	Troy Doezie	(630) 244-4244	nsautah@yahoo.com
Vermont	Steve Collins	(978) 937-5515	Steve@northeastnsa.com www.northeastnsa.com
Virginia	Tommy Zehmer	(757) 592-2817	NSAVA@AOL.COM www.virginiansa.com
Washington	Dale Gellner	(425) 741-9761	Dalesports@aol.com
West Virginia	Tommy Zehmer	(757) 592-2817	NSAVA@AOL.COM www.virginiansa.com
Wisconsin	Jim Valentine	(262) 862-7165	wisconsinNSA@gmail.com www.wisconsinnsa.com
Wyoming	Marty Lalley	(702) 896-3053	mlalley3@cox.net

Senior Softball — USA

Founded in 1988, Senior Softball—USA (SSUSA) is an organization devoted exclusively to softball for men over 50 and women over 45. Unlike other organizations that sponsor both adult and youth softball, the SSUSA focuses solely on adults. It offers age group divisions for men from 50+ to 70+ and for women from 45+ to 60+ in five year increments. SSUSA has 1,500 teams registered in 2008.

Senior Softball—USA
2701 K Street Suite 101A
Sacramento, CA 95816
(916) 326-5303
frand@seniorsoftball.com
http://www.seniorsoftball.com

The SSUSA operates through a series of regional directors which are listed in Table 18 3. SSUSA publishes a bi-monthly newsletter, Senior Softball News, with an annual subscription of $15.

Table 18–3
State Affiliates of the Senior Softball Association

Region	Contact	Phone	E-mail
South California	Paul Cochet	(805) 566-1036	ussa93109@yahoo.com
California	Fran Dowell	(916) 326-5303	frand@seniorsoftball.com
Southwest	Rick Seifman	(623) 776-3525	tournsport@aol.com
Northwest	Mike Sisavic	(503) 314-3967	fsisavic@hotmail.com
North	Steve Simmons	(952) 239-7674	stnlsimmons@aol.com
Mid-South	Keith Parker	(903) 315-6374	eagleat13@yahoo.com
Great Lakes	None Listed		
Southeast	Mark Ogletree	(913) 319-0669	twig_ssusa@twlakes.net
East	Steve Simmons	(952) 239-7674	stnlsimmons@aol.com
Florida	John Truitt	(563) 505-7301	truittjo@aoll.com

Independent Softball Association

The Independent Softball Association (ISA) calls itself the most progressive association in softball and supports 15,000 teams involving approximately 250,000 players. Founded in 1984, the ISA has initiated or adopted a number of innovative rules to speed up the game and make it more exciting. It allows stealing after the ball has crossed the plate or hit the ground. Its leagues and tournaments are organized by gender, age group, and skill level and operate in 31 states.

Independent Softball Association
670 W. Main St.
Bartow, FL 33830
(853) 519-7127
www.isasoftball.com

The list of state contacts and e-mail addresses is shown in Table 18–4.

Table 18–4
State Affiliates of the Independent Softball Association

State	Contact	E-mail
Alabama	http://www.alabamaisa.com/	al@isasoftball.com
Arizona	http://www.arizonaisa.com/	az@isasoftball.com
Arkansas	http://www.arkansasisa.com/	ak@isasoftball.com
California	http://www.isacalifornia.com/	ca@isasoftball.com
Colorado	http://www.isacolorado.com/	co@isasoftball.com
Deleware	http://www.delewareisa.com/	de@isasoftball.com
Florida	http://www.isaflorida.com/	fl@isasoftball.com
Georgia	http://www.isageorgia.com/	ga@isasoftball.com
Iliinois	http://www.illinoisisa.com/	il@isasoftball.com
Indiana	http://www.indianaisa.com/	in@isasoftball.com
ISA National Office	http://www.isasoftball.com/	isa@isasoftball.com
Kansas	http://www.kansasisa.com/	ks@isasoftball.com
Kentucky	http://www.kentuckyisa.com/	ky@isasoftball.com
Maryland	http://www.isamaryland.com/	md@isasoftball.com
Massachusetts	http://www.isamass.com/	ma@isasoftball.com
Michigan	http://www.michiganisa.com/	mi@isasoftball.com
Minnesota	http://www.minnesotaisa.com/	mn@isasoftball.com
Mississippi	http://www.isamississippi.com/	mi@isasoftball.com
Missouri	http://www.missouriisa.com/	mo@isasoftball.com
Nevada	http://www.nevadaisa.com/	nv@isasoftball.com
New Jersey	http://www.newjerseyisa.com/	nj@isasoftball.com
New Mexico	http://www.newmexicoisa.com/	nm@isasoftball.com
New York	http://www.nyisa.com/	ny@isasoftball.com
North Carolina	http://www.isanc.com/	nc@isasoftball.com
Ohio	http://www.isaohio.com/	oh@isasoftball.com
Oregon	http://www.oregonisa.com/	or@isasoftball.com
Pennsylvania	http://www.isapenn.com/	pa@isasoftball.com
Rhode Island	http://www.rhodeislandisa.com/	ri@isasoftball.com
South Carolina	http://www.carolinaisa.com/	sc@isasoftball.com
Tennessee	http://www.tennesseeisa.com/	tn@isasoftball.com
Texas	http://www.txisa.com/	tx@isasoftball.com
Utah	http://www.utahisa.com/	ut@isasoftball.com
Virginia	http://www.virginiaisa.com/	vi@isasoftball.com
Washington	http://www.isawashington.net/	wa@isasoftball.com
West Virginia	http://www.isawv.com/	wv@isasoftball.com

Softball Players Association

The Softball Player Association (SPA) was founded in 1992. One of the goals of the SPA is to "protect the integrity of the game of softball" through classifying the teams fairly and providing opportunities for senior softball players.

Softball Players Association
925 W. State Highway 152
Mustang, OK 73064
www.spasoftball.com

The SPA's team registration includes men's and women's teams in five-year increments from 35+ to 80+. It reports that it has 400+ teams and 10,000+ players.

The International Senior Softball Association

Among the goals of the International Senior Softball Association (ISSA) is "to foster productive working relationships among other senior softball organizations." In this role it appears to serve other organizations rather than to directly serve individuals or teams. However, it does sponsor the ISSA World Championship.

The International Senior Softball Association
9401 East St.
Manassas, VA 20110
(703) 368-1188
http://www.seniorsoftball.org/about/
issa@seniorsoftball.org

The Las Vegas Senior Softball Association

The Las Vegas Senior Softball Association (LVSSA) was founded in 2000 and is incorporated in the state of Nevada. It sponsors local (Las Vegas) recreational play and several tournaments including a world masters championship. It currently has 300 members and membership dues are $50 per year. Interestingly, dues are waived for members of 80 years of age.

The Las Vegas Senior Softball Association
PO Box 371135
Las Vegas, Nevada 89137
LVseniorsoftball@aol.com
http://www.lvssa.com/

The Huntsman Games

A full description of the Huntsman Games is included in Chapter 28. To contact the Huntsman Games:

Huntsman World Senior Games
1070 West 1600 South, A-103
St. George, Utah 84770
(435) 674-0550 or
(800) 562-1268
http://www.seniorgames.net
hwsg@seniorgames.net

North American Senior Circuit Softball

The North American Senior Circuit Softball (NASCS) was incorporated in 1985 and one of the goals of the organization is to dismiss the myths about aging by offering competitive outlets to athletes 50 and older at the national and international levels. It promotes the Senior Softball World Series and a series of regional tournaments.

North American Senior Circuit Softball
2510 Champions Way
Lansing, MI 48910
(517) 393-0505
www.nascs.org
kennascs@aol.com

Women's Senior Softball

As the list of softball national champions in Appendix A shows, only the SSUSA, the Huntsman Games, and the LVSSA offer age group softball competition for women over 40. However, the interest in women's softball is strong and growing. It is likely that this will change in the near future. For women interested in playing softball, Women's Senior Softball.Com (WSSC) at http://www.womensseniorsoftball.com/ seeks to help women players find competitive opportunities. Women's Senior Softball's directors can be reached at:

Connie Stewart
(702) 275-3937 — Cell
grannysoftball@aol.com

Cindi Winslow
(702) 813-4331
cyndi1@cox.net

Betti Garnett
(727) 459-5613
softball2eag@aol.com

Competitive Opportunities

The sport of softball has several disciplines:

- Fast Pitch has no restriction on the trajectory of the ball or the motion of the pitcher. Pitchers use a windmill motion to achieve pitch speeds of 70 mph or more. With the pitcher's mound only 46 feet from the batter, hitting the ball is, to say the least, challenging.
- Slow Pitch requires that the pitch have at least a three-foot arc, allowing more hitting. A popular variation of slow pitch softball uses a 16-inch ball rather than the standard 12-inch ball.
- Modified Slow Pitch restricts the motion of the pitcher (no windmilling) resulting in a pitch speed between the typical pitching speed of the two other disciplines.

The decentralization of organized softball, as well as the enthusiasm of its players, coaches, and administrators, has resulted in a broad network of leagues and tournaments.

With multiple organizations supporting softball in the United States, there is no shortage of opportunities to compete. However, local leagues, organized by municipalities, are the grassroots foundation of the sport. The best way to explore competitive opportunities is to contact your local parks department or recreation department. If there are no leagues in your area, contact one of the national organizations and they will be delighted to help you, or your local parks department, organize a league.

Leagues are typically organized by skill level, gender, and age. Seasons usually culminate in tournaments which may lead to participation in one of the national or international tournaments.

The breadth of the competitive landscape is truly astonishing. The ASA offers more than 100 national tournaments. The ASA has a Find a Local Tournament function on its web site at http://www.asasoftball.com/tournaments/_getLocalTournaments.asp. The NSA lists more than a dozen playing categories, including indoor softball, Native American softball, Hispanic softball, and Military-Industrial softball.

The summary of the major softball tournaments in Table 18–5 only hints at the breadth of the competitive landscape. All these tournaments included age group categories, men's and women's divisions, and, in many cases, skill-level divisions and fast and slow pitch. For more information, consult the sponsor's web site.

Table 18–5
2008 National Softball Tournaments

Sponsor	Gender/Age Group (1)	Location	Date
ASA	Men Fast Pitch 40+	Minot, ND	Aug. 20–24
ASA	Men 40+	Dallas, TX	Aug. 22–24
ASA	Men Fast Pitch 45+	Springfield, MO	Aug. 14–17
ASA	Men 40+	Roseville, CA	Sept. 5–7
ASA	Men East, All Ages	Burlington, NC	Aug. 29–Sept. 1
ASA	Men West, All Ages	Spokane, WA	Aug. 29–Sept. 1
ASA	Men Fast Pitch 50+	Ft. Worth, TX	Sept. 26–28
NSA	Men Winter World Series, All Ages	Naples, FL	Feb. 15–17
SSUSA	Men & Women, All Ages	Polk County, FL	Feb. 15–17
ISA	Men Senior Worlds, All Ages	Bridgeton, MO	Aug. 1-3
SPA	Men Nationals, All Ages (2)	Dalton, GA	Sept. 4–18
SPA	Men Nationals, 50+, 55+, 60+ (2)	Tulsa, OK	July 18–20
ISSA	Men & Women, All Ages	Manassas, VA	Aug. 15–17
LVSSA	Men & Women, All Ages	Las Vegas, NV	Aug. 29–Oct. 5
WSSC	Women, All Ages	Phoenix, AZ	Oct. 17–19
Huntsman	Men & Women, All Ages	St. George, UT	Oct. 6–18
NASCS	Men, All Ages	Lincoln, NE	Aug. 2–10

1 All games are slow pitch unless otherwise noted.

2 The SPA Nationals in Dalton include all divisions except the Major Plus, Major for 50+, 55+, and 60, which were held in Tulsa, OK.

Competitive Landscape

At the highest levels of competition, softball is extremely competitive. However, with the wide range of competitive categories, including softball disciplines, age groups and skill levels, an individual or team should find a reasonable level of competition. Table 18–6 summarizes the number of age group divisions and the number of teams in the various softball national championships and world series.

Table 18–6
Age Group Divisions in the 2007 Softball Championships and World Series

Sponsor	Number of Age Group Divisions	Age Range	Number of Teams
ASA	21	Men 50+ to 70+	104

Sponsor	Number of Age Group Divisions	Age Range	Number of Teams
NSA	8	Men 40+ to 70+	25
SSUSA	30	Men 40+ to 80+	290
		Women 40+ to 65+	31
ISA	8	Men 50+ to 60+	NA
ISSA	12	Men 50+ to 65+	55
SPA	24	Men 50+ to 80+	174
Huntsman	44	Men 50+ to 74+	266
		Women 50+ to 70+	56
LVSSA	25	Men 50+ to 75+	NA
		Women 40+ to 60+	NA

The list of national champions for the ASA, NSA, ISSA, SPA, Huntsman Games, and LVSSA is in Appendix A.

Estimates of the number of softball players in the United States range from two to five million, depending on whether you want to include recreational softball such as charity events, local weekend tournaments, and pick-up games. Given the breadth of softball opportunities available in the United States, both the rank beginner and the elite player should be able to find an appropriate competitive level.

How to Get Started

Skills

Having some experience playing baseball or softball is obviously a plus. However, at the lowest levels of the sport, there is great tolerance for rookies. Grit and enthusiasm can make up for a lack of playing experience.

Equipment

You'll need a glove which can cost from less than $100 to more than $400 new. The cost of a used glove will depend on the condition. There is nothing like the smell and feel of a newly broken-in glove. Most teams provide bases, bats and balls.

Coaching

There is almost no formal coaching, but most experienced players are willing—sometimes too willing—to provide tips to a novice player.

Venues

The team fee generally includes access to a softball field, as well as qualified umpires for league and tournament games.

Recognition

Awards

Leagues and tournaments typically provide awards for the top two or three teams and often name most valuable players and all-tournament teams.

National Teams

Given the number of national organizations, there is no single national team or national champion, but every organization crowns a champion in the various competitive categories. The list of national champions for the various sponsors of adult softball is in Appendix A.

Rankings

Although no organization ranks softball teams, The National Senior Softball Summit rates 1,908 softball teams by age group. The ratings are based on the previous year's performance and place teams in a competitive class—Major Plus, Major, AAA, and AA. The ratings are supported by nine organizations: ASA, ISA, LVSSA, NSA, SSUSA, SPA, ISSA, ISF, and the Huntsman Games. Table 18–7 shows the number of teams rated by age group, as of February 29, 2008. The ratings can be found at http://www.softballrating.com/.

Table 18–7
National Senior Softball Summit Team Ratings

Age Group	Team Ranked
50+	552
55+	382
60+	437
65+	308
70+	200
75+	29

Resources

Softball Skills and Drills, Judi Garman, Human Kinetics, 2001.
Softball Fundamentals, Rick Noren, Human Kinetics, 2005.
In addition to the publications available through the various sponsoring organizations, *Softball Magazine* (http://www.softballmag.com/) covers all aspects of the game for an annual subscription of $20 per year.

Speedskating

Introduction

All sports thrive on technological advances. Whether it's a shorter ski, a lighter shoe, or a racquet with more feel, elite athletes, and equipment manufacturers, are always looking for the next evolutionary or revolutionary leap forward. For speedskating, the two important technological leaps have occurred in the past fifty years. In 1960, racing on manmade ice became the Olympic standard, and in 1996 the clap skate was adopted by Olympic skaters. Although the concept of the clap skate may have been around since the early 1900s, it wasn't until the 1980s when the Faculty of Human Movement Sciences at Vrije Univeriteit of Amsterdam developed a competitive skate. The clap skate has a hinge between the toe of the boot and the skate blade so that the skater can use a longer stride and maximize the contact between the blade and the ice. Virtually every serious speedskater today uses the clap skate.

A few speedskaters over 40 may compete for spots on the U.S. Olympic Team, but most of the Masters speedskaters compete in age group divisions which are supported by the national sponsoring organization.

National Sponsoring Organization

The National Sponsoring Organization for speedskating is U.S. Speedskating (USS).
U.S. Speedskating
5662 South 4800 West
Kerns, UT 84118
(801) 417-5360
Executive Director: Bob Crowley
pkinder@usspeedskating.org
http://www.usspeedskating.org/

A first-year USS membership for competing athletes is $30 and is $55 thereafter. An electronic newsletter, *iBlade*, and a print newsletter, *Ice Chips*, are both available online at the USS web site.

Most U.S. speedskating clubs and competitions are located in the northern tier of the country. Table 19–1 lists the 15 speedskating associations in the U.S. and the number of member clubs in each association. For information on the individual clubs, go to the USS club locator under Clubs & Programs.

Table 19–1
U.S. Speedskating Associations and Clubs

Association	E-Mail	Clubs
Greater Minnesota Speedskating Association	jvondrasek@ankenykell.com	6
Amateur Skating Association of Illinois	cusosk8@hotmail.com	9
Wisconsin Speedskating Association	bob.c.neville@cummins.com	6
Missouri Speedskating Association	mospeedsk8@sbeglobal.net	3
Wasatch Speedskating Association	drewsymi@yahoo.com	3
Northern California Speedskating Association	sk8sicle@comcast.net	3
Southern California Speedskating Association	rdrusk@gmail.com	2
Michigan Speedskating Association	betcbedford@aol.com	7
Ohio Speedskating Association	ccurley@metrohealth.org	5
Chesapeake Speedskating Association	doinhome@comcast.net	9
Mid-Atlantic Speedskating Association	georso@optonline.net	7
Western New York Speedskating Association	Doherty_realty@hotmail.com	2
Northern New York Speedskating Association	rstrauss@nycap.rr.com	9
Connecticut Speedskating Association	seriousspeed007@yahoo.com	1
Northeast Speedskating Association	jim3775710@attbi.com	4

Competitive Opportunities

Speedskating competitions base competitive classes on:

- Gender—men and women
- Age—Currently 10-year age groups: 40–49, 50–59, 60–69, and 70+
- Distance—From 500 meters to 3,000 meters for long track races and 25 kilometers or more in marathon races. There are no over–40 age groups in short track racing.

The associations listed in Table 19–1 sponsor many adult speedskating meets and publicize them on their web site. Table 19–2 lists the 2008 major competitions that included age group competition.

Table 19–2
2008 Speedskating Major Competitions

Event	Location	Date
National Long Track Championships	Lake Placid, NY	Feb. 2–3
Masters International Long Track Championships	Milwaukee, WI	Feb. 16–17
North American Marathon Championships	Edmonton, AL (CAN)	Feb. 16–17
US Speedskating National Marathon	Bemidji, MN	Feb. 23–24

The results of these competitions are presented in Appendix A.

Competitive Landscape

The youngest age group for Masters Speedskating is 30–39, but, as noted above, only age groups over 40 are included here. Table 19–3 shows the number of competitors at the 2008 USS National Marathon and Long Course Championships.

Table 19–3
Number of Competitors at the 2007–2008
National Speedskating Championships[1]

Event	Gender	Age Group	Competitors
Marathon[2]	Men	40–49	14
Marathon[2]	Men	50–59	9
Marathon[2]	Men	60–69	2
Marathon[2]	Women	40–49	2
Marathon[2]	Women	50–59	5
Long Track[3]	Men	40–49	39
Long Track[3]	Men	50–59	45
Long Track[3]	Men	60–69	42
Long Track[3]	Men	70+	15
Long Track[3]	Women	40–49	35
Long Track[3]	Women	50–59	20
Long Track[3]	Women	60–69	5

1 These data refer to the 2008 National Marathon Championship in Bemidji, MN, on February 23 and 24 and the 2008 National Long Track Championship in Lake Placid, NY, on February 2 and 3.

2 Includes results from both the 25k and the 50k races

3 Includes results from the 500m, 800m, 1000m, 1500m, and 3000m races

Of the 233 competitors, 29 percent were women and 27 percent were over 60.

How to Get Started

Skills

In addition to basic skating skills, speedskating requires strength and, for longer races, endurance. Basic skating skills can be learned and practiced on any ice rink. Racing calls for refining these skills under the tutelage of a good coach.

Equipment

Beginners should start with a good used hockey or figure skate, which can often be purchased for less than $100. Modern clap skates can cost $500 or more.

Coaching

Some basic instruction is available on the USS web site and the USS certifies three levels of coaching and offers coaching clinics throughout the year.

Venues

The Find a Club section of the USS web site identifies ice skating facilities that support speedskating throughout the country.

Recognition

Awards

The first three places in each event generally receive medals.

National Teams

The USS does not select any age group national teams.

Rankings

The USS does not rank or rate age group racers.

Resources

A Basic Guide to Speedskating (An Official Olympic Committee Sports Series), Griffin Publishing, 2001.

Speed on Skates: A Complete Technique, Training, and Racing Guide for In-Line and Ice Skaters, Barry Publow, Human Kinetics, 1999.

Complete Handbook of Speed Skating, Dianne Holum, Enslow Publishing, 1984.

Squash

Introduction

The sport of squash evolved from other racquet sports played in England by boys at the Harrow School in the late 19th century. From a makeshift game played against the walls of campus buildings using a crude rubber ball and sawed-off racquets, squash has grown into a sport with more than 500,000 players in the United States.

The four-walled court forces competitors into a fierce intimacy that calls for both quickness and deep reserves of fitness. Although it is a fast, demanding sport, it also involves a measure of guile and cunning that has prompted individuals 60 years of age and older to compete. Sixty-seven men over 60 and 13 over the age of 75 competed in squash's 2006 Age Group Nationals.

Over the past 70 years squash in the United States has undergone a painful and expensive transition from the hardball game to the international softball game. James Zug, in his excellent history of the sport, likened the two games to fraternal twins "sharing the same genetic material, yet having trifling altered appearance." The games shared a four-wall court, a rubber ball, and strung racquet of basically the same size. The trifling differences were the ball—harder in the U.S. softer in England—and the width of the court—18.5 feet in the U.S. and 21 feet in England. What a difference 30 inches and the density of rubber can make. The U.S. game was faster with very little margin for error. The English game resulted in longer rallies, more finesse, and basically more squash-playing skills. The softball game spread throughout the non–U.S. world and, in order to compete in international competitions, Americans finally capitulated. The cost of rebuilding hundreds of courts in the U.S. and marginalizing several generations of hardball players has not been calculated. Today, those struggles are over and the sport—softball squash—is simply squash.

National Sponsoring Organization

The official national governing body of squash racquets is US Squash (formerly USSRA) and its mission is "to promote, develop, and increase participation in squash throughout the United States."

US Squash
555 Eighth Avenue Suite 1102
New York, New York 10018
(212) 268-4090
office@us-squash.org
www.us-squash.org

For administrative purposes, US Squash divides the United States into 43 District Squash Racquets Associations (SRAs). Table 20–1 lists the districts and their web sites.

Table 20–1
US Squash Districts

District SRA	Web site or Contact
Alaska	Bob Landau; rlandau@gei.net
Alaska	membership@ussquash.cmo
Albany (NY)	www.cds.org
Arizona	http://arizona.us-squash.org/news/
Buffalo	www.buffalosquash.org
Cincinnati	www.cincinnatisquash.com
Columbus (OH)	http://squashclub.org/csra/
Connecticut	membership@ussquash.cmo
Dallas (TX)	www.dallassquash.org
Florida	www.floridasquash.com
Hawaii	membership@ussquash.cmo
Houston	www.hsra.us-squash.org/
Idaho	membership@ussquash.cmo
Iliinois	www.illinoissquash.org/
Indiana	membership@ussquash.cmo
Iowa	membership@ussquash.cmo
Kentucky	www.kysra.org/
Maryland	www.mssra.net/

District SRA	Web site or Contact
Massachusetts	www.ma-squash.org/
Michigan	www.michigansquash.org/html/index.html
Minnesota	www.mnsquash.org
Mississippi	membership@ussquash.cmo
Montana	membership@ussquash.cmo
Nebraska	membership@ussquash.cmo
Nevada	membership@ussquash.cmo
New Mexico	www.nmsra.us-squash.org/
New York City (NY)	www.msra.net/
Northern California	www.norcalsquash.org/
Northern New Jersey	www.nnjsra.org/nnjhome.asp
Philadelphia (PA)	www.phillyboast.org
Pittsburgh (PA)	http://fp.cs.cmu.edu/boxleague/squash.php
Rhode Island	www.risra.org/risra/risra.php
Rochester (NY)	www.squashrochester.org/
Seattle (WA)	www.seattlesquash.com/
South Dakota	membership@ussquash.cmo
Southern California	www.socalsquash.com/
Southeastern	www.sesra.org/index2.html
St. Louis (MO)	www.stlsquash.org/
Tennessee	membership@ussquash.cmo
Virginia	www.vsra.us-squash.org
Washington DC	membership@ussquash.cmo
West Virginia	membership@ussquash.cmo
Wisconsin	membership@ussquash.cmo
Wyoming	membership@ussquash.cmo

If you do not find an SRA near you, you can contact the US Squash office for help.

US Squash annual membership fees are assessed according to the district and vary with the SRA, but range from $45 to $65. One of the member benefits is a subscription to *Squash Magazine*, a monthly publication.

Competitive Opportunities

The transition from hardball to softball is still going on and US Squash offers competition in both disciplines, although today softball squash is significantly more popular. Competitions are based on one or more of the following criteria:

- Game type—singles and doubles. Unlike racquetball, the other major indoor racquet sport, the doubles court in squash is larger than the singles court.
- Age group—Age groups are divided into 5–year increments beginning at age 35 for both men and women. The top age group for men is 85+ and the top age group for women is 75+
- Gender—men, women, and mixed for some doubles competitions
- Ratings—The US Squash ratings are based on a number scale from 2.0 (least likely to win any given match) to 6.5 (most likely to win any given match). The rating uses an algorithm to calculate the probability of winning any given match and is recalculated after each match. Distinctions among players of similar ratings are clear because ratings are calculated to the fifth decimal point (e.g., 4.55671). The rating algorithm is similar to that used by the US Chess Federation. For more information on ratings see http://www.us-squash.org/ratings/.

The ten national championship tournaments sponsored by US Squash for adults in 2007 and 2008 are listed in Table 20–2.

Table 20–2
US Squash 2007–2008 National Championships for Adults

Tournaments	Dates	Location
US Open Championships (Men)	9/27–10/4 2007	New York, NY
US Women's Team Championship	11/2–11/4 2007	Boston, MA
US Mixed Doubles Championship	2/1–2/3 2008	Boston, MA
US Hardball Championship	2/22–2/24 2008	Philadelphia, PA
US Century Doubles Championship	2/29–3/2 2008	New York, NY
US Open Age Division Championship	3/13–3/16 2008	Atlanta, GA
US Doubles Championship	3/28–3/30 2008	Philadelphia, PA
US Squash Skill Level Championship	4/10–4/12 2008	New Haven, CT
US Father-Son Championship	4/18–4/20 2008	New York, NY
US Mother-Daughter Championship	5/2–5/4 2008	Locust Valley, NY

The regional SRAs offer hundreds of local and regional tournaments that can be found on their web sites.

To find a club or other facility with squash courts, the US Squash web site has a Squash Court Locator at http://www.us-squash.org/tools/club-listing.php.

Competitive Landscape

By its very nature as a fast-paced sport in a confined space, squash competitions are typically intense. While squash is certainly a national game, the historic centers of squash are east of the Mississippi River and north of the Mason-Dixon Line. Most of the national championships are played in the northeast and most of the ranked players are from this part of the country as well.

Table 20–3 shows the number of players who competed in the 2007 National Squash Open in the over–40 age group divisions.

Table 20–3
Number of Competitors in the
2007 Squash Nationals Over 40 Age Groups

Gender	Age Group	Number of Competitors
Women	45+	11
Women	50+	6
Men	40+	8
Men	45+	22
Men	50+	23
Men	55+	16
Men	60+	10
Men	65+	9
Men	70+	8
Men	75+/80+	7

Of the 120 competitors in the over–40 age groups, 14 percent were women and players over 60 years of age accounted for 28 percent of all over–40 competitors. The names of the national champions are listed in Appendix A.

The 2007 Skill Level Championship was played in New York City and drew 322 players. A look at both the age group rankings and the skill level ratings show that men outnumber women competitors by more than 2 to 1. Table 20–4 shows the number of players in each of the rating categories.

Table 20–4
2007 Skill Level Ratings

Rating	Men	Women
2.0	8	19
2.5	148	68
3.0	383	114
3.5	549	76
4.0	465	57
4.5	330	27
5.0	158	8
5.5	78	2
6.0	28	0
6.5	6	0

US Squash also ranks players by age group and the number of ranked players in each division over 40 is shown in Table 20–5.

Table 20–5
U.S. Squash 2006/2007 Age Group Rankings

Age Group	Ranked Players
Women Over 40	6
Women Over 45	7
Women Over 50	5
Men Over 40	140
Men Over 45	73
Men Over 50	131
Men Over 55	52
Men Over 60	55
Men Over 65	26
Men Over 70	20
Men Over 75	3

Approximately 3 percent of the ranked players in age groups over 40 are women and players over 60 years of age account for 20 percent of all ranked players over 40.

How to Get Started

Skills

Squash requires a demanding combination of fitness and guile. The basics of the game can be learned in an afternoon, but understanding the intricacies of position and angles takes much longer. There is a great deal of starting and stopping which places demands on the knee and ankle joints. Of course, racquet-ball-eye coordination is essential.

Equipment

A good racquet, proper shoes, and protective eyewear are all you need to bring to a match. A new squash racquet can cost from $100 to over $300, but used racquets can often be found in the closets or garages of long-time players.

Coaching

Most venues with squash courts—private clubs, schools, or colleges—can provide lessons and individual coaching, or can put you in touch with a coach. A lesson or two is always a good idea and is essential for a beginner.

Venues

The US Squash web site has a Court Finder feature that includes the locations of squash courts in every state except Arkansas. The list indicates name, address, and phone number, as well as which type(s) of courts can be found at each location—hardball singles, hardball doubles, softball singles, softball doubles, or converted racquetball court.

Recognition

Awards

Typically, the winner and runner-up in each competitive class receive awards.

Rankings

US Squash ranks competitors by both age group competitors and skill level. The top ranked players in each age group, as well as the national champions, are listed in Appendix A.

National Teams

Although US Squash does select and publish national teams for men, women, boys, and girls, it does not select or publish national age group teams.

Resources

The definitive history of squash, *Squash: A History of the Game*, by James Zug was published by Scribner in 2003.
There are many instructional books, including:
Winning Squash Racquets, by John Barnaby; Allyn and Bacon, 1979.
Smart Squash: How to Win at Softball, Austin M. Francis, The Lyons Press, 1995.
Heather McKay's Complete Book of Squash, by Heather McKay, Ballantine Books, 1979.

Swimming

Introduction

Although swimming is the most elemental of sports—just you and a body of water—the popularity of the sport and modern commercial ingenuity has developed an incredible range of training aids. Some, such as pull buoys, kick boards, and hand paddles are relatively conventional. More sophisticated are the Hydro Hip ("to build power for hip rotation"), the

Turbo Limfinz ("an aquatic power device ... designed to give the user increased velocity and power"), and the Tech Toc ("the swimmer's metronome ... to hear and feel the rotation of the hips"). This training equipment may help you swim faster, but there's nothing like a swimmer in the next lane thrashing down the pool to get your competitive juices flowing. Swimming is one of the largest, best-organized sports for Masters Athletes.

National Sponsoring Organization

The national governing body of swimming in the United States is USA Swimming, with the broad objective of building membership, promoting swimming, and achieving competitive success, particularly in international competitions such as the Olympics.

USA Swimming
One Olympic Plaza
Colorado Springs, CO 80909
(719) 866-4578
www.usswim.org

USA Swimming focuses on competition at the highest levels, particularly at the junior levels and the Olympics, not adult swimmers.

The national organization for adult swimmers is United States Masters Swimming (USMS).

United States Masters Swimming
National Office
PO Box 185
Londonderry, NH 03053
National Office Coordinator: Tracy Grilli
Phone: (800) 550-7946
Fax: (603) 537-0204
usms@usms.org
www.usms.org

The USMS provides workouts, competitions, clinics, and workshops for adults aged 19 and over. Membership to USMS is administered through the Local Masters Swim Committees (LMSC). The 2003 adult annual membership fees ranged from of $25 to $30, depending on the location and services provided by the LMSC. Membership benefits include access to coaching, clinics, on-line workout plans, permission to compete in sanctioned meets and a subscription to the bi-monthly *USMS Swimmer Magazine*. Less than half of USMS members enter competitions.

Founded in 1970, USMS is organized into eight zones, 52 local masters swim committees and 500 clubs throughout the United States. Table 21–1 shows the eight USMS zones, the affiliated states, their coordinators and web sites and e-mail addresses.

Table 21–1
USMS Zones

Zone	States	Coordinator	E-mail/Web site
Breadbasket	ND, SD, MN, IA, KS, MO, CO, WY, NE	Lori Payne	Breadbasket@usms.org
Colonies	ME, NH, VT, MA, CT, RI, NY, NJ, DE, DC, MD, WV, eastern PA	Debbie Morrin-Nordlund	Colonies@usms.org www.colonieszone.org

Zone	States	Coordinator	E-mail/Web site
Dixie	NC, SC, GA, FL, MS, AL, LA, TN	Debbie Cavanaugh	Dixie@usms.org www.dixiezone.org
Great Lakes	MI, WI, IL, IN, OH, KY, western PA	Nadine Day	GreakLakes@usms.org www.greatlakeszone.org
Northwest	MT, WA, OR, ID, UT, AK	Wes Edwards	Northwest@usms.org www.northwestzone.org
Oceana	HI, northern CA, parts of NV	Leianne Crittenden	Oceana@usms.org
South Central	TX, AR, OK	Jill Gellatly	SouthCentral@usms.org
Southwest	AZ, NM, southern CA, parts of NV	Mary Hull	Southwest@usms.org www.southwestzone.org

Regions and local clubs can be found on the USMS web site or by contacting the zonal coordinator.

Competitive Opportunities

Swimming is one of the most popular sports for adults, with some estimates of participation as high as 150 million people. Most of these swimmers do not enter competitions, but a good many do and for them, there are many opportunities to test themselves.

Competition in masters swimming can be organized into three broad categories: pool competitions, postal meets, and open water events.

Pool competitions generally take place in short course, 25-yard pools, or long course, 50-meter pools. Classes in pool competitions are based on:

• Gender—men's and women's individual, relays and mixed relays
• Age Groups—from 19 to 90+ in five-year increments
• Stroke—freestyle, backstroke, breaststroke, butterfly, individual medley, and relays
• Distance

Table 21–2 presents the strokes and distances in both the 2007 Short Course National Championships and 2007 Long Course National Championships.

Table 21–2
Swimming Strokes and Distances
2007 USMS National Course Distances

Stroke	Short Course—Yards	Long Course—Meters
Freestyle	50, 100, 200, 500, 1000, 1650	50, 100, 200, 400, 800, 1000
Backstroke	50, 100. 200	50, 100, 200
Breaststroke	50, 100. 200	50, 100, 200
Butterfly	50, 100. 200	50, 100, 200
Individual Medley	100, 200, 400	200, 400
Relay (Freestyle)	200	200
Relay (Medley)	200	200

All events were offered for both men and women. The relay events were offered for men, women, and mixed teams. The national champions in all events are listed in Appendix A.

Postal meets are competitions in which the results are mailed into a sponsoring organization. This allows competitors to swim in their own pools, yet compete with other swimmers across the country. Postal meets may be based on a set time (e.g., who can swim the farthest in 1 hour?) or a set distance (e.g., who can swim 5 kilometers in the fastest time?).

Most postal meets offer age group classes for men and women, as well as relays. The winners of the USMS 1-Hour Postal Swim National Championship are listed in Appendix A.

Open water events are held in lakes, rivers, or ocean front venues and may cover 1/2-mile to 10 miles or more. These competitions offer age group classes for men and women. The winners of the USMS 1-Mile Open Water National Championship are listed in Appendix A.

There are hundreds of local and regional swim meets throughout the year and, as noted above, these can be identified through the zone or state coordinator. The USMS also has a Places to Swim Locator on its web site at http://www.usms.org/placswim/.

For those aiming to swim at the highest competitive levels, the USMS sponsored eleven national championships in 2008 and they are listed in Table 21-3.

Table 21–3
USMS 2008 National Championships

Championship	Location	Date
USMS 1-Hour Postal Championship[1]	N/A	January 1–31
USMS Short Course Yards Nationals	Austin, TX	May 1–4
USMS 5K/10K Postal Championship[1]	N/A	May 15–September 15
USMS 6+ Mile Open Water Championship	Clemson, SC	June 14
USMS 1-Mile Open Water Championship	Madison, CT	June 21
USMS 2-Mile Cable Championship	Charlottesville, VA	July 12
USMS 25k Open Water Championship	Noblesville, IN	July 19
USMS 3–6 Mile Open Water Championship	Bend, OR	August 3
USMS Long Course Meters Nationals	Mt. Hood, OR	August 14–17
USMS 1–3 Mile Open Water Championship	Madison, WI	August 23
USMS 3000/6000 Postal Championship[1]	N/A	September 15–November 15

1 In postal meets, the competitors swim the required distance/duration in their home pool and mail the results to the sponsor.

Competitive Landscape

If you want you measure yourself against the current crop of swimmers, the USMS publishes qualifying times for the long course and short course championships. They provide an idea of how competitive swimming is at this level of the sport. Despite the label, swimmers need not achieve the qualifying times to enter the national meets. They are used for only those swimmers who want to enter more than three events. Table 21–4 presents a selection of qualifying times for the 2008 Short Course Nationals. For the full list of qualifying times, see the USMS web site at http://www.usms.org/comp/scnats08nqt.pdf.

Table 21–4
Selected Qualifying Times for the 2008 Short Course Nationals

Event	Gender and Age Group	Qualifying Time[1]
100 yard Freestyle	Women 40–44	1:01.46
100 yard Backstroke	Women 55–59	1:29.93
100 yard Breaststroke	Women 65–69	1:57.03
100 yard Butterfly	Women 75–79	2:52.48
200 yard Individual Medley	Women 50–54	2:54.32
1650 yard Freestyle	Men 45–49	20:17.88
200 yard Backstroke	Men 60–64	2:55.71
50 yard Breaststroke	Men 75–79	0: 42.42
100 yard Butterfly	Men 80–84	3:49.36
100 yard Individual Medley	Men 40–44	1:03.07

1 Any USMS swimmer may enter up to three events in the national meets. To enter more than three events, the swimmer must have swum a time equal or better to the qualifying times for those events in the past two years.

Another gauge of the sport's competitiveness is the number of participants at national championship meets. The USMS 2007 National Short Course (Yards) Championships were held at the Weyerhaeuser King County Aquatic Center in Federal Way, Washington, from May 17 to 20. The total number of competitors over 40 was 3,782, of which 1,557 or 41 percent were women. Approximately 30 percent of the competitors were over 60 years old— 695 men and 447 women. Keep in mind that competitors is defined here as the number of participants in each event. Many, probably most, swimmers competed in more than one event and therefore, these individuals became multiple competitors.

Table 21–5 presents the number of competitors in the age groups over 40 for both the Long Course Nationals and the Short Course Nationals in 2007.

Table 21–5
Competitors, by Age Group, in the
2007 Long Course and Short Course Nationals

Gender	Long Course Nationals	Short Course Nationals
Men		
40–44	244	296
45–49	301	507
50–54	244	444
55–59	190	283
60–64	173	229
65–69	112	162
70–74	86	99
75–79	85	95
80–84	29	90
85–89	10	20
90–94	4	0
Subtotal	1,478	2,225
Women		
40–44	145	296
45–49	227	361
50–54	228	265
55–59	125	176
60–64	103	170
65–69	85	123
70–74	87	65
75–79	23	31
80–84	21	31
85–89	12	27
90–94	12	0
Subtotal	1,068	1,545

The winners of all events at the USMS 2007 Long Course and Short Course Nationals are listed in Appendix A.

For those swimmers who wish to begin at a less competitive level, hundreds of local and regional meets are sponsored by LMSC and regional organizations. According to the USMS, there are more than 500 local and regional competitions around the country and these can range from modest, informal meets to large inter-club meets. Regional competitions include both pool meets and open water swims. A selection of 2008 local and regional meets from across the country is shown in Table 21–6.

Table 21–6
Selected 2008 Local and Regional Competitions

Zone	Meet	Location	Date
Northwest	ORCA 2008 Swim Meet	Seattle, WA	March 8
Southwest	Caltech Pentathlon	Pasadena, CA	March 9
Breadbasket	Minnesota Short Course	Minneapolis, MN	March 14–17
Colonies	March Madness	Princeton, NJ	March 29
Great Lakes	Ohio Masters Championship	Columbus, OH	April 12
Oceana	Spring Lake 1-Mile	Santa Rosa, CA	May 17
South Central	Northwest Arkansas Invitational	Bentonville, AR	June 13
Dixie	Swim Around Key West	Key West, FL	June 21

The USMS maintains a comprehensive database of meet results which is used for annual USMS rankings. Rankings are published for short course (yards), long course (meters), and short course (meters). Rankings are organized by:

- Age groups in five-year increments from 18–23 to 100–104 years,
- Gender—Men and women, and
- Five strokes (freestyle, backstroke, breaststroke, butterfly, and individual medley).

Current, and historical rankings can be searched on the USMS web site at http://www. usms.org/comp/meets/toptimes.php. Although a summary of all the rankings maintained by USMS would be too cumbersome for this guide, Table 21–7 presents, as an example, the number of ranked swimmers, by age group and gender, for the Short Course, 100 yard freestyle.

Table 21–7
2006–2007 USMS Ranked Swimmers Short Course, 100 Yard Freestyle

Age Group	Ranked Men	Ranked Women	Total
40–44	202	137	339
45–49	264	139	403
50–54	214	128	342
55–59	149	74	223
60–64	100	61	161
65–69	66	32	98
70–74	42	34	76
75–79	31	25	56
80–84	22	8	30
85–89	7	8	15
90–94	1	2	3

In this table, women represent about 37 percent of the ranked swimmers and 25 percent of the ranked swimmers are 60 years or older.

How to Get Started

Skills

Swimming is a skill that can be learned at any age.

Equipment

Despite the long list of swimming aids listed in the catalogues of swimming equipment manufacturers, swimming actually requires very little equipment. A swim suit and a pair of goggles should do it. Goggles can be purchased for $15 to over $35. The current rage among competitive swimmers is full-length suits that promise to cut drag by 4 or more percent. If reducing your racing time by 4 percent is significant to you, you're probably already looking into one of these suits.

Coaching

Some kind of coaching is almost essential in learning to swim. Once you have a solid stroke, you can train by yourself. The newsletter of the New England Masters Swim Club has a column called "The Self-Coached Swimmer." But if you don't have the background or discipline to coach yourself you'll want to find a coach. The USMS and LMSCs have lists of active coaches. Working with a group under a coach is also a good way to make training more fun.

Venues

Not only does swimming require specific venues, but swimming competitions—at least well-organized ones—require lots of volunteers as starters, timers, and other officials. For this reason, it is a good idea to become affiliated with a club or team if you plan to compete.

Recognition

Awards

USMS and swimming does an excellent job of recognizing outstanding competitive performances. Swim meet awards may be given to the top three, or more, places in each event.

National Teams

The swimmers with the ten top times each year for each event, as well as the winners of the long-distance events, are named all-Americans. The person in each age group with the most All-American awards is selected as that age group's all-star. In addition, the USMS keeps a comprehensive list of the world and national records in all events.

Rankings

As noted above, the USMS keeps a detailed and comprehensive database of meet results on which swimmers are ranked.

Resources

The USMS web site has a library of training videos for rent, training articles, and books and videos for sale. The USMS bookstore is associated with Amazon.com. Terry Laughlin's "Total Immersion" program has been very popular and several books associated with the program are on the USMS web site at http://www.usms.org/merch/bookstore/.

Table Tennis

Introduction

The origins of table tennis are obscure. A version of indoor tennis was played in the early 1800s by British officers in India and South Africa, using lids from cigar boxes as paddles and rounded corks from wine bottles as balls with rows of books set up across the middle of the table as the net. As the sport spread to England, it became known as whiff whaff and gossima. The use of hollow celluloid balls began in the early 1900s and the name Ping Pong—representing the sound of these balls hitting the paddles and the table. Ping Pong was registered as a trade name by an English sporting goods firm in 1901.

Table tennis slowly evolved from a social diversion to a true sport. The first world championship tournament was held in London in 1927 and from that time until World War II, Hungary dominated the sport. Table Tennis became an Olympic sport in 1988. According to USA Table Tennis (USATT), more than 14 million Americans play table tennis, making it one of the most popular competitive activities in the country. There are more than 30 million competitive players worldwide with many more playing at a recreational level. Today, the powers in international table tennis are China, Sweden, and South Korea.

National Sponsoring Organization

USA Table Tennis is the national organizing body for table tennis in the United States.
USA Table Tennis (USATT)
One Olympic Plaza
Colorado Springs, CO 80909
(719) 866-4583
Michael D. Cavanaugh—executive director
usatt@usatt.org
http://www.usatt.org/

The goal of the USATT is to promote table tennis and to provide all participants with the best possible experience by advancing the sport in a variety of ways. The 2008 adult annual membership fee was $40. Membership benefits include permission to play in any of the USATT's sanctioned tournaments, a copy of the official rule book, and a subscription to *USA Table Tennis Magazine*.

The USATT serves almost 8,000 members and 240 clubs. Table 22–1 shows the states with the largest number of members and USATT member clubs.

Table 22–1
States with the Largest Number of USATT Members and Clubs

State	Members	Clubs
California	1,484	47
New York	625	30
Florida	472	21
Texas	418	14
New Jersey	391	7
Pennsylvania	342	14
Maryland	329	6

State	Members	Clubs
Illinois	329	12
Arizona	234	5
Ohio	250	12
United States	7,952	306

A map showing the number of active members and member clubs in each state can be found on the USATT web site at http://www.usatt.org/_member_by_state.shtml.

The web site also lists the clubs in each state, the USATT-sanctioned tournaments by region, and a chart showing the number of players by ranking. (See below for an explanation of the USATT ranking system.)

The eight regional coordinators through which the USATT operates oversee tournaments and are listed in Table 22–2.

Table 22–2
USATT Regional Coordinators

National Coordinator: Allen Barth   520 Elise Drive
Cordova, TN 38018
(901) 758-3278

Region	States	Coordinator	Telephone
East	ME, VT, NH, MA, CT, NY, PA, NJ, RI, DE, MD, WV, VA		(860) 416-5399
Midwest	MI, IL, IN, OH, KY	Ed Hogshead	(815) 965-8505
Mountain	CO, WY, UT, NM, NE	Larry Rose	(719) 685-0141
North	MN, ND, SD, IA, WI	Greg Miller	(763) 755-8691
Northwest	MT, WA, OR, ID, AL	George Kawamoto	(425) 672-3585
Pacific	CA, NV, AZ, HI	Ichiro Hashimoto	(818) 700-0948
South Central	TX, KS, OK, MO, AR, LA	Eugene Atha	(501) 835-5291
South East	TN, MS, AL, GA, NC, SC, FL	Larry Thoman	(615) 452-6470

Competitive Opportunities

Most USATT competitions are based on ratings, which is the way the USATT levels the competitive playing field. Ratings can range from 100 (novice) to 2800 (world class player). A player's rating may change, up or down, based on that player's tournament results. Defeat a higher rated player and your rating goes up. Be defeated by a lower rated player and your rating goes down. Most USATT tournaments provide rating events in which participants must have a rating of a certain level to participate. For example a tournament may be an under 1400 event which requires that all competitors have a rating of 1399 or below. A bell curve of USATT ratings at http://www.usatt.org/member_rankings.shtml shows that the average USATT member rating is between 1500 and 1700 with 613 members achieving a rating of at least 1600.

In addition to ratings, adult table tennis classifications are based on the following criteria:

- Gender—men, women
- Number of Competitors—singles or doubles
- Age Groups—from 30 to 70+ in 5-year or 10-year increments

• Hardbat—a competition based on the type of racquet, bat or paddle used. For information on hardbat competition, see the USATT web site.

Since 2003, the USATT has supported a program of table tennis leagues, encouraging local clubs to organize leagues. For more information, see the USATT web site at http://www.usatt.org/league/singles/.

A recent competitive innovation by the USATT is the Senior Masters Table Tennis Program for table tennis players over 50. Developed in conjunction with the National Senior Games Association (see Chapter 28), the program offers sanctioned competition without consideration for ratings. A list of the Senior Masters National Open Champions is presented in Appendix A.

Competitive Landscape

The local table tennis clubs are an excellent place to begin participating in table tennis competitions. The USATT sponsors more than 350 sanctioned table tennis tournaments each year, in addition to league play and exhibitions.

The 2007 Table Tennis National Championships were held in Las Vegas, Nevada, from December 15 to 18. A total of 790 players participated over four days in 61 events.

Ratings are the way that the USATT measures the competitive landscape. Table 22–3 shows the number of active members and their ratings for 2007.

Table 22–3
2007 Active USATT Members and Ratings

Rating Range	Active Members	Classification
100–500	477	Novice
501–1000	1,269	Novice
1001–1500	2,312	Intermediate
1501–2000	2,794	Intermediate/Advanced
2001–2500	699	Advanced/Elite
2501–2800	27	Elite

The ratings of the age group national champions over 40 are presented in Table 22–4.

Table 22–4
Ratings of 2007 Age Group National Champions Over 40

Age Group	Champion	Rating
Women Singles 40+	Diane Dongye Chen	2249
Women Singles 50+	Charlene Liu	2120
Women Singles 60+	Ann Alvarez	1947
Women Singles 70+	Jane Magras	1049
Men Singles 40+	Cheng Yinghua	2674
Men Singles 50+	Daniel Seemiller	2506
Men Singles 60+	Richard Hicks	2145
Men Singles 70+	Richard Hicks	2145
Men Singles 80+	Byng Forsberg	1521

A list of 2007 USATT national champions and open champions is presented in Appendix A.

How to Get Started

Skills

Table tennis requires quick reflexes, good hand-eye coordination, and a command of table tennis strokes. Given the relatively small space allotted for a match, quickness of foot and hand is critical. Tournaments may involve as many as half a dozen matches per individual in a day, so fitness is also important. Practice, as always, is what raises the rating of a novice.

Equipment

Aside from comfortable, rubber-soled shoes, a regulation table, table tennis racquet (also called a bat or a blade), and several table tennis balls (the balls tend to crack rather quickly) are the only equipment a novice will need. The local table tennis club will have regulation tables, which may cost $500 or more new, but second-hand tables can be purchased for less. A table tennis blade can cost from $35 to more than $100 depending on materials, construction, and design. For the serious player, there are also a variety of robotic training devices that allow a single player to practice against a machine. The cost of these may be several hundred dollars or more.

Coaching

Proper stroke technique is most easily acquired from a capable coach. Coaches can be found through your local club. The USATT also has an active coaching certification program and certifies table tennis coaches at five different levels. More than 400 certified coaches from across the county are listed on the USATT's web site at http://www.usatt.org/coaching/coaches_list.shtml.

Venues

As noted above, the best play to learn and practice table tennis is a local table tennis club and these are listed on the USATT web site at http://www.usatt.org/admin/ClubsList.aspx.

Recognition

Awards

Typically, prizes are awarded to the winners and runners-up for each competitive class in table tennis tournaments.

Fourteen age group divisions were included in the 2007 USATT National Championships, plus other divisions based on gender, game-type, and rating. The 2007 national champions are listed in Appendix A

National Teams

Although the USATT does name a national team, there are no national teams specifically for age group competitors.

Rankings

The USATT ranks players, based on the USATT Rating System, for the following age groups for players over 40:

- Men and women over 40
- Men and women over 50
- Men and women over 60
- Men and women over 70
- Over 75
- Over 80

Resources

Winning Table Tennis; Skills, Drills, and Strategies, Dan Seemiller and Mark Holowchak, Human Kinetics, 1996.
Sports Illustrated Book of Table Tennis, Dick Miles, Harper Collins, 1974.
How to Play Table Tennis: A Step-by-Step Guide, Malcolm Ryan, Jarrold Sports, 1993.

Tennis

Introduction

Although the origins of a tennis-like game go back as far as the Greeks and Romans, France can make a legitimate claim to inventing the game as we know it. The name of the game today (originally "jeu de paumme" or game of the palm) derives from the exclamation "Tenez!" shouted as a player was about to serve. The term is the imperative of the French verb "tenir" ("to hold" in English). The score at the beginning of each game, love, originates from the French word "l'oeuf" for egg or zero. The game scoring—15, 30, 40—comes from the quarters of the clock; at some point the "45" morphed to "40."

All this helps to explain Shakespeare's reference to the game in the first act of *Henry V*. In the second scene, the Dauphin of France sends Henry some tennis balls as a gift. For dramatic purposes, the Bard meant to suggest that this was an insult, chiding Henry for his youth and the French origin of the game. However, historians point out that this could not have actually been the case, since Henry already had served in several military campaigns and was a genuine threat to France. King Henry V died at the age of 35, just old enough to qualify as a Masters.

National Sponsoring Organization

The national governing body of tennis is the United States Tennis Association (USTA), which governs everything from junior programs and novice activities to the Pro Tour. Its mission is "to promote and develop the growth of tennis from the grassroots to the professional level."

United States Tennis Association
70 West Red Oak Lane
White Plains, NY 10604
(914) 696-7000
memberservices@usta.com
http://www.usta.com/home/default.sps

An individual adult membership in the USTA for one year is $35 and includes a 10-issue subscription to *Tennis Magazine* and six issues of *USTA News*, the organization's newsletter.

The USTA is organized into 17 regional sections and within these sections are state or local organizations. For information on your local organizations you can contact the appropriate region, listed in Table 23–1.

Table 23–1
USTA Regional Sections

Name/Address	Name/Address
USTA/New England 110 Turnpike Rd Westborough, MA 01581 (508) 366-3450 www.newengland.usta.com	USTA/Midwest 1310 East 96th St. Suite 100 Indianapolis, IN 46240 (317) 577-5130 www.midwest.usta.com
USTA/Caribbean Box 40439 San Juan, PR 00940 (787) 726-8782 www.caribbean.usta.com	USTA/Mid-Atlantic 7926 Jones Branch Dr. Suite 120 McLean, VA 22102 (703) 556-6120 www.midatlantic.usta.com
USTA/Eastern 4 West Red Oak Land Suite 300 White Plains, NY 10604 (914) 697-2300 www.eastern.usta.com	USTA/Middle States 1288 Valley Forge Rd. Suite 74 PO Box 987 Valley Forge, PA 19482 (610) 935-5000 www.middlestates.usta.com
USA Tennis Florida 1 Deuce Court Suite 100 Daytona Beach, FL 32124 (386) 671-8949 www.usatennisflorida.usta.com	USTA/Missouri Valley 6400 W. 95th St. Suite 102 Overland Park, KS 66212 (913) 322-4800 www.missourivalley.usta.com
USTA/Hawaii Pacific 1500 S. Berelania St. Suite 300 Honolulu, HI 96826 (808) 955-6696 www.hawaii.usta.com	USTA/Northern 1001 W. 98th St. Suite 101 Bloomington, MN 55431 (952) 887-5001 www.northern.usta.com
USTA/Intermountain 1201 S. Parker Rd. #200 Denver, CO 80231 (303) 695-4117 www.intermountain.usta.com	USTA/Northern California 1350 S. Loop Road, Suite 100 Alameda, CA 94502 (510) 748-7373 www.norcal.usta.com
USTA/Pacific Northwest 4840 S.W. Western Ave. Suite 300 Beaverton, OR 97005	USTA/Southern California PO Box 240015 Los Angeles, CA 90024

(503) 520-1877   (310) 208-3838
www.pnw.usta.com   www.scta.usta.com

USTA/Southern   USTA/Southwest
Spaulding Woods Office Park   7010 E. Acoma Dr. #201
5685 Spaulding Drive   Scottsdale, AZ 85254
Norcross, GA 30092   (480) 289-2701
(770) 368-8200   www.southwest.usta.com
www.southern.usta.com

USTA/Texas
8105 Exchange Dr.
Austin, TX 78754
(512) 443-1334
www.texas.usta.com
ghuntress@texas.usta.com

Competitive Opportunities

The USTA offers its 700,000 members a stunning array of competitive opportunities, particularly for the Masters Athlete. For competitors between 40 and 90, there are more than 200 national championships. Tennis uses the following criteria to determine competitive events:

- Age Groups—13 5-year increments from 30 to 90
- Skill Levels—2.5 to 7.0
- Game Type—Singles and doubles
- Gender—men, women, mixed (for doubles competition)
- Playing Surface—grass, clay, hard court, and indoor

Players over 60 years of age may also compete in the Super Senior division of leagues and tournaments.

The USTA offers two broad competitive opportunities: leagues and tournaments. In both cases, each player's skill level may be used to equalize the competition. The National Tennis Rating Program (NTRP) ratings range from 2.5 (novice) to 7.0 (world class) and are described in terms of general characteristics and experience at http://dps.usta.com/usta_master/usta/doc/content/doc_13_7372.pdf?12/6/2004%204:12:22%20PM. Players who compete for a year will be given an NTPR computer rating based on their results for that year.

The USTA Tennis League matches teams of five to eight players with similar skill levels throughout the country. More than 295,000 players participate in these competitions. Leagues are based on NTPR ratings and USTA Section League Coordinators (found at http://www.usta.com/leagues/custom._sps?iType=930&icustompageid=6704) can help new players locate a team.

In 2008, there were more than 40 age group national championship tournaments for players over 40. These tournaments are held across the country and take into account playing surfaces (grass, clay, indoor, and hard court), age groups, gender (men, women), and game-types (singles, doubles, mixed doubles). Table 23–2 lists the locations and dates of the 2008 championship events.

Table 23–2
2008 USTA National Age Group Championships

Event[1]	Location	Date
Men, Clay Court—40	Savannah, GA	Sept. 26–Oct. 2
Men, Clay Court—45	Ft. Lauderdale, FL	April 21–27
Men, Clay Court—50	Sarasota, FL	Sept. 28–Oct. 5
Men, Clay Court—55	Duluth, GA	Sept. 28–Oct. 5
Men, Clay Court—60	Duluth, GA	Sept. 21–28
Men, Clay Court—65	New Orleans, LA	April 7–13
Men, Clay Court—70, 85, 90	Pinehurst, NC	Sept. 8–14
Men, Clay Court—75, 80	Virginia Beach, VA	Aug. 25–31
Women, Clay Court, 40, 50	Pensacola, FL	April 1–5
Women, Clay Court, 45, 55, 65, 75, 85	Houston, TX	March 3–9
Women, Clay Court, 60, 70, 80	Huntsville, AL	April 19–25
Women, Clay Court, 90	Forest Hills, NY	July 6–13
Men, Hard Court—40	La Jolla, CA	Dec. 1–7
Men, Hard Court—45	Westlake Village, CA	June 28–July 4
Men, Hard Court—50	Santa Barbara, CA	July 6–12
Men, Hard Court—55	Indian Wells, CA	Nov. 3–9
Men, Hard Court—60, 90	Rancho Mirage, CA	April 7–13
Men, Hard Court—65, 70	Irvine, CA	June 16–22
Men, Hard Court—75, 80, 85	Rancho Santa Fe, CA	May 19–24
Women, Hard Court—40	La Jolla, CA	Dec. 1–7
Women, Hard Court—45, 55, 65, 75, 85	Salinas, CA	Sept. 15–21
Women, Hard Court—50, 60, 70, 80, 90	La Jolla, CA	May 12–18
Men, Grass Court—40	TBD	TBD
Men, Grass Court—45, 50	Philadelphia, PA	Aug. 24–30
Men, Grass Court—55, 60	Lawrence, NY	Sept. 8–14
Men, Grass Court—65	Rumson, NJ	Sept. 2–7
Men, Grass Court—70	Philadelphia, PA	Sept, 15–21
Men, Grass Court—75, 80	South Orange, NJ	Sept. 2–7
Men, Grass Court—85, 90	Chestnut Hill, MA	Aug. 31–Sept. 5
Women, Grass Court—40, 50, 60, 70, 80, 90	Forest Hill, NY	July, 6–13
Women, Grass Court—45, 55, 65, 75, 85	Philadelphia, PA	July 14–19
Men, Indoor—40	Park City, UT	April 7–11
Men, Indoor—45	Park City, UT	Nov. 10–16
Men, Indoor—50	Portland, OR	June 17–22
Men, Indoor—55	Boise, ID	May 5–10
Men, Indoor—60	Seattle, WA	Aug. 18–23
Men, Indoor—65	San Francisco, CA	Aug. 4–10
Men, Indoor—70, 75	Houston, TX	March 24–30
Men, Indoor—80, 85, 90	Vancouver, WA	May 6–10
Women, Indoor—40, 50	St. Clair Shores, MI	June 4–8
Women, Indoor—45, 55	Homewood, IL	May 14–18
Women, Indoor—60	Seattle, WA	Aug. 18–23
Women, Indoor—65, 75, 85	Shawnee Mission, KS	May 27–June 1
Women, Indoor—70, 80, 90	Portland, OR	Aug. 21–26

1 *All events include both singles and doubles competition.*

In addition, there are a variety of family-based tournaments, including husband-wife, father-son, mother-daughter, mother-son, father-daughter, grandfather-grandson ... you get the idea. In short, there are plenty of opportunities for competition in tennis and the USTA makes it easy to find a match.

Competitive Landscape

It is to be expected that, with the large number of tennis players in the United States, competition at the top is fierce. Serious players seek national rankings and there were 3,698 players with national rankings in singles and doubles in 2005—2,667 men and 1,031 women between the ages of 30 and 90 who are nationally ranked in singles and doubles, including more than 130 men and 40 women over 80 who have a singles ranking. Table 23–3 presents the number of ranked players in each age group for 2006, the last year for which data was available.

Table 23–3
2006 USTA—Number of Ranked Players

Age Group	Gender	Ranked Singles Players	Ranked Doubles Teams[1]
40–44	Men	212	77
45–49	Men	230	78
50–54	Men	219	89
55–59	Men	194	85
60–64	Men	182	84
65–69	Men	162	83
70–74	Men	124	56
75–79	Men	103	42
80–84	Men	72	37
85–69	Men	40	18
90+	Men	18	15
40–44	Women	59	42
45–49	Women	75	44
50–54	Women	78	54
55–59	Women	57	51
60–64	Women	76	58
65–69	Women	57	47
70–74	Women	44	36
75–79	Women	36	37
80–84	Women	23	19
85–69	Women	14	14
90+	Women	3	—

1 The USTA also ranks individual doubles players for many age groups.

The number competitors for each age group in the 2007 National Championships is presented in Table 23–4.

Table 23–4
Number of Competitors in Each Age Group for the 2007 National Championships

| Age Group | Gender | Number of Competitors | | | | |
		Clay	Hard	Grass	Indoor	Total
40–44	Men	130	190	70	65	455
45–49	Men	133	139	162	71	505
50–54	Men	155	115	183	79	532
55–59	Men	111	174	112	46	443
60–64	Men	136	152	79	81	448
65–69	Men	142	121	160	118	541
70–74	Men	118	98	110	85	411

Age Group	Gender	Clay	Hard	Grass	Indoor	Total
75–79	Men	88	70	73	61	292
80–84	Men	80	34	56	26	196
85–89	Men	53	33	41	19	146
90+	Men	24	39	21	23	107
Subtotal	Men	1,170	1,166	1,067	674	4,077
40–44	Women	29	68	20	35	152
45–49	Women	73	54	65	41	233
50–54	Women	29	124	59	48	260
55–59	Women	70	37	69	45	221
60–64	Women	58	95	63	45	261
65–69	Women	85	51	59	70	265
70–74	Women	42	71	40	59	212
75–79	Women	61	32	25	32	150
80–84	Women	30	33	22	27	112
85–89	Women	20	7	8	—	35
90+	Women	—	8	—	7	15
Subtotal	Women	497	580	430	409	1,916

Of the total of 5,993 competitors, 32 percent were women and 53 percent were over 60 years of age. The list of 2007 USTA National Champions in tennis can be found in Appendix A.

How to Get Started

Skills

Good tennis players are fit and have good hand-eye coordination. Both fitness and coordination can be developed with practice. Once the forehand and backhand strokes have been learned, other more sophisticated shots—lobs, drop shots, half-volleys—can be added and a fascinating mental dimension is added to the game.

Equipment

Besides proper shoes, you will need a tennis racquet. Although these come in an ever more sophisticated range of designs and materials, a local professional can help you select a racquet appropriate to your game and your wallet. Today a new racquet can be purchased for $100 to $200, or more of course.

Coaching

Playing tennis is not instinctive and a few lessons with a qualified coach will be a great help in getting you familiar with the game and your way around the court. Professional coaches are available at all private clubs and many public courts. One of the best ways to improve your game is to play with players who are more skilled than you—if you can coax them into it.

Venues

The USTA web site has a web-based tool for locating tennis courts, programs, and partners, using your ZIP code. The site is http://www.finder.usta.com/communitycenter/Find-ACourtHome.aspx?zip=01027.

Recognition

Awards

Typically, prizes are awarded to the winners and runners-up for each competitive class in tennis tournaments.

As noted above, the USTA offers more than 200 national championships. The 2007 National Tennis Champions for men and women in all age groups on the four surfaces are listed in Appendix A

Rankings

The USTA ranks players by gender and age, in both singles and doubles. The number of ranked players for 2006 for each age group is shown in Table 23–3. The rankings are available on the USTA web site.

National Team

The USTA does not select a national team for age groups.

Resources

There are many instructional books on tennis skills, including:
Tennis Skills: The Player's Guide, Tom Sadzeck, Firefly Books, 2001.
The Tennis Drill Book, Tina Hoskins, Human Kinetics, 2003.
Winning Ugly: Mental Warfare in Tennis Lessons from a Master, Brad Gilbert and Steve Jamison, Fireside, 1994.

Track and Field

Introduction

One account of the origins of track and field has a cook named Koroibos winning a foot race of 600 feet at the first Olympics in 776 B.C. Furthermore, this account claims that the 600-foot run was the only event for the next 13 Olympic Games. Hard to believe with the number and variety of events that now constitute track and field, from running, to jumping, to throwing. Add to this the popularity of track and field with Masters Athletes from ages 30 to 95+ and record-keeping can become a career. One example: the 2006 rankings for Outdoor Track & Field events (for both men and women) require more than 24 pages in the March 2007 issue of *National Masters News*. These rankings do not include indoor events, long distance running, or race walking. Track and field offers a popular, highly competitive, and varied set of opportunities for adult athletes.

National Sponsoring Organization

The first national governing body for track and field was the Amateur Athletic Union, which was formed in 1878. The organization underwent various changes over time, but in 1992 the body sanctioning track and field in the United States was changed to USA Track & Field (USATF). The USATF oversees track and field, long distance running, and race walking.

USA Track & Field
132 East Washington St. Suite 800
Indianapolis, IN 46204
Doug Logan, CEO
Phone—(317) 261-0500
Fax—(317) 261-0513
membership@usatf.org
http://www.usatf.org/

Other informative web sites include www.masterstrack.org, www.runningusa.org, and www.world-masters-athletics.org.

USA Track & Field has more than 100,000 individual members and sanctions more than 4,000 events each year. The organization is administered, in part, through 57 regional associations which are listed in Table 24–1. More than 2,500 local clubs offer an opportunity for athletes to participate in track and field at all levels.

Table 24–1
USA Track & Field Regional Associations

Region	Web site	Phone
Maine	www.meusatf.org/	(207) 474-8876
New England	www.usatfne.org/	(617) 566-7600
Adirondack	www.usatfadir.org/	(518) 273-5552
Niagara	www.usatf-niagara.org/	(585) 421-9626
Connecticut	www.usatf-ct.org/	(860) 704-4503
Metropolitan NY	www.mactrack.org/	(212) 620-5419
New Jersey	www.usatfnj.org/	(610) 647-2201
Mid-Atlantic	www.mausatf.org/	(215) 343-5838
Alabama	www.eteamz.com/alabamausatf/	(251) 661-1567
Potomac Valley	www.usatf.org/assoc/pva/	(410) 381-3743
Three Rivers (PA)	www.usatf.org/assoc/threerivers/	(724) 941-5639
Virginia	virginia.usatf.org/	(804) 353-9348
North Carolina	www.ncusatf.org/	(919) 772-6119
Florida	florida.usatf.org/	(305) 439-7064
Tennessee	startuck@earthlink.net (e-mail)	(615) 255-5802
Indiana	www.inusatf.org/	(317) 835-0161
Ohio	www.usatf.org/assoc/oh/	(937) 235-9436
Lake Erie	www.lakeerie.org/	(440) 842-2142
Michigan	michigan.usatf.org/	(313) 623-3029
Wisconsin	www.wiusatf.org/	(608) 274-4270
Illinois	www.usatfillinois.org/	(630) 512-0727
Ozark	www.usatf.org/assoc/ozark/	(314) 434-3397
Arkansas	www.arkansasrunner.com/usatf-ar.htm	(479) 824-3476
Southern	www.usatfsouthern.org	(225) 270-3322
Gulf	htosports.com/?USATFGULF	(713) 666-8133
Southwestern	www.swusatf.org/	(972) 283-1451
Oklahoma	www.usatf.org/assoc/ok/	(918) 770-0168
Missouri Valley	www.usatf.org/assoc/mv/	(913) 579-8722
Nebraska	www.nebraskausatf.org/	(402) 423-0515
Minnesota	www.usatfmn.org/	(651) 330-8847
Montana	www.mtusatf.org/	(406) 466-9146

Region	Web site	Phone
Colorado	www.usatf-co.org/	(719) 282-3052
Southern California	www.scausatf.org/	(562) 941-2621
Utah	utah.usatf.org/	(801) 277-7405
Inland Northwest	sites.google.com/site/inlandnwtrackandfield/	(509) 468-8211
Pacific Northwest	www.pntf.org/	(206) 433-8868
Oregon	www.usatf-oregon.org/	(541) 504-1077
Pacific	www.pausatf.org/	(916) 983-4715
Hawaii	www.usatf-hi.org/	(808) 792-3888
Iowa	www.usatf-iowa.org/	(563) 940-4297
Kentucky	kentucky.usatf.org/	(502) 229-9336
New Mexico	www.usatfnm.org	(505) 797-7482
South Texas	www.usatfsouthtexas.org/	(210) 520-9678
San Diego—Imperial	www.sdusatf.org/	(619) 275-6542
Georgia	www.usatfga.org	(404) 935-9046
Central California	central-california.usatf.org/	(559) 355-1133
West Texas	west-texas.usatf.org/	(432) 272-4136
Arizona	www.usatf.org/assoc/az/	(480) 949-1991
Nevada	www.usatfn.org/	(702) 432-0750
Wyoming	www.usatf.org/	(317) 261-0500
West Virginia	leaguelineup.com/welcome.asp?url=wvusatf	(304) 345-0497
Dakotas	dakotas.usatf.org/	(701) 642-4606
Border	www.usatf.org/assoc/border/	(915) 873-1951
Snake River	www.usatf.org/assoc/sr/	(208) 386-9392
South Carolina	www.scusatf.org	(803) 980-0059
Alaska	www.usatf.org/assoc/ak/	(907) 332-1543
Long Island	long-island.usatf.org/	(516) 349-9157

The cost of an individual one-year membership in USA Track & Field is $29.95. Member benefits include a subscription to *Fast Forward*, a quarterly magazine; sport accident insurance; and discounts on various types of merchandise.

The most comprehensive publication of Masters track and field is *National Masters News*, a monthly publication of results, technical discussions, records, schedules, and other information. A one-year subscription is $28. For more information go to www.nationalmastersnews.com.

Competitive Opportunities

The USATF Masters programs offer a variety of competitive opportunities. Age divisions for track and field and race walking begin at age 30 and for long distance running at age 40.

These sports are actually a constellation of events and competitors in Masters events are classed on the basis of:

• Gender (men and women)
• Age Groups
• Events (see Table 24–2)

The events offered in track and field depend on the gender and age of the participants. Table 24–2 shows the events.

Table 24–2
Track and Field Events

Track & Field	Long Distance Running	Race Walking
Pole Vault	Road races, trail runs, cross country runs from 1 mile to 100 miles	Track and road races from 1,500 meters (1 mile) to 50 km (50 miles)
Long, Triple, and High Jump Weight and Super Weight Throws Running Events (60 m to 10,000 m)		

The USATF sanctioned at least sixteen 2008 national championship events for Masters, which are listed in Table 24–3.

Table 24–3
USATF 2008 National Championship Events for Masters

Event	Date	Location
50K Race Walking Championships	Jan. 6	Houston, TX
USA Cross Country Championships	Feb. 16	San Diego, CA
50 km Championships	March 2	Huntington, NY
Masters Indoor Heptathlon Championships	March 8	Kenosha, WI
Masters Indoor T&F Championships	March 28	Boston, MA
Masters 10 km Championships	April 5	Austin, TX
20 km Masters Race Walk Championships	April 27	Orlando, FL
15 km Masters Race Walk Championships	May 18	Riverside, CA
Marathon Trail Championship	June 8	Deadwood, SD
50 Mile Trail Championships	July 28	Crystal Mountain, WA
Masters Outdoor T&F Championships	Aug. 7	Spokane, WA
Masters 100 km Trail Championships	Aug. 18	Eugene, OR
Masters Weight Pentathlon Championships	Aug. 23	New London, CT
Masters Marathon Championships	Oct. 5	Minneapolis, MN
Masters 5 km Cross Country Championship	Oct. 12	Greensboro, NC
Masters Ultraweight Pentathlon	Sept. 6	Seattle, WA

In addition to these events, there are hundreds of local and regional meets and races posted on the regional web sites (see Table 24–1).

Competitive Landscape

Competition for Masters Athletes in track and field is broad and deep. The April 2007 issue of *National Masters News* lists 93 national and regional competitions in track and field, long distance running, and race walking. There are many more local events, particularly in long distance running.

The USATF 2008 Masters National Indoor Track and Field Championships and 2007 Outdoor Track and Field Championships indicate the level of competition at the national level. The 2008 Masters National Indoor Championship was held in Boston, Massachusetts, from March 28 to 31. More than 800 athletes, ages 30 to 90+ participated.

The 2007 Masters National Outdoor Championship was held in Orono, Maine, from August 2 to 5. Table 24–4 presents a summary of the entries to these two national championship meets.

Table 24–4
Competitors at the USATF 2008 National Indoor and
2007 Outdoor Masters Championships (Men and Women)

Competitors[1]	2008 Indoor	% Competitors	2007 Outdoor	% Competitors
Total Over 40	1,223	100%	2,044	100%
Total Men Over 40	874	71%	1,366	67%
Total Women Over 40	349	29%	678	33%
Competitors 60+	635	52%	1,060	52%
Men 60+	460	31%	746	36%
Women 60+	175	7%	314	15%

1 Competitors are the number of participants in each event. In most case, individuals entered more than one event. Therefore, a single individual may accounts for multiple competitors.

As Table 24–4 shows, the total number of competitors over 60 years of age represented approximately 52 percent of all competitors over 40. While the number of female competitors over 60 is smaller than the number of male competitors over 60, it should be remembered that these women were at least 23 in 1972 when Title IX was passed. In this light, the level of participation is remarkable. A list of the 2007–2008 National Masters Indoor and Outdoor Champions is presented in Appendix A.

Finally, some of the winning times at the two Masters Track and Field Championships should provide some targets for aspiring competitors. Table 24–5 shows the winning times and distances for selected events and age groups.

Table 24–5
Selected Winning Times from the
2007 USATF Masters National Championships

Event	Gender and Age Group	Winning Time/Distance
Indoor—1 Mile Run	Women 50–54	6:13.20
Indoor—200 Meter Dash	Men 75–79	0:30.50
Indoor—3000 Meter Run	Women 40–44	10:08.89
Indoor—High Jump	Men 65–69	1.45 meters
Indoor—Long Jump	Women 55–59	4.39 meters
Indoor—Triple Jump	Men 45–49	13.00 meters
Indoor—Shot Put	Women 90–94	3.62 meters
Indoor—Super Weight Throw	Men 85–89	5.72 meters
Outdoor—100 Meter Dash	Women 65–69	0:14.45
Outdoor—5000 Meter Run	Men 40–44	15:55.18
Outdoor—Hammer Throw	Women 75–79	17.86 meters
Outdoor—Discus Throw	Men 50–54	44.21 meters
Outdoor—Pole Vault	Women 70–74	1.83 meters
Outdoor—2,000 Meter Steeplechase	Men 60–64	7:39.78
Outdoor—10,000 Meter Run	Women 50–55	45:53.74

For a full list of the winning times and distances for all age groups, see the US Track & Field web site.

How to Get Started

Skills

The range of skills involved in the various track and field events is very broad. Some, such as long distance running, can be learned at almost any age. Others, such as the weight events and pole vault, are very specialized. For the beginner, running is often the simplest way to begin competing.

Equipment

From running shoes to javelins, the equipment needed for track and field can range from the simple to the extremely sophisticated. A couple of places to start are http://www.everythingtrackandfield.com/, http://www.ontrackandfield.com/, and http://www.shapeupshop.com/athletic_equipment/track/index.html. Local track clubs and coaches will be able to help guide the aspiring track and field athlete to find the appropriate equipment.

Coaching

As always, good coaching can speed development, especially for the track and field skills. For events such as shot put and javelin, it is particularly critical. But even running can become more efficient and injury free under the tutelage of a good coach. Local running clubs and track and field clubs can provide access to coaches and equipment.

Venues

High schools and colleges typically have the track and other facilities needed to run a track and field program. Access to these venues is often available through the local running club.

Recognition

USATF recognizes outstanding performances by Masters Athletes in many ways.

Awards

Typically, awards at individual meets are given to the first three finishers for each event. National champions are crowned at each of the national championship meets. The National champions in track and field (indoor and outdoor) are listed in Appendix A.

At the end of each year, USATF presents awards to Masters Athletes for achievements in track and field, long distance running, and race walking. Table 24–6 summarizes these awards.

Table 24–6
USA Track and Field Annual Awards to Masters Athletes

Award	Qualification
Masters Age Group Athletes	Track and field—male and female in each age group over 40
Masters Athlete of the Year	Track and field—male and female over 40
Outstanding Performance	Track and field—male and female over 40
Masters Age Division Runners	Long distance running—male and female in each age group over 40
Paul Spangler Award	Long distance running—outstanding running in the oldest age category
Masters Harriers of the Year	Long distance running—outstanding male and female cross-country runners over 40
Masters Ultrarunners of the Year	Long distance running—male and female over 40
Masters Race Walker of the Year	Race walking—male and female over 40

National Teams

There is no national team of Masters Athletes.

Rankings and Records

USA Track & Field keeps detailed records of outstanding performances by Masters Athletes in seven categories:

- Indoor track and field,
- Outdoor track and field,
- Race walking—indoor track,
- Race walking—outdoor track,
- Race walking—road,
- Long distance running—track, and
- Long distance running—road

For a full listing of the current American and world records, see http://www.usatf.org/statistics/records/.

The *National Masters News* publishes rankings for indoor and outdoor track and field events by age group. The 2006 Outdoor Track & Field Rankings are published in the March 2007 issue and the U.S. Track & Field Age Records are published in the February 2007 issue.

The National Masters News also publishes a set of age-graded tables which allows athletes at any age or sex to compare their performance with any other athlete in any event. For example, a 70-year-old, running the 200 meter run in 37 seconds flat will find that her time is 84.17 percent of the standard for her age group. This is an invaluable tool to Masters Athletes to gauge their performance and improvement as they age.

Resources

Fundamentals of Track & Field, Gerald A. Carr, Human Kinetics, July 1999.

Beginner's Guide to Long Distance Running, Sean Fishpool, Barron's Educational Series, November 2005.

Complete Guide to Race Walking: Technique and Training, Dave McGovern, World Class Publications, January 1998.

Triathlon

Introduction

Multi-sport events date from the first Olympic Games in the 9th century B.C. when a pentathlon, consisting of competitions in discus, javelin, jumping, running, and wrestling, was held. Since that time, multi-sport events have proliferated to combine events in all manner of sports. A few of the most common events include the following:

- Duathlon—Running, swimming, running; http://rankings.usatriathlon.org/Duathlon/duathlon_commission.htm

- Biathlon—Nordic skiing, shooting; http://www.usbiathlon.com/
- Triathlon—Swimming, cycling, and running; http://www.usatriathlon.org/
- Quadrathlon—Swimming, kayaking, cycling, running; http://www.quadrathlon.com/index.html
- Modern Pentathlon—Swimming, running, shooting, fencing, and riding; http://www.pentathlon.org/index.php?id=31
- Heptathlon—100 meter hurdles, high jump, shot put, 200 meters run, long jump, javelin, 80 meter run; http://www.usatf.org/heptathlon/
- Decathlon—100 meter run, long jump, shot put, 400 meter run, 110 meter hurdles, discus, pole vault, javelin, 1500 meter run; http://www.decathlonusa.org/nature.html

There are also multi-sports events involving other sports such as canoeing, alpine skiing, and mountain biking. These events have begun to meld with the multi-sport events called adventure racing.

Of these events, the traditional triathlon offers the greatest opportunities for Masters Athletes. The growth of the triathlon over the past 32 years has been explosive, from an informal event in Mission Bay, California, in 1975 with 46 competitors to an Olympic sport with more than 100,000 members of USA Triathlon in 2008. This may be the fastest growing sport for Masters Athletes in the country.

National Sponsoring Organization

USA Triathlon is the national governing body of triathlon. The organization coordinates grass-roots and elite triathlon events across the country for its members. Over the past six years, the annual membership has grown by an average of 24 percent, a remarkable rate of growth. Last year, USA Triathlon sanctioned over 2,000 events.

USA Triathlon
1365 Garden of the Gods Road Suite 250
Colorado Springs, CO 80907
Phone: (719) 597-9090
Fax: (719) 597-2121
info@USATriathlon.org
http://www.usatriathlon.org/

USA Triathlon is organized into ten regional federations. The states in each region and the regional contact are shown in Table 25-1.

Table 25–1
USA Triathlon Regions

Region/Web site	States	Representative
Pacific Northwest www.usat-pnw.com	AL, HI, ID, OR, MT, WA	John Hoskins president@usat-pnw.com
Southwest www.usat-southwest.org	AZ, CA, NV	Kevin Trock
Midwest www.usat-mw.org	IA, KS, MN, MO, NE, ND, SD, WI	Kris Swarthout
South Midwest www.SMWtriathlon.org	AR, LA, OK, TX	David Young
Mideast www.usatmideast.com	IL, IN, KY, MI, OH	Greg Elsnic

Region/Web site	States	Representative
Southeast www.usat-se.org	AL, FL, GA, MS, SC, TN	Richard Anton
Mid Atlantic www.usat-ma.org	DE, MD, NJ, NC, PA, VA, DC, WV	Robert Vigorito
Northeast www.usat-ne.org	CT, MA, ME, NH, RI, NY, VT	Pam Zawada
Rocky Mountain www.usat-rockymountain.org	CO, NM, TX, UT, WY	Jose Valdez
Florida www.usat-florida.com	FL	Rebecca Meyer

The 2004 Bronze adult membership for USA Triathlon is $39 and you can apply online, by fax, or by mail. Benefits include eligibility in all national events, inclusion in the national ranking system, and a subscription to the bi-monthly *USA Triathlon Times*. USA Triathlon reported 100,674 members in 2007. More than 11 percent of all members are women over 40 and 37 percent of the members are over 40.

To help promote participation in age group triathlon, USA Triathlon has appointed an Age Group Commission to be a source of information and advice to the board of directors on issues of concern to age group multi-sport athletes.

The Age Group Commission has 21 members and is chaired by Lee Zohlman (leezee@bodyzen.com). The projects undertaken by the Age Group Commission include a study on how getting older affects performance. This study compares the performance in ten national and international events for age groups from 20–24 to 80–84 for both men and women. Table 25–2 shows the results of this study and indicates the effect of aging on performance in triathlons.

Table 25–2
Effect of Aging on Triathlon Performance

Age Group	Men[1]	Women[1]
35–39	2.9%	3.8%
40–44	4.8%	6.6%
45–49	8.4%	10.3%
50–54	13.7%	17.3%
55–59	18.4%	23.7%
60–64	26.4%	30.7%
65–69	40.0%	44.0%
70–74	41.6%	64.8%
75–79	82.7%	N/A
80–84	96.3%	N/A

1 Percent slower than overall winner. For example, if the overall winning men's time was eight hours and 10 minutes (490 minutes), then the winner of the men's 55–59 age group is estimated to be 9 hours 40 minutes (580+ minutes).

There are several caveats to this table and for a full explanation of the study go to http://www.bradsport.com/agegroupcommission/men.htm.

Competitive Opportunities

Although the word triathlon is derived from the Latin meaning three events, participants are often referred to more generally as multi-sport athletes. The traditional triathlon is an event that includes swimming, biking and running. The distances vary depending on the event. For example, a sprint triathlon typically includes a swim of 1/4 mile to 1 mile, a bike leg of 5 to 15 miles, and a run of 3 to 8 miles. The elite winning time in a sprint triathlon is typically under an hour.

The distances for an intermediate event, such as the Age Group Nationals, are a swim of 1500 meters, a bike leg of 40 kilometers and a run of 10 kilometers.

The Ironman distances, made famous by the competition held each year in Kona, Hawaii, are a swim of 2.4 miles, a bike leg of 125 miles, and a run of 26.2 miles. The winning men's time for the 40–45 age group for the 2006 World Ironman Championships was 8 hours 58 minutes and 55 second for the men (Brent Anderson of Denmark) and 10 hours 3 minutes and 6 seconds for the women (Donna Kay-Ness of the US).

The criteria used to establish classes in a triathlon event are:
- Gender—men and women
- Age—Age groups are in five-year increments from 20 to 80+
- Weight—Many competitions offer a Clydesdale class (for men over 200 lbs) and an Athena class (for women over 145 lbs). These competitors have their own web site at http://www.usa-clydesdale.com/.

At the national level, triathlon is a quite competitive. USA Triathlon lists eight national championships, with the Age Group Nationals being the premier event. In addition, there were ten regional championships for 2008, and hundreds of local competitions. Table 25–3 lists the information on the national championships for adults for each category. Competitors for the Age Group Nationals must qualify in USA Triathlon (USAT) sanctioned competitions. For information on regional qualifiers and local events in each category, contact the regional representative or check the USAT web site.

Table 25–3
USA Triathlon 2008 National Championships

Championship Event	Date of National	Location of National	Distance[1]
Age Group	September 20	Portland, OR	1.5 k (s), 40 k (b), 10 k (r)
Club	October 18	Boulder City, NV	500 m (s), 18 mi (b), 3 mi (r)
Collegiate	April 19	Tuscaloosa, AL	1.5 k (s), 19.9k (b), 10 k (r)
Long Course/Halfmax	October 18	Boulder City, NV	1.2 mi (s), 56 mi (b), 13.1 mi (r)
Spring	August 3	Trumansburg, NY	500 m (s), 12 mi (b), 5 k (r)
Winter Nationals	February 9	Bend, OR	8 k (r), 15 k (b), 10 k (ski)

1 (s) = swim; (b) = bike; (r) = run

The USTA lists several hundred local and regional events on its web site at http://www.usatmembership.com/EventCalendar/. The events can be searched by state, race type, or distance.

Competitive Landscape

The 2006 National Age Group Championships were held in Kansas City, Missouri, on July 11. A total of 724 competitors participated, 441 men and 282 women. The winning times for the age groups over 40 are listed in Table 25–4.

Table 25–4
Winning Times and Number of Competitors for 2006
Age Group Nationals (1500m swim; 40k bike, 10k run)

Age Group	Winning Men's Time	# of Competitors	Winning Women's Time	# of Competitors
40–45	2:02:36	54	2:16:08	40
46–49	2:07:06	36	2:22:34	33
50–54	2:11:43	34	2:21:59	23
55–59	2:16:14	28	2:45:45	16
60–64	2:22:13	24	2:50:37	9
65–69	2:34:06	26	2:59:40	5
70–74	3:07:23	5	3:31:54	3
75–79	3:26:33	2	5:13:15	1
85+	5:31:16	1		
Clydesdale <40	2:25:33	1		
Clydesdale 40+	2:13:40	5		
Athena <40			2:40:09	3
Totals		216		133

The names of the 2006 age group national champions are presented in Appendix A.

Another gauge of the competitiveness of age group triathlon is USA Triathlon's national rankings which rank triathletes based on their performances the previous year. Table 25–5 presents a summary of the 2007 Triathlon Rankings by age group.

Table 25–5
2007 Age Group Triathlon Rankings

Age Group	Men Ranked	Women Ranked	Total	% Women
40–44	3,345	1,606	4,951	32%
45–49	2,408	1,094	3,502	31%
50–54	1,520	630	2,150	29%
55–59	836	274	1,110	25%
60–64	435	101	536	19%
65–69	188	50	238	21%
70–74	75	12	87	14%
75–79	28	3	31	10%
80–84	5	1	6	17%
85+	1	0	1	0%
Total	8,841	3,771	12,612	30%

Ranked triathletes over 40 represent about 13 percent of the total USA Triathlon membership. Although women account for 30 percent of the total number of ranked age group competitors over 40, it is interesting to note that the percentage of women is greatest in the younger age groups and diminishes in the older age groups. This may reflect the influence of Title IX and the growing number of young women in competing in serious endurance sports.

How to Get Started

Skills

Triathlon is an endurance sport in which fitness, as well as specific athletic skills, is a key to success. Good swimmers must learn to bike and run efficiently; runners need to learn to swim well, and so on. Training in all three disciplines is important and part of the fun in this sport. Coaching helps improve your times quickly.

After training enough to complete the distances in each discipline—swim a half-mile, bike 10 to 12 miles, and run 3 to 4 miles—you might try a local sprint triathlon. Do not be intimidated by the veteran racers; compete to complete and have fun. You may find the challenge of multi-sport competition just the thing.

Equipment

The most costly piece of a triathlete's equipment is the bike, but, in the beginning, any decent road bike or even mountain bike will work. A good pair of running shoes is obviously important. In most races, swim goggles are also useful and, if you plan to race in the spring in the northern half the U.S., you'll probably want a wet suit to protect you from cold water during the swim.

One of the critical skills in triathlon is the transition. Making the change quickly from the swim to the bike to the run can shave seconds, or even minutes, off your time. Also, as in any endurance competition, it is important to get plenty of fluids.

Coaching

The USAT has a coaching certification program with three levels and requires coaches to be recertified periodically. The USAT web site has a state-by-state coach locator on its web site which includes the resumes and certification levels of the coaches.

Venues

Triathlons require a considerable amount of organization to provide suitable locations for swimming, biking and running, to keep track of all the competitors, and record the times. Experience in running these events is very important. There are a number of professional organizations that develop, organize, and put on triathlons. All events sanctioned by USAT will be well run with suitable locations.

Recognition

Awards

Triathlon meets typically present awards to the first three places in each competitive division.

National Teams

The USTA selects national age group triathlon teams—Team USA—to represent the United States in international competition in short course triathlon and long course triathlon, as well as duathlons, aquathlons, and winter triathlon.

Rankings

The USAT publishes age group rankings and the 2007 age group rankings are summarized in Table 25–5.

Resources

There are hundreds of books on triathlon training and history. Here are a few to start with.

Triathlon 101: Essentials for Multisport Success, John M. Mora and Karen Smyers, Human Kinetics, 1999.

Triathlons for Women: Training Plans, Equipment, Nutrition, Sally Edwards, Velo Press, 2002.

25 Years of the Ironman Triathlon Championship, Bob Babbit, Meyer & Meyer Fachverlag und Buchhandel GmbH, 2003.

Serious Training for the Endurance Athlete, Rob Sleamaker, Human Kinetics, 1996.

Volleyball

Introduction

Mintonette was invented by William G. Morgan at Holyoke (Massachusetts) YMCA in 1895, but the name was soon changed to volleyball. Morgan created the game for his classes of businessmen who were looking for a sport with less physical contact than basketball, which had been invented by Dr. James Naismith in 1891. The first game of volleyball was played at Springfield College in 1896. Today, more than 800 million people worldwide play the game.

The essence of volleyball is team play. No other team sport packs so many players into so small a space—one player for each 150 square feet of playing area. These people *must* play together. A volleyball team never possesses the ball. It is a non-contact sport that demands quickness and agility, puts a premium on height, and rewards selflessness.

At the same time, volleyball is a simple game to understand and one can begin to enjoy it a few minutes after learning the rules. The equipment is inexpensive and any open space with an even surface may be used as a court. The close coordination the game requires typically develops strong bonds among the players.

National Sponsoring Organization

The sport's governing body in the United States is USA Volleyball and is recognized by the Federation International de Volleyball (FIVB) and the United States Olympic Committee. FIVB is volleyball's international governing body.

USA Volleyball
715 S. Circle Dr.
Colorado Springs, CO 80910
Phone: (719) 228-6800
Fax: (719) 228-6899
postmaster@usav.org
http://www.usavolleyball.org

USA Volleyball is a decentralized organization. For administrative and competitive purposes, the country is divided into four zones each of which has two sections. Each section has three to seven regional volleyball associations (RVA). There are a total of 39 RVAs with their own commissioners, offices, and web sites. They are the primary sources of information and services to USA Volleyball members. In some cases, the RVAs support small sub-associations. For example, the New England Region Volleyball Association includes Green Mountain Volleyball for players in Vermont and the Maine State Volleyball Association. The various activities and relatively large number of regional and sub-regional associations are a testament to the sport's widespread popularity. To join USA Volleyball and obtain information on volleyball programs, competition, and instruction, contact your RVA. The RVAs are listed, with contact information, in Table 26–1.

Table 26–1
Regional Volleyball Associations

Region (RVA)	Web site	Phone
New England	www.nevolleyball.org/	(781) 449-5696
Iroquois-Empire (NY)	www.ireva.org/	(800) 251-9811
Garden-Empire (NJ/NYC)	www.geva.org/	(800) 338-4382
Chesapeake (MD/DE)	www.chrva.org	(703) 451-3082
Old Dominion (VA)	www.odrvb.org/	(804) 358-3000
Carolina (NC)	www.carolinaregionvb.org/	(336) 766-3581
Palmetto (SC)	www.palmettovb.com/	(864) 576-3700
Florida	www.usavfl.org/	(352) 742-0080
Southern	www.srva.org/	(800) 571-9810
Pioneer (KY)	www.pioneervb.org/	(502) 473-1200 ext. 11
Ohio Valley	www.ovr.org/	(888) 873-9478
Keystone (PA)	www.krva.org/	(717) 927-9161
Western Empire (NY)	www.wevavolleyball.org/	(585) 259-6557
Lakeshore (MI)	www.lakeshorevolleyball.org/	(517) 337-2049
Hoosier (IN)	www.indianavolleyball.org/	(574) 262-9211
Badger (WI)	www.badgervolleyball.org/	(414) 443-1011
Great Lakes (IL)	www.greatlakesvolleyball.org/	(708) 254-7200
Gateway (MO)	www.gatewayvb.org/	(314) 849-1221
Delta (AR/LA)	www.deltavolleyball.net/	(870) 933-8110
Gulf Coast (AL/FL)	www.gulfcoastvolleyball.org/	(251) 979-4287
Bayou (LA)	www.bayouvolleyball.com/	(504) 452-9522
North Country (MN/ND/SD)	www.ncrusav.org/	(952) 831-9150
Iowa	www.iavbreg.org/	(515) 727-1860
Heart of America (KS)	www.hoavb.org/	(913) 233-0445
Oklahoma	www.okrva.com/	(405) 285-6622
North Texas	www.ntrvolleyball.org/	(972) 247-3002
Lone Star (TX)	www.lsvolleyball.org/	(210) 945-4365
Great Plains (NE)	www.gpvb.org/	(402) 593-9670
Rocky Mountains (CO)	www.rmrvolleyball.org/	(800) 503-0969
Sun Country (NM/TX)	www.suncountryvb.org/	(806) 793-7089
Evergreen (MT, ID, WA)	www.evergreenregion.org/	(509) 235-6285
Intermountain (UT/NV)	www.imvolleyball.org	(801) 534-1933
Arizona	www.azregionvolleyball.org/	(602) 454-1367
Puget Sound (WA)	www.pugetsoundvb.org/	(425) 673-4103
Columbia Empire (OR)	www.columbiaempirevb.com/	(503) 644-7468
Northern California	www.ncva.com	(415) 550-7582
Southern California	www.scvavolleyball.org/	(714) 917-3595
Alaska	www.alaskavolleyball.com/	(907) 360-2042
Aoha (Hi)	www.aloharegion.com	NA

The cost of an RVA membership varies by region and all regions offer membership categories, such as adult and junior. Typically, the annual membership for a single adult is in the range of $30 to $45. Most regions also offer short-term memberships for about $5, which allows an individual to play in one-day tournament without joining for the entire year.

Competitive Opportunities

The National Sporting Goods Association estimates that approximately 11.1 million Americans played volleyball more than once in 2006. This is more than those that engaged in tennis, skiing (alpine and cross-country combined), or racquetball. Although many variations are played in backyards and parks, the sport has two major disciplines: (1) indoor and (2) outdoor, both of which offer many competitive opportunities for adults.

On page one of the 2007–2008 Official Volleyball Rules, it states, "Volleyball is a team sport played by two teams on a playing court divided by a net. The object of the game is for each team to send the ball regularly over the net to ground it on the opponent's court, and to prevent the same effort by the opponent."

Indoor volleyball pits two teams of six players against each other. The rules for outdoor volleyball allow for teams of 2, 3, 4, or 6, but 95 percent of the outdoor game is doubles, either on grass or on sand. The game on sand, beach volleyball, has mushroomed in popularity since the early 1990s and now has a professional circuit and appears regularly on television.

Volleyball games are played to 11 or 15 points. A team must win by two points with no maximum. Only the serving team can score. Teams change sides every 4 points (if the game is to 11) or 5 points (if the game is to 15) points. A system called rally point scoring (RPS) is now being used in some places. In RPS, a team need not be serving to win a point. Games are played to 25 and the winning team must win by 2 points or be the first team to win the 30th point. Like most team sports, volleyball has a whole set of rules governing everything from the size of the court to the conduct of the players.

In the two volleyball disciplines, competitive divisions can be defined by:

• Gender—men, women, and co-ed
• Skill Levels—AA, A, BB, B, CC, C
• Age Group—Usually in five- or ten-year increments from 30 to 75+

Volleyball is popular throughout the United States. The center of recreational volleyball is California, but strong volleyball teams from New England, the Midwest, and the South compete regularly in the national championships. Beach volleyball first took hold in coastal areas, but it has grown in popularity and many locations far from the nearest beach have constructed beach volleyball courts in parks and other public areas.

Volleyball demands quickness, jumping ability and good hand-to-eye coordination. As in many sports, strong teamwork can overcome a lack of individual skills in individual players. Teams that have played together for a long time have a distinct advantage. Because strategy can play a big part in competitive volleyball, experience and good coaching are important.

In addition to gender and age, volleyball uses a skill rating to classify competitors. Although competitors are asked to first classify themselves, RVA officials, rating committees, and other players will adjust the self-administered rating if they believe it is unfair.

There are eight ratings ranging from AA (the very best) to D (beginner). Tournaments usually include divisions for AA, A, BB, B, CC, and C. Ultimately, ratings are based on the player's skills in passing, setting, hitting, and defense. Players are encouraged to identify another player with similar skills and adopt that player's rating. Although the rating system is loosely defined, it seems to work because everyone seeks to develop competitions which are fair. Teams are often composed of players with different ratings. Formulas for determining the mix of ratings that are allowed for a team to compete in, for example a CC division, are spelled out by the tournament sponsor or the RVA.

The national championships also include the following types of tournaments which have their own set of eligibility requirements:

- U-Volley—imposes a height restriction on all players. Men may be no taller than approximately 6'1" inches and women may be no taller than 5'9" inches
- Co-Ed Volleyball—requires that males and females alternate service and when the ball is played more than once by a team, a female must make at least one of the contacts.
- Reverse Co-Ed Volleyball—requires that males and females alternate service and when the ball is played more than once by a team, a male must make at least one of the contacts.

With a sport as widespread and popular as volleyball, there are opportunities for competition at all levels. Local and regional tournaments can be found on the appropriate regional volleyball association's web site. International and national championships take place each year in both volleyball disciplines, for men and women, and for various skill levels and age groups. Table 26–2 lists the location and dates of the 2008 National Volleyball Championships for Adults.

Table 26–2
2008 National Volleyball Championships for Adults

Event	Location	Date
U.S. Adult Open National Championship	Atlanta, GA	May 24–31
U.S. Open Beach Volleyball Championship	Huntington Beach, CA	Sept. 21–23

Entry fees for the National Open Championship range from $675 to $900 per team for the age group divisions.

Information on thousands of local and regional tournaments are published in RVA newsletters and posted on their web sites.

Competitive Landscape

Volleyball offers challenging competition at all levels of skill, at all age levels, for men, women, and co-ed teams, and for players with disabilities.

Skill Ratings

The 2007 Open Volleyball Championships in Austin, Texas, offered competition in 29 separate divisions for men, women, and co-ed teams. Age group teams included eight divisions of men's teams (ages 40 to 75) and seven divisions of women's teams (ages 40 to 70). In the age group divisions, a total of 792 men and 424 women competed. Approximately 41 percent of the men and 32 of the women were over the age of 60.

An Open division, as well as four rating divisions—AA, A, BB, and B—were offered with the Men's BB division and Women's B division having the most teams competing.

To indicate the variety of competitive opportunities available in a championship volleyball tournament, Table 24–3 below shows the divisions, the number of teams and the estimated number of players that competed in the United States 2007 Open Volleyball Championships which were held in Austin, Texas.

The "Libero"

One of the more interesting recent changes in volleyball rules is the addition of a new type of player. In an effort to limit the dominance of offenses by strengthening team defenses, volleyball has added a new category of player, called the libero. The libero is a defensive specialist whose role is to keep the ball in play so that teammates can return it. The libero cannot serve, block, attack (e.g., hit the ball when it is above the net), or leave the back line. The team's regular substitution limits do not apply to the libero who may enter and leave the game freely (hence the name "libero"). To help referees identify this player, the libero's uniform must be a different color from his or her teammates. The libero rule was introduced in the United States in the 2001 National Championships.

Table 24–3
Competitors in the 2007 National Adult
Open Volleyball Championship

Division	Gender	# of of Players[1]	Gender	# of Players[1]
Open	Women	96	Men	96
AA	Women	144	Men	232
A	Women	192	Men	288
BB	Women	416	Men	424
B	Women	280	Men	400
40 & Over	Women	96	Men	64
45 & Over	Women	56	Men	64
50 & Over	Women	88	Men	160
55 & Over	Women	48	Men	176
60 & Over	Women	64	Men	120
65 & Over	Women	40	Men	96
70 & Over	Women	32	Men	72
75 & Over	Women	—	Men	40
U-Volley	Women	104	Men	—
Subtotal	Women	1,656	Men	2,232
Regular Co-Ed		136		
Reverse Co-Ed		112		
Special Olympics		80		
Total Competitors		4,216		

1 Assumes that each team had an average of eight players.

Almost 29 percent of the total number of competitors, an estimated 1,216 players, entered the age group classes in the 2007 National Adult Open Volleyball Championships. Women accounted for approximately 35 percent of the age group competitors. Players over 60 accounted for 38 percent of the age group players. It is likely that many players over 40 also played in the open and skill level divisions, but data on their ages was not available.

How to Get Started

Besides USA Volleyball and its RVAs, competitive volleyball is available through hundreds of other organizations, such as fitness clubs, parks departments, schools, and the YMCA.

Skills

To be played well, volleyball demands a high level of fitness and a good sense of the game. The best way to acquire and improve your skills is by playing on a team with good coaching on a regular basis. Weight training, running, and jumping are useful in building a good base for volleyball fitness. Certain skills, such as serving and setting, can be practiced alone, but nothing builds teamwork, a court sense, and sense of strategy like playing the game. In fact, because team play is so important in volleyball, spending a lot of time practicing volleyball alone is a questionable investment of time and energy.

Equipment

Volleyball requires very little equipment. An individual will need shorts, a t-shirt, and a good pair of light, rubber-soled shoes. The player's equipment for beach volleyball is even less expensive, just a bathing suit and bare feet. Most players wear kneepads for protection while diving for balls. Volleyballs can cost from $30 to $40. Nets and supports will cost several hundred dollars, with the exact cost determined by the sophistication of the system.

Coaching

USA Volleyball has a coaching accreditation program and offers clinics across the country for aspiring coaches. At the recreational level, informal coaching from other players is quite common; however, professional coaching is often found at the higher levels of competition.

Venues

Indoor volleyball is usually played on a basketball floor or other indoor athletic floor. The court is 29 feet 3 inches by 58 feet 6 inches and the net is 7 feet high. Courts can be erected, and disassembled quickly. Outdoor volleyball may be played on grass or sand and nets are easy to set up and take down.

Recognition

Awards

In most tournaments, the first two or three teams in each division typically receive awards. In larger tournaments, such as the national championships, an all-star or all-tournament team is named for each division. In the 2007 US Open, all-tournament teams were named for each division, including one for each of the age group divisions.

USA Volleyball annually recognizes all of its stakeholders, including coaches, players, referees, scorekeepers, the press, RVAs, and friends of volleyball. In 2006, USA Volleyball designated 17 separate awards.

National Teams

The National Volleyball Team consists of players who devote themselves full-time to the game. There are no age group national teams.

Rankings

USA Volleyball does not publish age group rankings.

Resources

VolleyballUSA is the quarterly publication of US Volleyball and is a free member benefit.

The publication *Volleyball* is a monthly magazine available at newsstands or online at: http://newsdirectory.com/go/?f=&r=spo&u=www.volleyballmag.com

Useful books include:

Volleyball Fundamentals, Joe Dearing, available through US Volleyball.
Volleyball Drills for Champions, Edited by Marty Wise, available through US Volleyball.
Complete Conditioning for Volleyball, Al Scates and Mike Linn, available through US Volleyball.

Weightlifting and Powerlifting

Introduction

Lifting weights, as a sport, probably began somewhere in the mists of prehistory when *Homo erectus* challenged his colleagues to carry a log or heft a stone. Of course there is no record of this, but we do know that recruits in the Zhou Dynasty (10th century B.C. to 256 B.C.) were required to pass tests of strength before they could enter the military. In 684 B.C., the great Greek wrestler, Milo of Crotona, introduced progressive weight training by lifting a calf each day until it grew into a bull and then, it is recorded, carried the four-year old heifer—whose weight might have been as much as 900 pounds—the length of the Olympic stadium. Milo was an Olympic champion for 28 years, past the age of 40—a true Masters Athlete. Records of these events are sketchy, but a boulder on the island of Santorini weighing almost 1,060 pounds and dating from the 6th century B.C. bears the inscription, "Eumastas, son of Kritobolos, lifted me from the ground."

From these beginnings, the sports of weightlifting and powerlifting have evolved. Both sports involve lifting weights and divide competitive classes by gender, body weight, and age. For this reason, they are considered together in this chapter. However, they differ in several important ways, including the types of lifts required, the body weight classes, and their sponsoring organizations.

Weightlifting

National Sponsoring Organization

Weightlifting, as currently practiced, began to appear in the late 19th century in Austria, Germany, and France. The first world weightlifting championships were held in 1891 and the first modern Olympic Games, held in 1896, included both one-handed and two-handed weightlifting events. By the 1920 Olympics (Antwerp, Belgium) weightlifting became a permanent Olympic event. One-handed events were dropped around the 1920s and women's competitions began to appear in the 1980s. The first women's world championship was held in 1987 and women's events were added to the Olympic program in 2000.

USA Weightlifting is the national governing body for Olympic weightlifting and a member of the International Weightlifting Federation with 120 member countries.

USA Weightlifting
Executive Director: Dennis Snethen
1 Olympic Plaza
Colorado Springs, CO 80909
Phone—(719) 866-4508
Fax—(719) 866-4741
usaw@usaweightlifting.org
www.usaweightlifting.org

The annual membership fee for USA Weightlifting is $40 for masters. A magazine, *Weightlifting*, is published four times a year for members.

Masters weightlifting has its own web site at http://www.mastersweightlifting.org/. Masters Weightlifting is a committee within USA Weightlifting and promotes the sport of Olympic weightlifting for people over the age of 35.

USA Weightlifting is affiliated with 46 Local Weightlifting Committees (LWCs) which are listed, along with contact information, in Table 27–1.

Table 27–1
Local Weightlifting Committees

LWC Name	E-Mail	Phone
Allegheny	regis.becker@verizon.net	(412) 276–7905
Arizona	joe@performanceone.net	(480) 247–3970
Arkansas/Louisiana	kyle.pierce@isus.edu	(318) 795–4241
Central	charlestonweightliftingclub@yahoo.com	(217) 258–6588
Colorado	rreichstein@faegre.com	(303) 467–7796
Florida	camargo57@gmail.com	(407) 221–9517
Georgia/Alabama	hcigar@juno.com	(912) 354–8072
Hawaii	miyamotom992@hawaii.rr.com	(808) 988–6698
Idaho	Conroy.mike@meridianschools.org	(202) 888–5846
Indiana	ggardis52@sbcglobal.net	(219) 614–0822
Iowa	ialifter@yahoo.com	(712) 792–2412
Kentucky	pursleymd@insightbb.com	(859) 223–5076
Maine	NA	(207) 796–2069
Maryland/Potomac Valley	swishytrishy@comcast.net	(410) 828–6070
Metropolitan	eleiko2@aol.com	(516) 520–0451
Michigan	frostie397@aol.com	(517) 627–3816
Middle Atlantic	doc.miller@comcast.net	NA
Minnesota	sadecki667@aol.com	(651) 490–0310
Missouri Valley	intersrv@inter-serv.org	(816) 238–1615
Montana	nowclear@aol.com	(406) 682–7676
Nevada	chillyi@me.com	(702) 454–4245
New England	renoswini@verizon.net	(617) 244–2845
New Jersey	jdelago@tpgphl.com	(856) 222–1378
New Mexico	smartbob@unm.edu	NA
Niagara	titusbyc@yahoo.com	NA
North Carolina	eflynndc@juno.com	NA
North Texas	torshammar@aol.com	(940) 696–0829
Ohio	kylejojones@yahoo.com	(440) 937–3086
Oklahoma	smiller113@cox.net	(405) 759–2786
Oregon	hvvath@aol.com	(541) 726–5651
Pacific	80olympn@LiftTilyaDie.com	NA
South Carolina	powmongo@yahoo.com	(803) 732–2619
South Dakota	pwrmn705@pie.midco.net	(605) 224–4812
South Texas	swords72@msn.com	(281) 316–2935
Southern	gaylehatch@cox.net	(225) 925–0078

LWC Name	E-Mail	Phone
Southern Pacific	dimcde@pacbell.net	(714) 334–8089
Tennessee	speedandstrength@aol.com	(423) 236–5088
Utah	row_well_and_live@yahoo.com	NA
Virginia	NA	(757) 851–6394
Washington	usawathietesrep@yahoo.com	(253) 350–8462
West Virginia	itusic@hotmail.com	(304) 455–6476
Wisconsin	gremore@centurytel.net	(920) 863–6888

Competitive Opportunities

Masters weightlifting uses three criteria to determine its competitive classes:

• Gender—Men and women
• Age—Five year increments, from the age of 35. Highest age class determined by entries.
• Body Weight—Six divisions for women from 48 kg to 75 kg and over; eight divisions for men from 53 kg to 105 kg and over.

Weightlifting competition requires two lifts*:

• The snatch, in which the weight is lifted over the head in one continuous motion, and
• The clean and jerk, in which the weight is pulled from the platform to the shoulders and then, in a second motion, lifted over the head.

In the 2007 National Masters Weightlifting Championships, a total of 82 different classes were offered—24 classes for women and 58 classes for men. The 25 classes for women included 8 age groups. In the men's competition, the 63 classes were divided into 10 age groups.

The Masters Weightlifting web site lists four national and international masters weightlifting competitions for 2008, as shown in Table 27–2.

Table 27–2
2008 National and International Weightlifting Competitions

Competition	Date	Location
National Masters Championships	Apr. 4–6	Savannah, GA
World Masters Championships	Sept. 27–Oct. 4	Argosloli Kefalonia, Greece

For local and regional Masters competitions, contact the LWC in your area.

Competitive Landscape

A combined total of 158 competitors over 40 entered the 2007 National Masters, held March 30 to April 1 in Savannah, GA. Of these 158 competitors, 19 percent were women and 81 percent were men. Also, approximately 41 percent were over the age of 60. The classes and entries are summarized in Table 27–3.

*A full description of the technical requirements for each of these lifts, as well as other rules, can be found at http://www.mastersweightlifting.org/

Table 27–3
Weightlifting American Masters and
National Masters—Entries and Classes

Gender	Age Group	Competitors
Men	40 & Over	14
Men	45 & Over	15
Men	50 & Over	17
Men	55 & Over	23
Men	60 & Over	17
Men	65 & Over	15
Men	70 & Over	12
Men	75 & Over	8
Men	80 & Over	6
Men	85 & Over	1
Women	40 & Over	8
Women	45 & Over	6
Women	50 & Over	4
Women	55 & Over	6
Women	60 & Over	2
Women	65 & Over	4

Each age group included multiple weight classes. As Table 27–3 shows, 18 percent of the age group competitors over 40 were women and 42 percent of these competitors were over 60. For more details, see the list of National Champions in Appendix A.

Powerlifting

National Sponsoring Organization

Powerlifting grew from the tradition of strength tests and strong men in the early part of the 20th century, but it wasn't until 1964 that it was officially recognized as a sport by the A.A.U. USA Powerlifting is a member of the International Powerlifting Federation with 83 member nations throughout the world. The stated goal of USA Powerlifting is "to promote drug-free powerlifting in the United States and around the world."

USA Powerlifting
Dr. Larry Maile, president
PO Box 668
Columbia City, IN 46725
Phone: (260) 248-4889
Fax: (260) 248-4879
http://www.usapowerlifting.com/home.shtml

The annual membership fee for USA Powerlifting is $40 and includes a quarterly newsletter.

USA Powerlifting has representative state chairs in 44 states which are listed, along with contact information, in Table 27–4.

Table 27–4
Powerlifting State Chairs

State	E-Mail	Phone
Alabama	BillyKeel@aol.com	(256) 761–3270
Alaska	Ron.AKD@AK.net	(907) 277–8212

State	E-Mail	Phone
Arizona	RICH.WENNER@asu.edu	(480) 688–7336
Arkansas	uspl_arkansas@stlff.com	(636) 219–3205
California	USPLCACHAIR.aol.com	(909) 880–2948
Colorado	gscuba@prodigy,net	(303) 973–5354
Connecticut	Contact the National Office	(260) 248–4889
Deleware	Contact the National Office	(260) 248–4889
Florida	rhk@verizon.net	(954) 790–2240
Georgia	NA	(770) 495–0787
Hawaii	NA	(808) 968–6431
Idaho	andesean@isu.edu	(208) 282–2540
Iliinois	smfit1@hotmail.com	(618) 252–0883
Indiana	powerhouse562@comcast.net	(765) 716–2587
Iowa	bgetch20@cableone.net	(712) 258–4965
Kansas	martytulry@gmail.com	NA
Kentucky	superpump07@yahoo.com	(270) 212–0282
Louisiana	NA	(223) 753–8586
Maine	NA	(207) 872–8921
Maryland	NA	(410) 997–1172
Massachusetts	NA	(781) 447–6714
Michigan	gbartotti@comcast.net	(517) 783–3383
Minnesota	NA	(651) 485–7353
Mississippi	NA	(288) 255–3887
Missouri	mens99meet@aol.com	(618) 451–4737
Montana	Bulletgym@centric.net	(406) 543–7800
Nebraska	pnsinde@megavision.com	(402) 986–1784
Nevada	Contact the National Office	(260) 248–4889
New Hampshipre	twweeks@verizon.net	(603) 924–6349
New Jersey	claytonw@ptd.net	(908) 496–4172
New Mexico	Contact the National Office	(260) 248–4889
New York	aeastma1@nycap.rr.com	(518) 424–4303
North Carolina	jennifer@132poundsofpower.com	(704) 483–6332
North Dakota	diane.siveny@ndakpl.com	(701) 852–9039
Ohio	gpage!@adesa.com	(330) 405–8972
Oklahoma	Contact the National Office	(260) 248–4889
Oregon	MoonLifter@aol.com	(541) 482–6318
Pennsylvania	garageinkpowerlifting@hotmail.com	NA
Rhode Island	moyen@nextlevel-fitness.com	(401) 934–2040
South Carolina	reginah6@bellsouth.net	(843) 552–1775
South Dakota	stevehowardbentbar@rap.midco.net	(605) 348–4039
Tennessee	abcampbell69@hotmail.com	(423) 725–2415
Texas	beckfish@netzero.net	(512) 560–2522
Utah	by-crom@msn.com	(801) 254–7814
Vermont	Contact the National Office	(260) 248–4889
Virginia	valifting@aol.com	(434) 985–3932
Washington	paulahouston@comcast.net	(206) 760–8724
West Virginia	wdcurrence@aep.com	(304) 550–5064
Wisconsin	bruce48@tds.net	(262) 639–3210
Wyoming	NA	(307) 778–2043

Competitive Opportunities

Like weightlifting, powerlifting uses three criteria to determine its competitive classes:

- Gender—men and women
- Age—Five year increments, from the age of 40. Highest age class determined by entries.
- Body Weight—Ten weight classes for men, from 56 kg to 125+ kg, and nine classes for women, from 48 kg to 90+ kg.

Powerlifting competition requires three lifts*:

• The squat, in which the barbell is placed on the competitor's shoulders and the competitor must lower himself or herself to a position where the top surface of the thighs is lower than the knees and then rise and stand erect.
• The bench press, in which the competitor lies on a bench with his feet on the floor with the barbell raised above the chest by extending the arms. The barbell is then lowered to the chest, and then raised, again extending the arms.
• The deadlift, in which the competitor grasps the barbell on the platform and then stands erect.

Table 27–5 lists the powerlifting events for 2008 which will include age group divisions.

Table 27–5
2008 Powerlifting Meets

Event	Location	Dates
USAPL Women's National Championship	Killeen, TX	Feb. 14–17
USAPL National Masters Championship	Miami, FL	May 2–4
USAPL Bench Press Nationals	Charlotte, NC	Aug. 30–31
USAPL Deadlift/Squat Nationals	Denver, CO	Oct. 18
USAPL Florida Senior Games	Cape Coral, FL	Dec. 6

There are more than 70 local and regional powerlifting meets on the USAPL web site at http://www.usapowerlifting.com/schedule.shtml.

Competitive Landscape

In 2007, a combined total of 183 competitors entered the Men's and Women's National Powerlifting Championships, 139 men and 34 women. The number of competitors in each weight class is listed in Table 27–6.

Table 27–6
Age Group Competitors in the
National Powerlifting Championships

Weight Class	Gender	Competitors
54.0 kg	Men	3
60.0 kg	Men	3
67.5 kg	Men	6
75.0 kg	Men	16
82.5 kg	Men	19
90.0 kg	Men	29
100.0 kg	Men	24
110.0 kg	Men	21
125.0 kg	Men	18
125.0+ kg	Men	10
48.0 kg	Women	2
52.0 kg	Women	3
56.0 kg	Women	3
60.0 kg	Women	5

*A full description of the technical requirements for each of these lifts, as well as other rules, can be found at http://www.powerlifting-ipf.com/IPF_rulebook_2007.pdf.

Weight Class	Gender	Competitors
67.5 kg	Women	8
75.0 kg	Women	5
82.5 kg	Women	3
90.0 kg	Women	2
90.0+ kg	Women	3

Table 27–6 shows that 19 percent of the age group competitors over 40 were women and that the competitors over 60 accounted for 13 percent of the over–40 competitors. The names of the national powerlifting champions are listed in Appendix A.

The USAPL also publishes an annual ranking of powerlifters, based on the previous year's performance. Table 25–7 lists the number of men and women powerlifters ranked in each age group.

Table 27–7
2007 Ranking of USAPL Powerlifters by Age Group

Age Group	Ranked Men	Ranked Women
40–44	229	48
45–49	177	45
50–54	132	37
55–59	75	13
60–64	71	6
65–69	24	9
70–74	20	0
75+	5	0

Of the 891 powerlifters in these rankings in the age group between 40 and 75+, approximately 18 percent are women and 15 percent are over the age of 60.

How to Get Started

Skills

Both weightlifting and powerlifting not only involve strength, but also flexibility and coordination. Because of the strains that competitive lifting can place on the body, it is critical that novices work with experienced coaches to learn and practice proper techniques. The lists of local weightlifting committees and powerlifting state chairs in Tables 25–1 and 25–4 are good starting points for finding good coaching.

Equipment

Weightlifting and powerlifting use barbells which consist of bars with a series of weighted plates on each end of the bar. Costs for barbells vary depending on the number and weight of plates. A competition set barbell and plates can cost $3,000 or more. Serious competitors also use special shoes, gloves and other accessories.

Coaching

USA Weightlifting has a five-level coaching certification program and a list of certified coaches is available on its web site.

USA Powerlifting offers a three-level coaching certification program and a list of these coaches is on the web site.

Venues

Training for these sports can be done at many local gyms, fitness clubs, and YMCAs. The weightlifting LVAs and powerlifting state chairs can help you locate a local venue. Also, USA Weightlifting publishes a college and club directory, available on its web site.

Recognition

Awards

Typically awards at each meet are given for the top three lifters in each weight class and age group.

National Teams

Neither USA Weightlifting nor USA Powerlifting selects age group national teams.

Rankings

Both USA Weightlifting and USA Powerlifting hold national masters championships and rank masters athletes. However, USA Weightlifting has not published rankings for Masters since 2005 and does not publish age group rankings. The 2007 Weightlifting Masters National Champions for men and women are presented in Appendix A.

USA Powerlifting publishes rankings by age group and gender. A summary of these rankings is presented in Table 25–7. The 2007 Powerlifting Masters National Champions for men and women are presented in Appendix A.

Resources

USA Weightlifting has a variety of training materials, books and videos, for sale on its web site. Also:

Essential of Weightlifting and Strength Training, Mohamed F. El-Hewie, Shaymaa Publishing, 2006.

Introduction to Olympic-Style Weightlifting, Cissik and Cissik. McGraw-Hill Primus Custom Publishing, 1998.

Powerlifting: A Scientific Approach, Frederick C. Hatfield, Contemporary Books, 1981.

Powerlifting Basics: Texas Style, Paul Kelso, Ironmind Enterprises, 1996.

Multi-Sport Events

Introduction

For those people who compete in sports, even at a very modest level, and would like to take a step forward in the competitive experience, I suggest one of the events described below. These are multi-sport festivals which bring together participants for a week or more of competition and socializing.

National Senior Games

Since 1987, the National Senior Games Association (NSGA) has offered a bi-annual summer competition in 18 sports for competitors over 50 years of age. The dates, locations, and estimated number of participants for these events are shown in Table 28–1.

Table 28–1
National Senior Olympics

Date	Location	# of Participants
1987	St. Louis, MO	2,500
1989	St. Louis, MO	3,400
1991	Syracuse, NY	5,000
1993	Baton Rouge, LA	7,200
1995	San Antonio, TX	8,000
1997	Tucson, AZ	10,300
1999	Orlando, FL	12,000
2001	Baton Rouge, LA	8,700
2003	Hampton Roads, VA	10,700
2005	Pittsburgh, PA	10,500
2007	Louisville, KY	12,100
2009	San Francisco, CA	—
2011	Houston, TX	—
2013	Cleveland, OH	—

The NSGA acts as the umbrella organization for the State Senior Olympic Organizations. The State Senior Olympic Organizations sponsor their own state games and the winners of these competitions are invited to compete in the National Senior Olympics. A list of the State Senior Olympic organizations is shown in Table 28–2.

Table 28–2
State Senior Olympic Organizations

State	Web site/Phone	E-Mail
Alabama	(334) 242–4496	None
Alaska	www.alaskaisg.org/	alaskaseniorgames@hotmail.com
Arizona	www.seniorgames.org/	irene.stillwell@phoenix.gov
Arkansas	www.srsports.org/	arsrolym@hotsprings.net
California	www.californiaseniorgames.com/	CynthiaR@pasadenaseniorcenter.org
Colorado	www.rmseniorgames.com	Sheri.Lobmeyer@greeley.gov
Connecticut	www.seniorgamesct.org/	allyson@nutmegstategames.org
Delaware	www.delawareseniorolympics.org/	admin@delawareseniorolympics.org
D.C.	www.dpr.dc.gov/dpr/site/default.asp	ben.butler@dc.gov
Florida	www.flasports.com/page_seniorgames.shtml	games@flasports.com
Georgia	www.georgiagoldenolympics.org/	goldenolympics.ga@gmail.com
Hawaii	www.hawaiiseniorolympics.org/	zeug@hawaii.rr.com
Idaho	www.idahoseniorgames.org/clients/idsenior/	http://jack.ward@ymcatvidaho.org/
Illinois	www.ilsenoly.org/	dstaley@springfieldparks.org
Indiana	www.indianaseniorgames.com	sslavens@hamiltoncountytowns.com
Iowa	www.iowaseniorolympics.com/	director@iowaseniorolympics.com
Kansas	www.topeka.org/prksrec/index.shtml	bsewell@topeka.org
Kentucky	www.kentuckyseniorgames.com	TStevens@cipaducah.ky.us
Louisiana	www.lsogn.net/	lsog@lsog.net
Maine	www.smaaa.org/	jdill@smaaa.org
Maryland	www.mdseniorolympics.org/	info@mdseniorolympics.org
Massachusetts	www.maseniorgames.org	Senior_games@spfldcol.edu

State	Web site/Phone	E-Mail
Michigan	www.michiganseniorolympics.org/	misrolympics@yahoo.com
Minnesota	www.mnseniorgames.com/	fritz.bukowski@mail.co.douglas.cmn.us
Mississippi	www.msseniorolym.org/	msseniorolym@aol.com
Missouri	www.smsg.org/senior_games/	stottr@missouri.edu
Montana	www.montanaseniorolympics.org/	kayjn@imt.net
Nebraska	www.nebraskaseniorgames.com/	amollring@kearneygov.org
Nevada	www.nevadaseniorolympics.com/	nevadaseniorgames@earthlink.net
New Hampshire	www.nhseniorgames.org/	nhgssg1@comcast.net
New Jersey	http://njso.us/	mjg129@aol.com
New Mexico	www.nmseniorolympics.org/	nmso@qwest.net
New York	www.empirestategames.org/	doherty@oprhp.state.ny.us
North Carolina	www.ncseniorgames.org/	ncsgbrad@mindspring.com
North Dakota	No State Games	Contact Minnesota or South Dakota
Ohio	www.ohioseniorolympics.org/	info@ohioseniorolympics.org
Oklahoma	www.oklahomaseniorgames.org/	douglas.paulsen@okc.gov;danamike98@yahoo.com
Oregon	No State Games	Contact California or Washington State
Pennsylvania	www.keystonegames.com/	Paseniorgames@aol.com
Rhode Island	www.riseniorolympics.org	mlyons@weei.com
South Carolina	www.scseniorgames.com	cmh@bellsouth.net
South Dakota	southdakotaseniorgames.org/	letsplay@iw.net
Tennessee	www.tnseniorolympics.com/	tnseniorolympics@comcast.net
Texas	www.tsga.org/	tsga@tsga.org
Utah	www.seniorgames.net/	hwsg@infowest.com
Vermont	(802) 824–6521	ardissmith@mymailstation.com
Virginia	www.virginiaseniorgames.org/	cra18@co.honrico.va.us
Washington	www.pugetsoundgames.com/	jack.kiley@comcast.net
West Virginia	www.wvssc.com	lonab@charter.com
Wisconsin	www.wiseniorolympics.com/	hramon@hbf.org
Wyoming	www.wyseniorolympics.com/	paul_prevdel@rswy.net

The National Senior Olympic Summer Games offer competition in the following eighteen sports.

Archery	Badminton	Basketball	Bowling
Cycling	Golf	Horseshoes	Race Walking
Racquetball	Road Racing	Shuffleboard	Softball
Swimming	Table Tennis	Tennis	Track & Field
Triathlon	Volleyball		

State organizations can, and do, offer sports in addition to these. For example, in addition to the 18 national games sports, the State of California offered 13 local sports including soccer, trapshooting, and rock climbing. Massachusetts also offered competition in billiards, bocce, and pistol shooting. A list of the dates and locations of the state games is presented in Table 28–3.

Table 28–3
2008 State Senior Games

State	Location	Dates
Alabama	Montgomery	May 2–4 (April 4–6 cycling; May 9, table tennis)
Alaska	Fairbanks	August 8–17
Arizona	Phoenix	Feb. 16–March 9
Arkansas	Hot Springs	Sept. 17–21 (Oct. 11 5K/10K RR)
California	Pasadena	June 7–22

State	Location	Dates
Colorado	Greeley	June 18–22
Connecticut	Hartford	May 30–June 1
Delaware	Statewide	Sept./Nov.
D.C.	Districtwide	May 6–9
Florida	Cape Coral	Dec. 6–14
Georgia	Warner Robins	Sept. 24–27
Hawaii	Honolulu	Various dates for different sports
Idaho	Boise	Aug. 16–17 (Aug. 20–24 softball, tennis, cycling)
Illinois	Springfield	Sept. 17–22, 27–28
Indiana	Hamilton Country	June 12–15
Iowa	Des Moines	June 5–8
Kansas	Topeka	Sept. 24–29 (Oct. 2–5 Team, Oct. 3 Golf)
Kentucky	Ashland	Sept. 17–21
Louisiana	Baton Rouge	Sept. 7–Oct. 26
Maine	Statewide	Aug. 23–Sept. 21
Maryland	Montgomery County	Sept./Oct.
Massachusetts	Springfield	Various dates for different sports
Michigan	Oakland County	Aug. 9–17
Minnesota	Alexandria	July 21–25
Mississippi	Clinton	May 3–17 (April 27–29 tennis)
Missouri	Columbia	June 19–22 (August 16–17 softball)
Montana	Butte/Missoula	June 12–14 (June 27–29 softball in Missoula)
Nebraska	Kearney	Aug. 7–10
Nevada	Las Vegas	Sept. 23–Oct. 19
New Hampshire	Manchester	July 30–Aug. 17
New Jersey	Woodbridge	Sept. 12–14
New Mexico	Several Locations	Various dates for different sports
New York	Cortland	June 3–8
North Carolina	Raleigh	Various dates for different sports
North Dakota	No state games	Contact Minnesota or South Dakota
Ohio	Dayton	July 27–Aug. 4
Oklahoma	Oklahoma City	Sept. 11–17
Oregon	No state games	Contact California or Washington State
Pennsylvania	York	July 21–27
Rhode Island	Providence	June 6–8
South Carolina	Florence	May 14–17
South Dakota	Mitchell	Sept. 4–7
Tennessee	Williamson County	July 18–24
Texas	Temple	Sept. 19–28
Utah	St. George	Oct. 6–18 (see Huntsman Games)
Vermont	Chester/Castleton	Various (summer)
Virginia	Virginia Beach	May 8–11 (May 16–18 swimming, softball)
Washington	Olympia	July 25–27
West Virginia	Morgantown	Various dates for different sports
Wisconsin	Milwaukee	Sept. 2–14
Wyoming	Sheridan	July 24–Aug. 16

Competitors placing 1st or 2nd in their State Senior Games, or meeting minimum performance standards, become eligible to compete in the National Senior Olympics. Minimum performance standards are set for certain sports based on age group and gender. For example, the minimum performance standard in swimming the 50-yard freestyle for men 70–74 was 0:34.40. For the five kilometer road race, the minimum performance standard for women 55–59 was 27:02. This means that a woman age 55–59 who runs the five kilometer race in less that 27:02 can compete in the National Senior Games, even if she did not place 1st or 2nd in her State Games. The complete list of minimum performance standards can be found on the NSGA web site. The NSGA also sponsors the Senior Olympic Hockey Championships which are described in Chapter 9 (Ice Hockey).

Six states—Connecticut, Massachusetts, Michigan, Montana, New York, and Wyoming —also hold winter games competitions.

For more information about the Winter or Summer Games, contact
The National Senior Games Association
PO Box 82059
Baton Rouge, LA 70884
www.nsga.com/virtualmall/index.mv
?Screen=SFNT@Store_Code=0022

The Huntsman World Senior Games

Started in 1987 as the World Senior Games, it became the Huntsman World Senior Games (HWSG) when Jon M. Huntsman became its principal sponsor in 1989. It is held every year in St. George, Utah. Participants must be at least 50 years old, but there are no minimum standards for entry into any of the sports. In 2007, it offered competition in 23 sports. In addition to more traditional sports, such as swimming, tennis, and track and field, the HSWG includes competition in square dancing, cowboy action shoot, and pickleball. The emphasis is on competition, socializing, and fun in equal measure. A variety of health screenings is available to participants and a full schedule of social events is an integral part of the HWSG.

Based on the list of medal winners posted on the HSSG web site, most competitors are from the western United States.

For more information, contact:
Huntsman World Senior Games
1070 West 1600 South, A-103
St. George, Utah 84770
(435) 674-0550 or
(800) 562-1268
www.hwsg.com

The World Masters Games

The World Masters Games are a quadrennial multi-sport event that have been held since 1985. Table 28–4 shows the location and estimated number of participants in the six games held since 1985.

Table 28–4
World Masters Games

Year	Location	# of Participants	Sports	# of Countries
1985	Toronto, Canada	8,305	22	61
1989	Herning, Denmark	5,500	37	76
1994	Brisbane, Australia	24,500	30	74
1998	Portland (OR), USA	11,800	28	102
2002	Melbourne, Australia	24,886	26	98
2005	Edmonton, Canada	21,600	27	88
2009	Sydney, Australia	—	28	—

The seventh World Masters Games will be held in Sydney, Australia from October 10 to 18, 2009.

The governing organization for the World Masters Games is the International Masters

Games Association (IMGA), a non-profit organization formed in 1995 and headquartered in Lausanne, Switzerland.

International Masters Games Association
Maison du Sport International
Avenue de Rhodane 54
1007 Lausanne
Switzerland
Phone: 41+ 21 60 18171
Fax: 41+ 21 60 18173
info@imga.ch
www.imga.ch/

The IGMA requires that 15 core sports be on the program at each World Masters Games. The competition in each sport is carried out according to the rules and regulations of the sport's international governing body. Table 28–5 shows the IGMA's 15 core sports and their governing bodies.

Table 28–5
IGMA Core Sports

Sport	International Governing Body	Website
Athletics	World Masters Athletics	www.world-masters-atheltics.org/
Badminton	International Badminton Federation	www.intbadfed.org/
Basketball	International Basketball Federation	www.fiba.com/
Canoeing	International Canoe Federation	www.canoeicf.com/
Football_ (Soccer)	Federation Internationale de Football Association	www.fifa.com/en/index.html
Golf	Professional Golf Association	www.pga.com/
Orienteering	International Orienteering Federation	www.orienteering.org/
Rowing	International Federation of Rowing Associations	www.worldowing.com/home/default.sps
Shooting	International Shooting Sport Federation	www.issf-shooting.org/
Squash	World Squash Federation	www.squash.org/
Swimming	La Federation Internationale de Natation	www.fina.org/
Table Tennis	International Table Tennis Federation	www.ittf.com/
Tennis	International Tennis Federation	www.itftennis.com/abouttheitf/
Triathlon	International Triathlon Federation	www.triathlon.org/
Weightlifting	International Weightlifting Federation	www.iwf.net/

In addition to these 15 sports, the host city may choose 10 or more optional sports. In the past these have included such sports as rugby, netball, and cycling. Aside from the minimum age requirements, there are no qualifying criteria. Anyone may participate. All sports offer age group classifications, typically using five-year intervals.

The next World Masters Games will include 28 sports and various disciplines. The sports and minimum ages for competitors are listed in Table 28–6.

Table 28–6
Sydney World Masters Games Sports

Sport	Discipline	Minimum Age
1. Archery		30
2. Athletics	Track and Field	30
	Half Marathon	30
	Race Walk	30

Sport	Discipline	Minimum Age
	Road Race	30
	Cross Country	30
3. Badminton		35
4. Baseball		30
5. Basketball		30
6. Canoe/Kayak	Canoe Polo	30
	Canoe Slalom	30
	Sprint (Flatwater)	30
	Marathon	30
7. Cycling	Criterium	30
	Road Race	30
	Time Trial	30
	Track	30
8. Diving		25
9. Football (Soccer)		30
10. Golf		35
11. Hockey (Field)		35
12. Lawn Bowling		35
13. Netball		35
14. Orienteering		35
15. Rowing		27
16. Rugby Union		35/Men, 30/Women
17. Sailing		35
18. Shooting	Clay Target	30
	Pistol and Air Pistol	30
	Small Bore & Air Rifle	30
19. Softball		35
20. Squash		35
21. Surf Lifesaving		30
22. Swimming	Open Water	25
	Pool	25
23. Table Tennis		35
24. Tennis		30
25. Touch Football		30
26. Volleyball	Indoor	30
	Beach	30
27. Water Polo		30
28. Weightlifting		35

Further information about the Sydney World Masters Games can be found at www.2009worldmasters.com

The excitement, enthusiasm, and fun of these events are difficult to explain. Seeing hundreds of other Masters Athletes competing in their respective sports is confirmation of the joy in adult sports. These events can be the highlight of a Masters Athlete competitive career.

Appendix A
National Champions

Alpine Skiing. MEN
2007 Masters Nationals—Big Sky, MT, March 10–16

Event	Age	Champion	# Competitors
Downhill	40–44	Steve Masur	6
Downhill	45–49	Erik Klemme	15
Downhill	50–54	Rees Palermo	13
Downhill	55–59	Bob Dreyer	12
Downhill	60–64	Pepi Newbauer	10
Downhill	65–69	Lee Kaufman	13
Downhill	70–74	Willie Schmidt	6
Downhill	75–79	Harold Wescott	7
Downhill	80+	Richard Calvert	1
Giant Slalom	40–44	Timothy Hill	14
Giant Slalom	45–49	Eric Klemme	21
Giant Slalom	50–54	Bill Zimmerman	21
Giant Slalom	55–59	Bob Dreyer	16
Giant Slalom	60–64	Pepi Newbauer	16
Giant Slalom	65–69	Steve Foley	18
Giant Slalom	70–74	John Bloomberg	10
Giant Slalom	75–79	Gaetano DeMattei	9
Giant Slalom	80–84	Duffy Dodge	5
Super G	40–44	Timothy Hill	11
Super G	45–49	Eric Klemme	20
Super G	50–54	Ken Dreyer	19
Super G	55–59	Bob Dreyer	14
Super G	60–64	Pepi Newbauer	17
Super G	65–69	Keith Thompson	20
Super G	70–74	Willie Schmidt	10
Super G	75–79	Gaetano DeMattei	9
Super G	80–84	Duffy Dodge	5
Slalom	40–44	Timothy Hill	12
Slalom	45–49	Kurt Belden	16
Slalom	50–54	Bill Skinner	20
Slalom	55–59	Bob Dreyer	15
Slalom	60–64	Pepi Newbauer	15
Slalom	65–69	Haldor Reinholt	16
Slalom	70–74	Carl Fullman	10
Slalom	75–79	Alphonse Sevigny	8
Slalom	80–84	Duffy Dodge	6
Slalom	85–89	Francis Balice	1

Alpine Skiing. WOMEN
2007 Masters Nationals (WOMEN)—Big Sky, MT, March 10–16

Event	Age	Champion	# Competitors
Downhill	40–44	Sherrie Glas	4
Downhill	45–49	Victoria Valar	1
Downhill	50–54	Deborah Lewis	5
Downhill	55–59	Rosemary Moschel	3
Downhill	60–64	Glenn McConkey	2
Downhill	65–69	Nancy Auseklis	4
Slalom	40–44	Chris Katzenberger	7
Slalom	45–49	Victoria Valar	8
Slalom	50–54	Deborah Lewis	7
Slalom	55–59	Carol Levine	6

Event	Age	Champion	# Competitors
Slalom	60–64	Glenn McConkey	3
Slalom	65–69	Nancy Auseklis	7
Slalom	70–74	Grace Oaks	3
Slalom	75–79	Virginia Reed	2
Giant Slalom	40–44	Sherrie Glas	7
Giant Slalom	45–49	Lisa Densmore	10
Giant Slalom	50–54	Deborah Lewis	8
Giant Slalom	55–59	Carol Levine	6
Giant Slalom	60–64	Glenn McConkey	4
Giant Slalom	65–69	Anne Nordhoy	7
Giant Slalom	70–74	Grace Oaks	3
Giant Slalom	75–79	Jane Cooke	2
Super G	40–44	Sherrie Glas	7
Super G	45–49	Lisa Densmore	8
Super G	50–54	Deborah Lewis	7
Super G	55–59	Charlene Braga	5
Super G	60–64	Glenn McConkey	3
Super G	65–69	Anne Nordhoy	7
Super G	70–74	Grace Oaks	3
Super G	75–79	Virginia Reed	2

Badminton. 2007 Badminton Senior Nationals — Manhattan Beach, CA, March 6–11

Event	Gender	Age-	Champion	Competitors
Singles	Men	40–44	Sandro Rossi	8
Singles	Men	45–49	Sandro Rossi	16
Singles	Men	50–54	Imre Bereknyei	10
Singles	Men	55–59	Bob Cook	10
Singles	Men	60–64	Bob Cook	3
Singles	Men	65–69	Dick Warnock	8
Singles	Men	70–74	Harry Orr	3
Singles	Men	75–79	James Bosco	4
Singles	Men	80–85	Bill Tom	5
Doubles	Men	40–44	Jonatan/Tok	6
Doubles	Men	45–49	Jonatan/Tok	32
Doubles	Men	50–54	Bereknyei/Jonatan	10
Doubles	Men	55–59	Gouw/Cook	4
Doubles	Men	60–64	Gouw/Cook	16
Doubles	Men	65–69	Lyons/Fishback	10
Doubles	Men	70–74	Teoh/Pang	8
Doubles	Men	75–79	Enochs/Bosco	8
Doubles	Men	80–85	White/Harvey	6
Singles	Women	40–44	Gena Fite	3
Singles	Women	55–59	Sue Dommeyer	3
Singles	Women	65–69	Margo Hurst	3
Singles	Women	75–79	Joyce Jones	3
Singles	Women	80–84	Lee Calvert	4
Doubles	Women	40–44	Kitzmiller/Briese	6
Doubles	Women	50–54	Lira/Acuna	8
Doubles	Women	55–59	Bowles/Dommeyer	8
Doubles	Women	60–64	Wilson/Matthieu	6
Doubles	Women	65–69	Warnock/Gray	6
Doubles	Women	70–74	Jones/Bohn	4
Doubles	Women	75–79	Jones/Skinner	6
Singles	Women	80–84	Calvert/McFarland	4
Doubles	Mixed	40–44	Fite/Rossi	10
Doubles	Mixed	45–49	Lira/Chen	8
Doubles	Mixed	50–54	Lira/Chen	10
Doubles	Mixed	55–59	Bowles/Anderson	10
Doubles	Mixed	60–64	Wilson/Fishback	10
Doubles	Mixed	65–69	Warnock/Warnock	32
Doubles	Mixed	70–74	Bohn/Orr	16
Doubles	Mixed	75–79	Jones/Harvey	10
Doubles	Mixed	80–84	Calvert/Witte	10

Baseball: Men's Senior Baseball League.
2007 MABL/MSBL World Series—Phoenix, AZ, Oct. 16–31

Event	Age Group	Champions	# Teams
National	45+	Long Island Mets	7
Mountain	45+	Jagermeister Warriors	10
Central	45+	San Antonio Red Sox	12
National—Wooden Bat	45+	So Cal Stars	6
American—Wooden Bat	45+	Rhode Island Salty Dogs	5
Central—Wooden Bat	45+	Las Vegas Rattlers	8
National—Wooden Bat	50+	Calzona Tribe	7
American—Wooden Bat	50+	Greenwood Ridge Dragons	8
National	55+	Kansas City Cubs	4
American	55+	Paladin 55'	4
Central	55+	Hollywood Stars	6
National—Wooden Bat	60+	Detroit 60's	4
American—Wooden Bat	60+	Terre Haute Volkers	6
World Series	65+	San Diego Padres	6

National Adult Baseball Association
2007 NABA World Series—Phoenix, AZ, Sept 30—Oct. 11
2007 NABA Over 50/60 World Series—Las Vegas, Oct. 22–26

Event	Age	Champion	Teams
NABA World Series—Wood	38+	San Diego Black Sox	5
NABA World Series—A	38+	Vancouver/Phoenix Pirates	6
NABA World Series—Rookie	38+	Denver Bears	12
NABA World Series—Wood	48+	San Diego Black Sox	5
NABA World Series—A	48+	Sotelo All Stars	5
NABA World Series—Wood	57+	USA Patriots	7
Over 50/60 World Series—AAAA	50+	South Dakota Jackalopes	3
Over 50/60 World Series—AAA	50+	Denver Browns	5
Over 50/60 World Series—AA	50+	Mariners 50	3
Over 50/60 World Series—A	50+	Team USA Red Crowley	3
Over 50/60 World Series AA	60+	South Dakota Phesants	3
Over 50/60 World Series—A	60+	Braves 60	3

Baseball. 2007 Roy Hobbs Baseball World Series

Event	Age	Champion	Teams
Roy Hobbs World Series—AAAA	38+	Pittsburgh	12
Roy Hobbs World Series—AAA	38+	DuPage Angels	13
Roy Hobbs World Series—AA	38+	Puerto Rico Cardinales	12
Roy Hobbs World Series—A	38+	Tidewater Drillers	13
Roy Hobbs World Series—AAAA	48+	Border City Brewers	11
Roy Hobbs World Series—AAA	48+	Minnesota Bulldogs	11
Roy Hobbs World Series—AA	48+	Toledo Paramount	11
Roy Hobbs World Series—A	48+	Salem-Pitt Warlocks	12
Roy Hobbs World Series—B	48+	Orlando Blazers B	11
Roy Hobbs World Series—AAAA	55+	Wshington Titans	9
Roy Hobbs World Series—AAA	55+	Chicago Fire	9
Roy Hobbs World Series—AA	55+	Houston Colt 45's	9
Roy Hobbs World Series—AAAA	60+	Detroit 60's	9
Roy Hobbs World Series—AAA	60+	Akron Classics	9
Roy Hobbs World Series	65+	Chicago Spirit	7

Baseball (MEN). 2007 Roy Hobbs Baseball World Series

Level	Age	Champion	Teams
AAAA	38+	Pittsburgh	12
AAA	38+	DuPage Angels	13
AA	38+	Puerto Rico Cardinales	12
A	38+	Tidewater Drillers	13
AAAA	48+	Border City Brewers	11
AAA	48+	Minnesota Bulldogs	11

Level	Age	Champion	Teams
AA	48+	Toledo Paramount	11
A	48+	Salem-Pitt Warlocks	12
B	48+	Orlando Blazers B	11
AAAA	55+	Wshington Titans	9
AAA	55+	Chicago Fire	9
AA	55+	Houston Colt 45's	9
AAAA	60+	Detroit 60's	9
AAA	60+	Akron Classics	9
Open	65+	Chicago Spirit	7

Basketball (MEN). 2007 Masters Basketball—Coral Springs, FL, May 18–22

Age	Champion	Teams
40+	Miami Old Timers (FL)	6
45+	Service America (OH)	8
50+	Baltimore (MD)	10
55+	Titans (FL)	4
60+	Sag Harbor Whalers (NY)	5
65+	Sambuca Jazz (TX)	8
70+	Sambuca Jazz (TX)	4

Basketball (MEN).
2007 Buffalo Masters Basketball—Buffalo, NY, March 14–16*

Age	Champion
40+	LCI Lazers
45+	Indy Allstars
50+ C†	Coles
50+ R†	Syracuse "Y"
55+ C	Oakland's Finest
55+ R	Hobbertoons
60+ C	New Dimensions
60+ R	Paragon
65+	Park Ohio
70+	Chicago 70

*Number of teams in competitions unavailable
† C = Competitive Division; R = Recreational Division

Canoeing. (ADULT SPRINTS).
2007 Marathon Nationals—Warren, PA, August 18–22

Event	Gender	Age	Champion	Competitors
C-1	Women	40+	Colleen Moore	4
C-1	Women	50+	Jan Whitaker	3
K-1	Women	40+	Sonja Gilman	2
K-1	Women	50+	Georgette Goonan	2
K-1	Women	60+	Kathy Kenley	1
C-2	Women	40+	Simpson/Moore	8
C-2	Women	60+	Henry/Whitaker	4
C-1	Men	40+	John Edwards	9
C-1	Men	50+	Ralph Vincent	11
C-1	Men	60+	Stan Machacek	18
K-1	Men	40+	Ron Kaiser	3
K-1	Men	50+	Lloyd Reeves	4
K-1	Men	60+	Tom Jones	5
C-2	Men	40+	Cummings/Dyka	4
C-2	Men	50+	Vincent/McAndrew	10
C-2	Men	60+	Johnson/Bradford	12
C-2	Mixed	40+	Edwards/Faloon	24

Canoeing. 2007 Marathon Nationals—Warren, PA, August 18–22

Event	Gender	Age	Champion	Competitors*
K-1 Touring	Men	40+	Will Smith	4
K-1 Touring	Men	50+	Jim Goochee	7
K-1 Touring	Men	60+	Ed Laszek	2
C-1	Men	40+	John Edwards	18
C-1	Men	50+	Joe Johnson	22
C-1	Men	60+	Tom Thomas	19
C-1	Men	65+	Richard Ulbrich	8
C-1	Men	70+	Dan King	6
C-1	Men	75+	Robert Gillings	4
C-2	Men	40+	Edwards/McNett	12
C-2	Men	50+	Larsen/Johnson	14
C-2	Men	60+	Thomas/Allen	16
C-2	Men	65+	Henry/Davis	2
C-2	Men	70+	Karig/Botzow	6
C-2	Men	75+	Fremont/Cole	2
K-1 Downriver	Men	40+	Matt Streib	3
K-1 Downriver	Men	60+	Ralph Scofield	4
K-1 ICF	Men	40+	James Mallory	5
K-1 ICF	Men	60+	Bill Baker	3
K-1 Sea Kayak	Men	50+	Steve Rosenau	2
K-1 Sea Kayak	Men	60+	Ed Laszek	4
K-1 Unlimited	Men	40+	Ron Kaiser	6
K-1 Unlimited	Men	50+	John Redos	4
K-1 Unlimited	Men	60+	Doug Bushnell	3
Standard C-2	Men	40+	Bennett/Tinsley	12
C-2	Mixed	40+	Limberg/Ellis	34
K-1 Touring	Women	40+	Sonja Gilman	1
K-1 Touring	Women	50+	Linda Volpe	1
K-1 Touring	Women	60+	Kathy Kenley	1
C-1	Women	40+	Colleen Moore	6
C-1	Women	50+	Karen Simpson	2
C-1	Women	65+	Beth Schulter	2
C-2	Women	40+	Moore/McNett	10
C-2	Women	50+	Faloon/Schulter	3
C-2	Women	60+	Henry/Whitaker	2
K-1 Downriver	Women	40+	Betsy Arnold	1
K-1 Downriver	Women	50+	Linda Volpe	2
K-1 ICF	Women	40+	Melissa Schmidt	3
K-1 Sea Kayak	Women	40+	Betsy Bellario	3
K-1 Sea Kayak	Women	60+	Anita Allen	1
K-1 Unlimited	Women	40+	Melissa Schmidt	4
K-1 Unlimited	Women	50+	Anita Allen	2

Certain classes were run with mixed age groups and awards given to the first paddler in the the age group. Complete data on the number of paddlers in the age group was not available.

Cross-Country Skiing. 2007 Masters Nationals—Bend, OR, March 22–25

Event	Gender	Group	Champion	Competitors
10k Classic	Men	60+	Del Pletcher	18
10k Classic	Men	65+	Gerhard Schopp	13
10k Classic	Men	70+	Irvin Servold	6
10k Classic	Men	75+	Norman Clark	3
10k Classic	Men	80+	Charley French	2
10k Classic	Men	85+	Daniel Bulkley	1
15k Classic	Men	40+	Eric Martin	11
15k Classic	Men	45+	Jack Hart	12
15k Classic	Men	50+	Brent Turner	17
15k Classic	Men	55+	David Christopherson	19
15k Freestyle	Men	75+	David Ayarra	7
15k Freestyle	Men	80+	Roger Guildersleeve	2
15k Freestyle	Men	85+	Charley French	1
15k Freestyle	Men	90+	Daniel Bulkley	1
15k Skiathlon	Men	40+	Eric Martin	8
15k Skiathlon	Men	45+	Scott Waichler	4

Event	Gender	Group	Champion	Competitors
15k Skiathlon	Men	50+	Gary Klingler	9
15k Skiathlon	Men	55+	David Christopherson	16
15k Skiathlon	Men	60+	Del Pletcher	15
15k Skiathlon	Men	65+	Gerhard Schopp	10
15k Skiathlon	Men	70+	Irvin Servold	7
15k Skiathlon	Men	75+	Norman Clark	2
15k Skiathlon	Men	80+	Charley French	3
20k Freestyle	Men	60+	Jon Berryman	19
20k Freestyle	Men	65+	Gerhard Schopp	12
30k Freestyle	Men	40+	John Spaude	20
30k Freestyle	Men	45+	Jack Hart	15
30k Freestyle	Men	50+	Larry Katz	26
30k Freestyle	Men	55+	David Christopherson	24
10k Classic	Women	40+	Laura McCabe	7
10k Classic	Women	45+	Muffy Ritz	6
10k Classic	Women	50+	Juliet Bradley	4
10k Classic	Women	55+	Carolyn Tiernan	4
10k Classic	Women	60+	Dagmar Eriksson	5
10k Classic	Women	65+	Hedda Anya	4
10k Classic	Women	70+	Barbara Lewis	3
15k Freestyle	Women	60+	June Lane	5
15k Freestyle	Women	65+	Louise Wholey	3
15k Freestyle	Women	70+	Barbara Lewis	2
15k Skiathlon	Women	40+	Laura McCabe	8
15k Skiathlon	Women	45+	Muffy Roy	5
15k Skiathlon	Women	50+	Juliet Bradley	3
15k Skiathlon	Women	55+	Carolyn Tiernan	3
15k Skiathlon	Women	60+	June Lane	3
15k Skiathlon	Women	65+	Hedda Anya	2
15k Skiathlon	Women	70+	Louise Goodman	1
20k Freestyle	Women	40+	Teresa Deprey	12
20k Freestyle	Women	45+	Ruth Williamson	10
20k Freestyle	Women	50+	Katie Meyer	7
20k Freestyle	Women	55+	Carolyn Tiernan	6

Road Cycling.
2007 USA Cycling National Festival—Seven Spring, PA, July 5–17

Event	Gender	Age	Champion	Competitors
20 km Time Trial	Men	55–59	Gordon Paulson	31
20 km Time Trial	Men	60–64	G. Turner Howard	23
20 km Time Trial	Men	65–69	Scott Tucker	20
20 km Time Trial	Men	70–74	Franz Hammer	8
20 km Time Trial	Men	75–79	Francois Mertens	4
20 km Time Trial	Men	80–85	Charles Martin	2
30 km Time Trial	Men	40–44	Michael Hutchinson	62
30 km Time Trial	Men	45–49	Thurlow Rogers	63
30 km Time Trial	Men	50–54	David Zimbelman	48
Criterium	Men	40–44	Michael Hutchinson	71
Criterium	Men	45–49	Skip Foley	74
Criterium	Men	50–54	Kent Bostwick	47
Criterium	Men	55–59	Kenny Fuller	31
Criterium	Men	60–64	John Elgart	32
Criterium	Men	65–69	Ed Lang	16
Criterium	Men	70–74	Franz Hammer	7
Criterium	Men	75–79	Francois Mertens	2
Criterium	Men	80–84	Charles Martin	1
Road Race	Men	40–44	Dirk Pohlmann	70
Road Race	Men	45–49	Thurlow Rogers	84
Road Race	Men	50–54	Wayne Stetina	58
Road Race	Men	55–59	David Leduc	31
Road Race	Men	60–64	G. Turner Howard	23
Road Race	Men	65–69	Robert Brooks	14
Road Race	Men	70–74	Franz Hammer	9
Road Race	Men	75–79	Francois Mertens	3

Event	Gender	Age	Champion	Competitors
30 km Time Trial	Tandem/Men	110+	Buck/Bernzny	10
30 km Time Trial	Tandem/Men	90+	Lofton/Wright	8
Road Race	Tandem/Men	110+	Elgart/Wolff	8
Road Race	Tandem/Men	90+	Amelburu/Schaefer	8
30 km Time Trial	Tandem/Mixed	110+	Ostenso/Paulson	14
30 km Time Trial	Tandem/Mixed	90+	Philips/Aimone	14
Road Race	Tandem/Mixed	110+	Ostenso/Paulson	8
Road Race	Tandem/Mixed	90+	Everett/Everett	8
30 km Time Trial	Tandem/Women	90+	Kaplan/Rock	6
Road Race	Tandem/Women	90+	Celecki/Thompson	4
20 km Time Trial	Women	45–49	Ruth Clemence	13
20 km Time Trial	Women	50–54	Marianne Holt	13
20 km Time Trial	Women	55–59	Elizabeth Tyrell	10
20 km Time Trial	Women	60–64	Particia Roberts	2
20 km Time Trial	Women	65–69	Julie Lockhart	5
20 km Time Trial	Women	70–74	Joyce Quadri	2
30 km Time Trial	Women	40–44	Jillian Behm	17
Criterium	Women	40–44	Mara Miller	15
Criterium	Women	45–49	Tracy Huber	18
Criterium	Women	50–54	Linda Schnepf	13
Criterium	Women	55–59	Kay Tsui	7
Criterium	Women	60–64	Particia Roberts	2
Criterium	Women	65–69	Julie Lockhart	3
Criterium	Women	70–74	Joyce Quadri	2
Road Race	Women	40–44	Terrie Clouse	15
Road Race	Women	45–49	Ruth Clemence	13
Road Race	Women	50–54	Linda Schnepf	12
Road Race	Women	55–59	Elizabeth Tyrell	6
Road Race	Women	60–64	Particia Roberts	2
Road Race	Women	65–69	Julie Lockhart	3

Track Cycling. 2007 Masters National Track Championship —Trexlertown, PA, Aug 27–31

Event	Gender	Age	Champion	Competitors
10km Points Race	Men	55–59	Chip Berezny	18
10km Points Race	Men	60–64	Thomas Lobdell	15
10km Points Race	Men	65+	Robert Lee	13
2000m Time Trial	Men	50–54	James Host	24
2000m Time Trial	Men	55–59	Steven Worley	12
2000m Time Trial	Men	60–64	Steven Lehman	15
2000m Time Trial	Men	65–69	James Murdock	9
2000m Time Trial	Men	70+	Richard Simons	5
20km Points Race	Men	45–49	Rich Meeker	27
20km Points Race	Men	50–54	Brent Emery	23
25km Points Race	Men	40–44	Kenneth Harris	34
26km Madison	Men	45+	Donaghy/Pearson	12
3000m Time Trial	Men	40–44	Simon Walker	31
3000m Time Trial	Men	45–49	Marco Hellman	24
4km Team Time Trial	Men	40+	Price/Saroff/Soma/Walker	18
4km Team Time Trial	Men	50+	Berezny/Black/Joseph/Butler	16
500m Time Trial	Men	50–54	James Joseph	28
500m Time Trial	Men	55–59	Bill Ziegler	22
500m Time Trial	Men	60–64	Ronald Hargrave	20
500m Time Trial	Men	65–69	Earl Henry	9
500m Time Trial	Men	70+	Luigi Fabbri	6
Kilometer Time Trial	Men	40–44	Stephen Hill	28
Kilometer Time Trial	Men	45–49	Grant Soma	31
Points Race Award	Men	70+	Luigi Fabbri	4
Sprint Final	Men	40–44	Stephen Hill	8
Sprint Final	Men	45–49	Warren Geissert	8
Sprint Final	Men	50–54	Kurt Sato	8
Sprint Final	Men	55–59	Art McHugh	8
Sprint Final	Men	60–64	Bobby Phillips	8
Sprint Final	Men	65+	Earl Henry	8

Event	Gender	Age	Champion	Competitors
Team Sprint	Men	40+	Mann/Waterman/Singleton	12
Team Sprint	Men	50+	Adams/Montongne/Millar/Simmons	13
10km Points Race	Women	40–44	Annette Hanson	16
10km Points Race	Women	50–54	Lucy Shannon Youngquist	5
10km Points Race	Women	55–59	Louella Holter	2
10km Points Race	Women	60–64	Marsha Marco	1
10km Points Race	Women	65+	Julie Lockhart	1
2000m Time Trial	Women	40–44	Kathryn Wilder	10
2000m Time Trial	Women	45–49	Annette Hanson	7
2000m Time Trial	Women	50–54	Jane Rinard	8
2000m Time Trial	Women	55–59	Terry Roach	4
500m Time Trial	Women	40–44	Linda Foti	14
500m Time Trial	Women	45–49	Annette Hanson	10
500m Time Trial	Women	50–54	Donna Smith	8
500m Time Trial	Women	55–59	Elizabeth Tyrell	3
500m Time Trial	Women	60+	Linda Miller	4
Sprint Final	Women	40–44	Cathy Keeley	8
Sprint Final	Women	45+	Donna Smith	8
Sprint Final	Women	50–54	Donna Smith	4
Sprint Final	Women	60–64	Linda Miller	1
Sprint Final	Women	65+	Julie Lockhart	1
Team Sprint	Women	45+	Love/Smith	4

Cycling (Cyclo-cross).
2007 Cyclo-cross Junior/Master Nationals—Kansas City, MO, Dec. 13–16

Gender	Age	Champion	Competitors
Men	40+ B	Partick Morrissey	118
Men	40–44	James Coats	163
Men	45–49	Steve Tilford	120
Men	50–54	Edmund Overend	71
Men	55–59	Fred Wittwer	45
Men	60–64	Lewis Rollins	12
Men	65–69	R. Willmore	11
Men	70+	Walt Axthelm	2
Women	40–44	Shannon Gibson	19
Women	45–49	Catherine Walberg	24
Women	50–54	Kathy Sarvary	11
Women	55–59	Diane Ostenso	7
Women	60+	Julie Lockhart	2

Mountain Biking.
2007 Mountain Bike National Championship—West Dover, VT, July 20—24

Event	Gender	Age	Champion	Competitors
Cross Country Beginner	Men	40–49	R. Scott Tedro	17
Cross Country Beginner	Men	50–99	Larry Russell	4
Cross Country Expert	Men	40–44	Samuel Wilcox	31
Cross Country Expert	Men	45–49	Johnny O'Mara	30
Cross Country Expert	Men	50–54	Henry Kramer	24
Cross Country Expert	Men	55–59	Timothy Messersmith	11
Cross Country Expert	Men	60–64	Bob Blatner	8
Cross Country Expert	Men	65–99	Charles Beristain	9
Cross Country Sport	Men	40–49	Vin Mancuso	42
Cross Country Sport	Men	50–99	Gary Musgrove	15
Downhill Beginner	Men	40–49	Tom Judy	1
Downhill Expert	Men	40–44	John Galli	10
Downhill Expert	Men	45–49	Anthony Watkins	6
Downhill Expert	Men	50–54	Scott Lideen	4
Downhill Expert	Men	55–59	Stefan Cihylik	2
Downhill Sport	Men	40–49	Dave Woodall	8
Downhill Sport	Men	50–59	Edward Smith	5
Dual Slalom Open	Men	40–99	Pierce/Pratt	7
Super D	Men	40–49	Rich Bartlett	15

Event	Gender	Age	Champion	Competitors
Super D	Men	50–59	Timothy Messersmith	14
Cross Country Beginner	Women	40–99	Theresa Carilli	5
Cross Country Expert	Women	40–44	Julia Violich	7
Cross Country Expert	Women	45–49	Linda Browand	4
Cross Country Expert	Women	50–54	Jane Finsterwald	2
Cross Country Expert	Women	55–99	Lydia Barter	2
Cross Country Sport	Women	40–99	Janice Morris	8
Downhill Expert	Women	40–49	Vicky Koch	1
Downhill Sport	Women	40–99	Kathy Salisbury	3
Super D	Women	40–99	Charlene Smith	6

Diving. 2007 U.S. Masters National Outdoor Diving Championship—Nassau County, NY, Sept. 15–17

Event	Gender	Age	Champion	Competitors
1 Meter	Men	40–44	Todd Muzlet	5
1 Meter	Men	45–49	Ken Vigiletti	6
1 Meter	Men	50–54	David Cotton	2
1 Meter	Men	55–59	Peter Jewell	1
1 Meter	Men	60–64	Richard Blough	2
1 Meter	Men	65–69	John Deininger	3
1 Meter	Men	70–74	Felix Grossman	1
1 Meter	Men	75–79	Robert Sherman	3
1 Meter	Men	80–84	Tom Hairabedian	1
3 Meter	Men	40–44	Todd Muzlet	4
3 Meter	Men	45–49	Ken Vigiletti	4
3 Meter	Men	50–54	David Cotton	2
3 Meter	Men	55–59	Peter Jewell	1
3 Meter	Men	60–64	Richard Blough	2
3 Meter	Men	65–69	John Deininger	2
3 Meter	Men	70–74	Felix Grossman	1
3 Meter	Men	75–79	John Conner	3
3 Meter	Men	80–84	Tom Hairabedian	2
Platform	Men	40–49	Alex Lapidus	5
Platform	Men	50–59	David Cotton	2
Platform	Men	60–69	Richard Blough	3
Platform	Men	70–79	Robert Sherman	2
Platform	Men	80–84	Tom Hairabedian	1
1 Meter	Women	40–44	Jennifer Mangum	2
1 Meter	Women	45–49	Karla Helder	7
1 Meter	Women	50–54	Gail Heaslip	3
1 Meter	Women	55–59	Mary Bennett	3
1 Meter	Women	60–64	Deborah Mynatt	1
1 Meter	Women	65–69	Marcia Thompson	1
1 Meter	Women	70–74	Helen Bayly	1
1 Meter	Women	75–79	Ibone Bel'g'tia	3
3 Meter	Women	40–44	Jennifer Mangum	3
3 Meter	Women	45–49	Karla Helder	5
3 Meter	Women	50–54	Margaret Cheney	2
3 Meter	Women	55–59	Mary Bennett	2
3 Meter	Women	60–64	Deborah Mynatt	1
3 Meter	Women	75–79	Ibone Bel'g'tia	1
Platform	Women	40–49	Jennifer Mangum	4
Platform	Women	50–59	Mary Bennett	2
Platform	Women	60–69	Deborah Mynatt	1
Platform	Women	70–79	Ibone Bel'g'tia	2
Synchro Diving	Women	50–64	Cheney/Bennett	4
Synchro Diving	Women	65+	Wood/Wilson	2
Synchro Diving	Mixed	50–64	Heaslip/Conner	4
Synchro Diving	Mixed	65+	Sherman/Wilson	6

Fencing. 2007 Summer Nationals—Miami, FL, June 29—July 8

Event	Gender	Age	Champion	Competitors
Epee	Men	40–49	Rick Watrall	60
Epee	Men	50–59	Walter Dragonetti	55
Epee	Men	60–69	William Reith	26
Foil	Men	40–49	Donald Davis	45
Foil	Men	50–59	Thomas Lutton	39
Foil	Men	60–69	James Adams	24
Saber	Men	40–49	Steven Heck	15
Saber	Men	50–59	Paul Hicha	24
Saber	Men	60–69	Paul Apostol	16
Epee	Women	40–49	Suzanne Simpson	24
Epee	Women	50–59	Marianne Bosco	26
Epee	Women	60–69	Diane Kallus	6
Foil	Women	40–49	Katalin Kenessey-Gasparin	33
Foil	Women	50–59	Jeanette Starks-Faulkner	26
Foil	Women	60–69	Diane Kallus	6
Saber	Women	40–49	Mary Wilkerson	14
Saber	Women	50–59	Delia Turner	17
Saber	Women	60–69	Ellen O'Leary	5

Handball (MEN).
2007 U.S. Masters Singles/Doubles 4—Wall Handball Championship
Singles—Dallas, TX; Doubles—Overland Park, KS, March 22–25

Event	Age	Champion	Competitors
Singles	40+	Vern Roberts	4
Singles	45+	Tracy Eubanks	7
Singles	50+	Jack Brady	15
Singles	60+	Greg Raya	10
Singles	65+	Wayne Neumann	12
Singles	70+	Buzz Shumate	9
Singles	75+	Bill Strawn	6
Doubles	40+	Esser/Pfannenstiel	14
Doubles	45+	Roberts/Roberts	12
Doubles	50+	Fox/Campbell	22
Doubles	55+	Carrillo/Fitzwater	32
Doubles	60+	Hulick/Kogan	28
Doubles	65+	Rohrer/Schulz	14
Doubles	70+	Chapman/DelGrande	16
Doubles	75+	Sleeper/Strawn	12

Handball (MEN). 2007 U.S. 4-Wall National Championship
Minneapolis, Minnesota, April 30–May 6

Event	Age	Champion	Competitors
Singles	40+	Ducksy Walsh	12
Singles	45+	Steve Christoff	13
Singles	50+	David Steinberg	19
Singles	50+ B	Ed Campbell	13
Singles	55+	Glenn Carden	19
Singles	60+	Greg Raya	14
Singles	60+ B	Dennis Grande	10
Singles	65+	Dennis Moser	21
Singles	70+	Jim Economides	8
Singles	70+ B	Lou Signer	7
Singles	75+	Bill Strawn	9
Singles	80+	Charlie Malone	4
Doubles	40+	Walsh/Jensen	18
Doubles	45+	Schaumann/Miller	16
Doubles	50	Corrigan/Kirk	18
Doubles	55+	Carrillo/Fitzwater	26
Doubles	60+	Nett/Hinkleman	22
Doubles	65+	Grossenbacher/Flowers	30

Event	Age	Champion	Competitors
Doubles	70+	Chapman/DelGrande	16
Doubles	75+	Sleeper/Strawn	10

Handball (MEN). 2007 U.S. 3-Wall National Championship
Maumee, Ohio, August 30–Sept. 3

Event	Age	Champion	Competitors
Singles	40+	Ron Lescinskas	10
Singles	40+ B	Scott Walker	14
Singles	45+	Alan Frank	13
Singles	50+	Dave Dohman	10
Singles	50+ B	Octavio Lemus	20
Singles	55+	Sean Conneely	15
Singles	60+	Greg Raya	12
Singles	65+	Kent Fullelman	12
Singles	70+	Larry Brown	9
Singles	75+	Ben Marguglio	5
Doubles	40+	Lescinskas/McDonough	24
Doubles	50+	Dohman/Sterrett	40
Doubles	60+	Miller/Smith	24
Doubles	70+	Sleeper/Marguulio	14

Ice Hockey (MEN). 2007 USA Hockey Adult National Championships
40 & Over, Naples, FL; 50/60 & Over, Bradenton, Fl, April 12–15*

Event	Age-Group	National Champion
No Checking	40 & Over	North Carolina Eagles (NC)
No Checking—USA	50 & Over	T's Pub (MA)
No Checking—Blue	50 & Over	Team IMS (FL)
No Checking—Light	50 & Over	Sons of Beach (FL)
No Checking	60 & Over	Minn Old Timers (MN)

*Number of competitors not available.

Ice Hockey (MEN). 2007 Hockey North American National Championships
40 & Over, Naples, FL; 50/60 & Over, Bradenton, Fl, April 12–15*

Event	Champion
Tier 1	Rockville Rattlers
Tier 2	Detroit Yellow Jackets
Tier 3	Detroit Moose
Tier 4 Level 1	New Jersey Stars
Tier 4 Level 2	Philadelphia Stars
Tier 4 Level 3	Philadelphia Ice Dragons
Tier 4 Level 4	Philadelphia Galaxy
Tier 4 Level 5	Detroit Outlaws

*Number of competitions not available

Orienteering. 2007 U.S. Individual Orienteering
National Championships—Triangle, Virginia, November 2–4

Event	Gender	Age	Champion	Competitors
Brown	Men	65+	Rich Parker	16
Brown	Men	70+	John Vallin	9
Brown	Men	75+	Tom Jahn	3
Brown	Men	80+	Kenneth Lew	2
Brown—Combined	Men	65+	Rich Parker	16
Brown—Combined	Men	70+	John Vallin	9
Brown—Combined	Men	75+	Tom Jahn	3
Brown—Combined	Men	80+	Kenneth Lew	2
Green	Men	40+	Gregory Balter	15
Green	Men	45+	Tom Hollowell	29
Green	Men	50+	Dave Linthicum	37

Event	Gender	Age	Champion	Competitors
Green	Men	55+	Jeffrey Saeger	23
Green	Men	60+	Peter Gagarin	31
Green—Combined	Men	40+	Gregory Balter	16
Green—Combined	Men	45+	Tom Hollowell	31
Green—Combined	Men	50+	Eric Weyman	38
Green—Combined	Men	55+	Jeffrey Saeger	23
Green—Combined	Men	60+	Peter Gagarin	32
Sprint—Brown	Men	65+	Fred Veller	7
Sprint—Brown	Men	70+	John Vallin	5
Sprint—Brown	Men	80+	Kenneth Lew	1
Sprint—Green	Men	40+	Eugene Mlynczyk	19
Sprint—Green	Men	45+	Clinton Morse	18
Sprint—Green	Men	50+	Memund Daltveit	23
Sprint—Green	Men	55+	Walter Siegenthaler	13
Sprint—Green	Men	60+	Peter Gagarin	17
Brown	Women	40+	Julie Cleary	10
Brown	Women	45+	Peggy Dickinson	12
Brown	Women	50+	Natalia Babeti	12
Brown—Combined	Women	40+	Julie Cleary	10
Brown—Combined	Women	45+	Peggy Dickinson	12
Brown—Combined	Women	50+	Natalia Babeti	12
Orange	Women	55+	Nadezhda Popova	6
Orange	Women	60+	Sharon Crawford	8
Orange	Women	65+	Judith Dickinson	7
Orange	Women	70+	Mette Tabur	4
Orange	Women	75+	Ruth Johnson	1
Orange—Combined	Women	55+	Beatrice Zucher	6
Orange—Combined	Women	60+	Sharon Crawford	8
Orange—Combined	Women	65+	Judith Dickinson	7
Orange—Combined	Women	70+	Mette Tabur	4
Orange—Combined	Women	75+	Ruth Johnson	1
Sprint—Brown	Women	40+	Gayle Ryan	2
Sprint—Brown	Women	45+	Peggy Dickinson	8
Sprint—Brown	Women	50+	Robyn Rennie	8
Sprint—Orange	Women	55+	Beatrice Zucher	6
Sprint—Orange	Women	60+	Sharon Crawford	2
Sprint—Orange	Women	65+	Lynette Walker	2
Sprint—Orange	Women	70+	Donna Cookin	1
Sprint—Orange	Women	75+	Ruth Johnson	1

Platform Tennis. 2007 U.S. Senior Platform Tennis Championships—Pelhamm NY, March 23–24 2008 U.S. Women's 50/70 National Championship—Scarsdale, NY, January 16–17*

Event	Gender	Age	Champions
2007 Natonals	Women	40+	Andrea/Sheri
2008 Natonals	Women	50+	Ford/Hays
2007 Natonals	Women	60+	Garrett/Simmers
2008 Natonals	Women	70+	Hummers/Mariani
2007 Natonals	Men	45+	Goodspeed/Todd
2007 Natonals	Men	55+	Adams/Hays
2007 Natonals	Men	65+	Dey/Spears

*Number of competitors for both championships available.

Racquetball. 2008 NMRA National Championship—Orem, UT, March 5–8

Event	Gender	Age	Champion	Competitors
Singles	Men	45+	Oscar Fierro	5
Singles	Men	50+	Stephen Wattz	16
Singles	Men	55+	Joe Lee	13
Singles	Men	60+	Michael Call	11
Singles	Men	65+	Steve Covey	11
Singles	Men	70+	Charlie Harmon	13

Event	Gender	Age	Champion	Competitors
Singles	Men	75+	Aaron Vederoff	6
Singles	Men	80+	Victor Sacco	6
Singles	Men	85+	Sam Harry	2
Singles	Men	90+	Ben Marshall	1
Doubles	Men	45+	Travers/Cain	16
Doubles	Men	50+	Bratt/Gunderson	24
Doubles	Men	55+	Saakian/Gonzalez	52
Doubles	Men	60+	Pawka/Hanson	48
Doubles	Men	65+	Davis/Letter	28
Doubles	Men	70+	Graff/Adams	24
Doubles	Men	75+	Vederoff/Mcelwee	24
Doubles	Men	80+	Bruner/Sacco	10
Doubles	Men	85+	Harry/Gillio	2
Doubles	Mixed	45+	Hollingsworth/Ellis	6
Doubles	Mixed	50+	Hiles/Luttner	14
Doubles	Mixed	55+	Weisbart/Cohen	8
Doubles	Mixed	60+	Northwood/Furaus	6
Doubles	Mixed	65+	Lawler/Schaefer	8
Doubles	Mixed	70+	Markus/Dorst	2
Singles	Women	45+	Marinane Walsh	4
Singles	Women	50+	Marcia Richards	6
Singles	Women	55+	Shirley Parsons	2
Singles	Women	60+	Mary Lou Furaus	4
Singles	Women	65+	Mildred Gwinn	2
Doubles	Women	45+	Walsh/Pawka	8
Doubles	Women	50+	Cameron/Shewfelt	6
Doubles	Women	60+	Neer/Sawyer	4
Doubles	Women	65+	Gwinn/Schaefer	4

Racquetball. 2007 National Singles Championship (Over-40)—Houston, TX, May 23–28

Gender	Age	Champion	Competitors
Men	40+	Jimmy Lowe	21
Men	40+ A	Dave Hibbard	20
Men	40+ B	Martin Quinones	15
Men	40+ C	Charlie Hayden	8
Men	45+	Tim Hansen	22
Men	45+ A	Russell Palazzo	16
Men	45+ B	David Stewart	17
Men	45+ C	Paul Gomberg	13
Men	50+	Ruben Gonzalez	21
Men	50+ A	Doug Kite	20
Men	50+ B	John Shubert	15
Men	50+ C	Lloyd Ferran	11
Men	55+	Russ Montague	19
Men	55+ A	John Lomonaco	17
Men	55+ B	Tony Vargas	10
Men	55+ C	Christopher Young	11
Men	60+	Ed Remen	18
Men	60A/65A	David Edwards	6
Men	60B/65B	John Bryant	6
Men	60C/65C	Ernesto Segura	8
Men	65+	Patrick Taylor	9
Men	70+	Michael Jackson	12
Men	75+	John O'donnell Jr	6
Men	80/85/90	Robert Mcadam	3
Women	40+	Debra Tisinger-Moore	9
Women	40A/45A	Melody Gorno	5
Women	40B/50B/55B	Jo Anna Reyes	4
Women	40C/45C/50C/60C/65C	Diana Starr Allen	3
Women	45+	Malia Bailey	6
Women	45+ B	Judy Ostoich	9
Women	50+	Linda Moore	5
Women	50A/55A	Shirley Parsons	6

Gender	Age	Champion	Competitors
Women	55+	Merijean Kelley	6
Women	60+	Merijean Kelley	6
Women	65/75	Mildred Gwinn	5

Racquetball. 2007 National Doubles Championship (Over-40) — Tempe, AZ, Sept. 26–30

Gender	Age	Champion	Competitors
Men	40+	Amatulli/Minor	40
Men	45+	Azuma/Travers	56
Men	45+ A	Cannon/Martucci	52
Men	45+ B	Dallsky/Koliczw	28
Men	45+ C	Heath/Hockenberry	4
Men	50+	Lubbers/Bonanno	76
Men	55+	Castelanelli/Ortega	52
Men	55+ A	Christ/Cohen	6
Men	55+ B	Verhaeghe/Lundy	6
Men	55+ C	Hubrich/Evans	6
Men	60+	Olsen/Mckie	40
Mixed	40+	Nance/Nomura	20
Mixed	45+	Bell/Bailey	36
Mixed	50+	Azuma/Dexter	56
Mixed	55+	Chaney/Vincent	18
Mixed	60+	Kelley/Pawka	12
Mixed	65+	Guerro/Funes	16
Women	45+ B	Velasquez/Richardson	4
Women	50+	Dexter/Moore	32
Women	55+	Kelley/Kronenfeld	20
Women	60+	Kelley/Funes	4
Women	65+	Schaefer/Gwinn	2

Road Racing. 2007 US Masters 5km Cross Country Championship Sarasota Springs, NY, October 14

Gender	Age	Champion	Competitors
Men	40–44	Kent Lemme	36
Men	45–49	Peter Magill	30
Men	50–54	David Cannon	42
Men	55–59	Richard Larsen	21
Men	60–64	William Dixon	20
Men	65–69	Tom Weddle	8
Men	70–74	John Leonard	7
Men	75–79	Ted Sullivan	5
Men	80–84	Michael Bartholomew	36
Men	90–94	Bob Matteson	1
Women	40–44	Marisa Hanson	18
Women	45–49	Charlotte Rizzo	10
Women	50–54	Suzanne Myette	13
Women	55–59	Kathryn Martin	5
Women	60–64	Sylvie Kimche	3
Women	65–69	Dorothy Little	1
Women	70–74	Edna Hyer	1
Women	75–79	Helen Bueme	2
Women	80–84	Regina Tumidajewicz	1

Road Racing. 2007 USA Masters 100km Trail Championship Crescent Lake, Oregon, August 18

Gender	Age	National Champion	Competitors
Men	40–44	Mark Lantz	9
Men	45–49	Eric Clifton	6
Men	50–54	Dave Stevenson	3
Men	55–59	Mike Burke	2

Gender	Age	National Champion	Competitors
Men	65–69	Kent Holder	1
Women	40–44	Beverley Anderson-Abbs	5
Women	45–49	Meghan Abrogast	4
Women	55–59	Marlis DeJongh	1

Road Racing. 2007 USA 8 km
Cross Country Championship—Boulder, CO, February 10

Gender	Age	Champion	Competitors
Women	40–44	Patty Murray	29
Women	45–49	Gil Mercedes	10
Women	50–54	Martha Buttner	4
Women	55–59	Kathryn Martin	3
Women	60–64	Marilyn Stapleton	6
Women	65–69	Betty Valent	3
Women	70–74	Lois Calhoun	3
Women	80–84	Nancy Smalley	1
Men	40–44	Dennis Simonaitis	41
Men	45–49	Peter Magill	30
Men	50–54	Steve Gallegos	26
Men	55–59	Doug Bell	13
Men	60–64	Richard Myers	15
Men	65–69	Thom Weddle	5
Men	70–74	John Brennand	3
Men	75–79	Donald Hayes	3
Men	80–84	Glen McIntosh	3
Men	85–89	Irving Weiss	1

Rowing (MEN). 2007 US Rowing Masters
National Championship—Oak Ridge, Tennessee. September 8–12

Event	Age	National Champion	Competitors
Coxed Four	36–42	Potomac Boat Club A	44
Coxed Four	43–49	Potomac Boat Club A	50
Coxed Four	50–54	Florida Athletic Club B	30
Coxed Four	55–59	Florida Athletic Club	60
Coxed Four	65–69	Occoquan International A	10
Coxed Four	70–74	Occoquan International	5
Coxed Four	80+	Treasure Coast Rowing Club	5
Coxed Four	36–42	Potomac Boat Club A	30
Coxed Four	60–64	Occoquan International	20
Coxed Four Club	43–49	Riverfront Recapture A	45
Coxed Four Club	50–54	Community Rowing Inc A	45
Coxed Four Club	55–59	Cambridge Boat Club A	15
Coxed Four Club	60–64	Cambridge Boat Club A	25
Coxed Four Club	65–69	Saugatuck Rowing Club B	5
Coxed Four Ltwt	43–49	Saugatuck Rowing Club	5
Coxed Four Ltwt	50–54	San Diego Rowing Club A	15
Coxed Four Ltwt	55–59	Syracuse Chargers Rowing A	5
Coxless Four	36–42	Potomac Boat Club A	8
Coxless Four	43–49	Occoquan International A	8
Coxless Four	50–54	Occoquan International A	16
Coxless Four	55–59	Occoquan International	12
Coxless Four	60–64	Occoquan International	4
Coxless Four	65–69	Occoquan International A	8
Coxless Four Scull	36–42	Chesapeake Boathouse A	16
Coxless Four Scull	43–49	Narragansett Boat Club	28
Coxless Four Scull	50–54	Whitemarsh Boat Club	12
Coxless Four Scull	55–59	Lightwave Rowing Assoc.	4
Coxless Four Scull	55–59	Occoquan International	20
Coxless Four Scull	60–64	Minneapolis Rowing Club A	4
Coxless Four Scull	60–64	Dallas Rowing Club	4
Coxless Four Scull	60–64	Occoquan International	12
Coxless Four Scull	65–69	Cygnet Rowing Club	4

Event	Age	National Champion	Competitors
Coxless Four Scull	65–69	Saugatuck Rowing Club	4
Coxless Four Scull	70–74	Occoquan International	4
Coxless Four Scull	80+	Treasure Coast Rowing Club	4
Coxless Four Scull	50–54	Occoquan International	20
Coxless Four Scull	65–69	Occoquan International	8
Coxless Four Scull Club	43–49	Saugatuck Rowing Club	4
Coxless Four Scull Club	50–54	Saugatuck Rowing Club	12
Coxless Four Scull Ltwt	43–49	Saugatuck Rowing Club A	4
Coxless Four Scull Ltwt	50–54	Whitemarsh Boat Club	16
Coxless Pair	36–42	Greater Columbus Rowing A	4
Coxless Pair	43–49	Swan Creek Rowing Club A	10
Coxless Pair	50–54	Swan Creek Rowing Club A	10
Coxless Pair	55–59	Occoquan International	10
Coxless Pair	60–64	New Haven Rowing Club A	6
Coxless Pair	65–69	Occoquan International	4
Coxless Pair	70–74	Occoquan International	2
Double Scull	36–42	Narragansett Boat Club A	16
Double Scull	43–49	Ecorse Rowing Club A	20
Double Scull	50–54	Saugatuck Rowing Club A	20
Double Scull	55–59	Narragansett Boat Club	22
Double Scull	60–64	Narragansett Boat Club	14
Double Scull	70–74	Occoquan International	8
Double Scull	75–79	College Boat Club	6
Double Scull	65–69	Cambridge Boat Club A	20
Double Scull Ltwt	36–42	Saugatuck Rowing Club A	6
Double Scull Ltwt	43–49	Chesapeake Boathouse	10
Double Scull Ltwt	50–54	Baltimore Rowing Club	16
Double Scull Ltwt	55–59	Minneapolis Rowing Club	10
Double Scull Ltwt	60–64	Jacksonville Rowing Club A	6
Double Scull Ltwt	65–69	College Boat Club	10
Double Scull Ltwt	70–74	College Boat Club	6
Double Scull Ltwt	75–79	Minneapolis Boat Club	2
Eights	55–59	Occoquan International	45
Eights	65–69	Occoquan International	18
Eights	36–42	Potomac Boat Club A	45
Eights	43–49	Potomac Boat Club A	63
Eights	50–54	Occoquan International	72
Eights	60–64	Occoquan International	9
Eights Club	36–42	Saugatuck Rowing Club A	27
Eights Club	43–49	Potomac Boat Club A	36
Eights Club	50–54	Community Rowing Club	27
Eights Club	55–59	Community Rowing Club A	27
Eights Club	60–64	Saugatuck Rowing Club A	9
Single Scull	36–42	G. Hartsuff	12
Single Scull	43–49	M. Bozenski	13
Single Scull	50–54	R. Miller	16
Single Scull	55–59	C. Selden	10
Single Scull	60–64	C. Hamlin	17
Single Scull	65–69	H. Hamilton	6
Single Scull	70–74	C. Zezza	7
Single Scull	75–79	D. Smith	2
Single Scull	75–79	C. Collins	6
Single Scull Ltwt	36–42	J. Griffith	6
Single Scull Ltwt	43–49	D. Gorriaran	6
Single Scull Ltwt	50–54	J. Sanders	7
Single Scull Ltwt	55–59	K. Juurakko	9
Single Scull Ltwt	60–64	D Bort	8
Single Scull Ltwt	65–69	H. Hamilton	5
Single Scull Ltwt	70–74	J. Heiden	4
Single Scull Ltwt	75–79	R. Kendall	5
Single Scull Ltwt	80+	D. Smith	1

Rowing (Mixed). 2007 USRowing Masters
National Championship—Oak Ridge, Tennessee, September 8–12

Event	Age	Champion	Competitors
Coxed Four	36–42	Greater Columbus Rowing A	25
Coxed Four	43–49	East Arm Rowing Club A	40
Coxed Four	50–54	Annapolis Rowing Club A	25
Coxed Four	55–59	Occoquan International	20
Coxed Four	60–64	Prince William Rowing Club	5
Coxless Four Scull	43–49	Saugatuck Rowing Club A	24
Coxless Four Scull	60–64	Cincinnati Rowing Club A	12
Coxless Four Scull	65–69	Occoquan International	8
Coxless Four Scull	36–43	Ecorse Rowing Club	24
Coxless Four Scull	50–54	Narragansett Boat Club	24
Coxless Four Scull	55–59	Fairmount Rowing Assoc. A	16
Double Scull	36–42	Narragansett Boat Club	16
Double Scull	43–49	Narragansett Boat Club A	36
Double Scull	50–54	Saugatuck Rowing Club A	28
Double Scull	55–59	Minneapolis Boat Club A	16
Double Scull	60–64	Lincoln Park Boat Club A	10
Double Scull	65–69	Fairmount Rowing Assoc. A	8
Double Scull	70–74	Saugatuck Rowing Club A	4
Eights	43–49	Saugatuck Rowing Club A	27
Eights	36–42	Rocky Mountain Rowing Club A	81
Eights	50–54	Syracuse Chargers Rowing Club	27
Eights	55–59	Occoquan International	18

Rowing (Mixed). 2007 USRowing Masters
National Championship—Oak Ridge, Tennessee, September 8–12

Event	Age	Champion	Competitors
Coxed Four	36–42	Rocky Mountain Rowing Club A	25
Coxed Four	43–49	Watercat Rowing Club A	40
Coxed Four	50–54	Watercat Rowing Club A	35
Coxed Four	55–59	Masters Coaching	30
Coxed Four	60–64	Masters Coaching	10
Coxed Four Club	36–42	Capital Rowing Club A	60
Coxed Four Club	43–49	Annapolis Rowing Club B	75
Coxed Four Club	50–54	Carnegie Lake Rowing Assoc. A	50
Coxed Four Club	55–59	Community Rowing Inc A	20
Coxed Four Club	60–64	Chester River Rowing Club A	10
Coxed Four Club	65–69	Oak Ridge Rowing Assoc.G	5
Coxed Four Ltwt	36–42	Community Rowing Inc A	15
Coxed Four Ltwt	43–49	Rocky Mountain Rowing Club A	15
Coxed Four Ltwt	50–54	Carnegie Lake Rowing Assoc A	15
Coxless Four	36–42	Saugatuck Rowing Club A	12
Coxless Four	43–49	Saugatuck Rowing Club A	8
Coxless Four Scull	36–42	Saugatuck Rowing Club A	16
Coxless Four Scull	43–49	Rocky Mountain Rowing Club	24
Coxless Four Scull	55–59	Miami Rowing Center	16
Coxless Four Scull	60–64	Potomac Boat Club A	8
Coxless Four Scull	50–54	Atlanta Rowing Club	28
Coxless Four Scull Ltwt	50–54	Saugatuck Rowing Club A	8
Coxless Four Scull Club	36–42	Saugatuck Rowing Club A	20
Coxless Four Scull Club	43–49	Rocky Mountain Rowing Club A	24
Coxless Four Scull Club	50–54	Lake Merritt Rowing Club A	16
Coxless Four Scull Club	55–59	Saugatuck Rowing Club A	12
Coxless Four Scull Club	60–64	Cincinnati Rowing Club A	4
Coxless Four Scull Ltwt	55–59	Oak Ridge Rowing Assoc. A	4
Coxless Pair	36–42	Minneapolis Rowing Club A	4
Coxless Pair	43–49	Lake Merritt Rowing Club A	4
Coxless Pair	50–54	Watercat Rowing Club A	4
Double Scull	36–42	Saugatuck Rowing Club A	22
Double Scull	43–49	Rivanna Rowing Club	14
Double Scull	50–54	Minneapolis Rowing Club A	16
Double Scull	50–54	Green Lake Crew	12

Event	Age	Champion	Competitors
Double Scull	55–59	La Baie Verte Rowing Club A	4
Double Scull	65–69	Potomac Boat Club A	6
Double Scull	60–64	Fairmount Rowing Assoc. A	8
Double Scull Ltwt	36–42	Saugatuck Rowing Club B	8
Double Scull Ltwt	43–49	Saugatuck Rowing Club B	14
Double Scull Ltwt	55–59	Cincinnati Rowing Club A	6
Double Scull Ltwt	60–64	Oak Ridge Rowing Assoc.	2
Eights	55–59	Saugatuck Rowing Club A	9
Eights	60–64	Masters Coaching	9
Eights Club	36–42	Community Rowing A	81
Eights Club	55–59	Syracuse Chargers A	18
Eights Club	60–64	Potomac Boat Club A	18
Eights	36–42	Capital Rowing Club A	27
Eights	43–49	Orlando Rowing Club A	63
Eights	50–54	Saugatuck Rowing Club A	45
Eights	50–54	Saugatuck Rowing Club A	54
Eights	55–59	Masters Coaching	36
Eights Club	43–49	Minneapolis Rowing Club A	117
Single Scull	36–42	E. Kennelly	12
Single Scull	43–49	E. Kennelly	8
Single Scull	50–54	M. Jekabsons	10
Single Scull	55–59	A. Cann	6
Single Scull	60–64	S. Sargent	3
Single Scull	65–69	J. Stone	2
Single Scull Ltwt	36–42	S. Conner	7
Single Scull Ltwt	43–49	P. Raila	8
Single Scull Ltwt	50–54	P. Meyer	7
Single Scull Ltwt	55–59	E. Hansen	4
Single Scull Ltwt	60–64	C.Kendle	1
Single Scull Ltwt	75–79	E. Green	1

Soccer. 2007 USASA Veteran's Cup—Bellingham, Washington, July 21–22

Event	Gender	Age	Champion	Competitors
Premier	Men	Over 40	Tri-Alliance 02' (Washington)	6
1st Division	Men	Over 40	Connecticut United	6
Division	Men	Over 50	Golden Oldies (California North)	10
Division	Men	Over 55	Golden Oldies (California North)	12
Division	Men	Over 60	Dallas Legends (North Texas)	9
Premier	Women	Over 40	San Francisco (California North)	5
1st Division	Women	Over 40	Team Field Turf (Washington)	6
Division	Women	Over 45	Camp Springs SC (Maryland)	4
Division	Women	Over 50	Holomua (Hawaii)	11
Division	Women	Over 55	California Kickin' (California North)	4
Division	Women	Over 60	Cascade Avalanche 60 (Washington)	5

Softball (MEN). 2007 Amateur Softball Association
National Champions—Multiple Locations and Dates

Event	Age	Champion	Teams
Slow Pitch	40-Over	JK Inc.	21
Slow Pitch	45-Over	Coutesy's/Kelly's Sports/Combat	7
Fast Pitch	50-Over	Memphis PO-10	
Slow Pitch AA	50	State College	2
Slow Pitch AAA	50	KJP Sales	7
Slow Pitch Major Plus	50	Damon's Grill	2
Slow Pitch Major	50-Over	Travelodge 55's	8
Slow Pitch AA	55	Southland Log Homes	6
Slow Pitch AAA	55	VA Vending/TGI Fridays	6
Slow Pitch Major Plus	55	Spicer's/33 1/2	2
Slow Pitch Major	55-Over	NJ Hit4	
Slow Pitch AA	60	Southern Sixties	3
Slow Pitch AAA	60	Tidewater 60's	4
Slow Pitch Major Plus	60	Spicer's/Turn Two	2
Slow Pitch Major	60-Over	Matador Club	5

Event	Age	Champion	Teams
Slow Pitch AA	65	Richmond Classics/Estes Express	4
Slow Pitch AAA	65	GA Nuggets	4
Slow Pitch Major Plus	65	Florida Legends/Human Kinetics	3
Slow Pitch Major	65-Over	Premium Seats	2
Slow Pitch AAA	70-Over	Hamel's 70	3
Slow Pitch Major	70-Over	Southern Pride	4

Softball (MEN). 2007 National Softball Association National Champions—Multiple Locations and Dates

Event	Age	Champion	Teams
Major	40+	Team Worth/40+	5
AAA	50+	Indiana Classics	8
Major	50+	Pensacola Merchants	2
Western World Series—Major	50+	MTC Softball Club	2
AA	55+	Birmingham 55's	3
AAA	55+	Georgia/Alabama Masters	2
Major	55+	Kayson 55	2
Major Plus	55+	Spicer's 33 1/2 55's	2
Western World Series—AAA	55+	Norcal Stixx	2
Western World Series—Major Plus	55+	MTC 55's	2
AA	60+	Border States Softball	5
AAA	60+	Teeters	5
Major	60+	Tapco	4
Major Plus	60+	Boaz/ASI	2
Western World Series—Major	60+	California Starzz	2
Western World Series—Major Plus	60+	Old A's/Miken	2
Western World Series AAA	60+	Mustang 60	2
AA	65+	Shelby Seniors	2
Western World Series—Major Plus	65+	Norcal Bluejays	2
AA	70+	Mid-Georgia Seniors	2
Major	70+	Joseph Chevrolet 70+	4

Softball (MEN). 2007 International Senior Softball Association National Championships—Manassas Virginia, June 22–24

Event	Age	Champion	Teams
Major	50+	Damon's Grill	2
A	50+	Coastal Masonry	6
B	50+	Goodman Softball	4
C	50+	Creative Builders	8
Major	55+	Unknown/Combat/Truncell	2
A	55+	Spicer 33 1/2	5
B	55+	High Street Bucs	5
C	55+	Northampton Produce	4
Major	60+	Spicer Properties/Turn Two	3
B	60+	Vacar Stars	5
C	60+	Michigan Express	6
Major	65+	Florida Legends/Human Kinetics	2

Softball (MEN). 2007 Softball Players Association National Championships—Multiple Locations and Dates

Event	Age	Champion	Teams
AA	50+	Springfield Express	4
AAA	50+	Cummings Texas Legends	13
Major	50+	Windy City Softball	10
Major Plus	50+	Kevitt/Ploog	6
AA	55+	KC Thunder	5
AAA	55+	GA/AL Masters	10
Major	55+	Kayson's Grill	10
Major Plus	55+	GFS	6
AA	60+	Tri-Cities 60's	9

Event	Age	Champion	Teams
AAA	60+	Texas Legends	16
Major	60+	Matador Club	12
Major Plus	60+	Spicer/Turn 2	8
AA	65+	Midwest Silverjox	9
AAA	65+	Chicago Black	13
Major	65+	Ed's Aluminum	4
Major Plus	65+	Florida Legends	3
AA	70+	Indiana Silver Foxes	7
AAA	70+	Dan Pfeiffer	9
Major	70+	Clearwater 70's	4
Major Plus	70+	San Francisco Seals	3
AA	75+	Old Gold	2
AAA	75+	Georgia Peaches	4
Major	75+	Texas Classics	2
	80+	Center for Sight	3

Softball 2007 Huntsman World Senior Games— St. George, Utah, October 6–18*

Event	Gender	Age	Champion
Major	Men	50+	Butch's Bulldogs
AAA	Men	50+	Mavericks
AA	Men	50+	X-Men
A	Men	50+	Francom Motors
B	Men	50+	Buzzards 50+
C	Men	50+	Silver A's
Major	Men	55+	Handeland Flooring
AAA	Men	55+	Toronto Softball
AA	Men	55+	BRL Investment 55+
A	Men	55+	Fire One Inc.
B	Men	55+	Sacramento Islanders
C	Men	55+	Nanaimo Independence II
Major Plus	Men	60+	Old A's
Major	Men	60+	The Bench Pub
AAA	Men	60+	Moulson's 60s
AA	Men	60+	Michigan Express
A	Men	60+	Mr. D's Chevron
B	Men	60+	St. Albert Lilydale White Sox
C	Men	60+	Brannon Tire Ravens
D	Men	60+	Copper Gang
Major	Men	65+	Pittsburgh Gold
AAA	Men	65+	California Angels
AA	Men	65+	Beef O'Brady's
A	Men	65+	Central Pennsylvania Seniors
B	Men	65+	Bradenton Bombers
C	Men	65+	Physiomotion
D	Men	65+	Molson Bull Dogs
Major	Men	70+	Joeseppi's
AAA	Men	70+	Hamel's
AA	Men	70+	Mesa Cardinals—70
A	Men	70+	Sierra Bees
B	Men	70+	Humboldt Classics
Major	Men	74+	Arizona 75s
AAA	Men	74+	Midwest Senior Softball 74+
Major	Women	50+	Maryland Roadrunners
AAA	Women	50+	Seniors Unlimited 50+
AA	Women	50+	California Rockers
Major	Women	55+	California Spirits 55s
AAA	Women	55+	Seniors Unlimited 55+
Major	Women	60+	Salt Chuckers
AAA	Women	60+	Florida Spirit 60s
Major	Women	65+	BC Swingers
AAA	Women	65+	Sportaculars Canada 65
Open	Women	70+	Freedom Spirit of Florida 70

*Number of teams not available

Softball. 2007 Las Vegas Senior Softball Association World Series Championship—Las Vegas, Nevada, Sept—October*

Event	Gender	Age	Champion
Major Plus	Men	50+	Seacrest Mavricks
Major	Men	50+	Windy City Softball
AAA	Men	50+	Wongs
AAA	Men	50+	South Florida Heat
Major Plus	Men	55+	Connecticut Sportplex
Major	Men	55+	Animals
AAA	Men	55+	Palm Springs Heat
AAA	Men	55+	Sonic Blast
Major Plus	Men	60+	Spicer Properties/Turn Two
Major	Men	60+	Nevada Gold
AAA	Men	60+	High Desert 60s
AAA	Men	60+	Rally Time Sports 60s
Major Plus	Men	65+	Nor Cal Bluejays
Major	Men	65+	Topgun 65s
AAA	Men	65+	Chicago Classic Black
AAA	Men	65+	Physiomotion 65s
Major	Men	70+	Texas Greyhounds 70s
AAA	Men	70+	So Cal Grizzlies
AAA	Men	70+	American Metal
Major Plus	Men	75+	Tiodize 99 75s
Major	Men	75+	Texas Classic
AAA	Men	75+	So Cal Jets
Open	Men	80+	Tremont Hotel Baltimore MD
Open	Women	40+	Arizona Dream Team
Open	Women	60+	Las Vegas Neons

Speed Skating. 2008 National Marathon Speed Skating Championship—Bemidji, MN, Feb. 23–24
2007–2008 Long Track National Championships—Lake Placid, NY, Feb. 2–3

Event	Gender	Age	Champion	Competitors
Marathon—25 km	Women	40–49	Carolyn Cone	2
Marathon—25 km	Women	50–59	Kathie Zapotocki	4
Marathon—25 km	Men	40–49	Mike Anderson	8
Marathon—25 km	Men	50–59	David Lawler	6
Marathon—25 km	Men	60–69	Ed Burns	1
Marathon—50 km	Women	50–59	Kathie Zapotocki	1
Marathon—50 km	Men	40–49	Mike Anderson	6
Marathon—50 km	Men	50–59	Ken Huss	3
Marathon—50 km	Men	60–69	Ed Burns	1
Long Track—500 meters	Women	40–49	Kim Young	7
Long Track—800 meters	Women	40–49	Suzy Osum	7
Long Track—1500 meters	Women	40–49	Suzy Osum	7
Long Track—1000 meters	Women	40–49	Kim Young	7
Long Track—3000 meters	Women	40–49	Kim Young	7
Long Track—500 meters	Women	50–59	Carol Moore	4
Long Track—800 meters	Women	50–59	Carol Moore	4
Long Track—1500 meters	Women	50–59	Carol Moore	4
Long Track—1000 meters	Women	50–59	Carol Moore	4
Long Track—3000 meters	Women	50–59	Kathie Zapotocki	4
Long Track—500 meters	Women	60–69	Mary Lou DiNicola	1
Long Track—800 meters	Women	60–69	Mary Lou DiNicola	1
Long Track—1500 meters	Women	60–69	Mary Lou DiNicola	1
Long Track—1000 meters	Women	60–69	Mary Lou DiNicola	1
Long Track—3000 meters	Women	60–69	Mary Lou DiNicola	1
Long Track—500 meters	Men	40–49	Brian Boudreau	9
Long Track—800 meters	Men	40–49	Marty Haire	10
Long Track—1000 meters	Men	40–49	Brian Boudreau	10
Long Track—3000 meters	Men	40–49	Brian Boudreau	10
Long Track—500 meters	Men	50–59	Mark Chrysler	9
Long Track—800 meters	Men	50–59	Mark Chrysler	9
Long Track—1000 meters	Men	50–59	Jonathan White	9

Event	Gender	Age	Champion	Competitors
Long Track—1500 meters	Men	50–59	Mark Chrysler	9
Long Track—3000 meters	Men	50–59	Jonathan White	9
Long Track—500 meters	Men	60–69	Chris Hawkins	6
Long Track—800 meters	Men	60–69	Chris Hawkins	9
Long Track—1000 meters	Men	60–69	Patrick Knox	9
Long Track—1500 meters	Men	60–69	Chris Hawkins	9
Long Track—3000 meters	Men	60–69	Chris Hawkins	9
Long Track—500 meters	Men	70+	Dick Klein	3
Long Track—800 meters	Men	70+	Dick Klein	3
Long Track—1000 meters	Men	70+	Dick Klein	3
Long Track—1500 meters	Men	70+	Dick Klein	3
Long Track—3000 meters	Men	70+	Dick Klein	3

Squash. Softball Singles. 2007 U.S. Squash Nationals (Over-40 Age Group Divisions)

Gender	Age	National Champion	Competitors
Women	45+	Kate LaGrand	11
Women	50+	Marjin Wall	6
Men	40+	Andre Maur	8
Men	45+	Dominic Hughes	22
Men	50+	David Perry	23
Men	55+	Gulmast Khan	16
Men	60+	Bert Kornyei	10
Men	65+	John Nelson	9
Men	70+	Robert Macdonald	8
Men	75+/80+	Charles Butt/Bud Fields	7

Squash. Softball Singles. 2006–2007 U.S. Squash Rankings (Over-40 Age Group Divisions)

Gender	Age	Champion	Competitors
Men	40+	Andre Maur	140
Men	45+	Diniar Alikhan	73
Men	50+	David Perry	131
Men	55+	Malcolm Davidson	52
Men	60+	William Berlinghof	55
Men	65+	John Nelson	26
Men	70+	Robert Macdonald	20
Men	75+	Lee Engler	3
Women	40+	Jeanne Blasberg	6
Women	45+	Kate LaGrand	7
Women	50+	Carole Grunberg	5

Swimming (WOMEN). 2007 Short Course National Championships— Federal Way, Washington, May 14–17

Event	Age	Champion	Competitors
50-Yard Freestyle	40–44	Lisa Rapuano	28
100-Yard Freestyle	40–44	Anna Scott	24
200-Yard Freestyle	40–44	Laureen Welting	25
500-Yard Freestyle	40–44	Birgit Lohberg	21
1000-Yard Freestyle	40–44	Laureen Welting	10
1650-Yard Freestyle	40–44	Amy Dantzler	6
50-Yard Backstroke	40–44	Janis Gebhart	16
100-Yard Backstroke	40–44	Janis Gebhart	10
200-Yard Backstroke	40–44	Birgit Lohberg	14
50-Yard Breaststroke	40–44	Susan Von der Lippe	18
100-Yard Breaststroke	40–44	Susan Von der Lippe	21
200-Yard Breaststroke	40–44	Susan Von der Lippe	14
50-Yard Butterfly	40–44	Anna Scott	17
100-Yard Butterfly	40–44	Susan Von der Lippe	8
200-Yard Butterfly	40–44	Susan Von der Lippe	6

Event	Age	Champion	Competitors
100-Yard IM	40–44	Elizabeth Nowak	25
200-Yard IM	40–44	Susan Von der Lippe	17
400-Yard IM	40–44	Laureen Welting	8
50-Yard Freestyle	45–49	Liz Hobbs	28
100-Yard Freestyle	45–49	Karlyn Pipes-Neilsen	30
200-Yard Freestyle	45–49	Karlyn Pipes-Neilsen	32
500-Yard Freestyle	45–49	Susanne Simpson	18
1000-Yard Freestyle	45–49	Susanne Simpson	7
1650-Yard Freestyle	45–49	Denise Brown	9
50-Yard Backstroke	45–49	Karlyn Pipes-Neilsen	20
100-Yard Backstroke	45–49	Karlyn Pipes-Neilsen	19
200-Yard Backstroke	45–49	Zena Courtney	12
50-Yard Breaststroke	45–49	Caroline Krattli	31
100-Yard Breaststroke	45–49	Caroline Krattli	26
200-Yard Breaststroke	45–49	Caroline Krattli	19
50-Yard Butterfly	45–49	Traci Granger	24
100-Yard Butterfly	45–49	Andrea Block	14
200-Yard Butterfly	45–49	Susanne Simpson	12
100-Yard IM	45–49	Karlyn Pipes-Neilsen	40
200-Yard IM	45–49	Kim Crouch	14
400-Yard IM	45–49	Lisa Pace	15
50-Yard Freestyle	50–54	Leianne Critenden	25
100-Yard Freestyle	50–54	Leianne Critenden	17
200-Yard Freestyle	50–54	Charlene O'Brien	17
500-Yard Freestyle	50–54	Charlene O'Brien	16
1000-Yard Freestyle	50–54	Terry Latham	9
1650-Yard Freestyle	50–54	Charlene O'Brien	10
50-Yard Backstroke	50–54	Patty Landers	17
100-Yard Backstroke	50–54	Patty Landers	10
200-Yard Backstroke	50–54	Patty Landers	10
50-Yard Breaststroke	50–54	Leianne Critenden	21
100-Yard Breaststroke	50–54	Karen Melick	16
200-Yard Breaststroke	50–54	Karen Melick	15
50-Yard Butterfly	50–54	Karen Rosner	14
100-Yard Butterfly	50–54	Mary Lippold	11
200-Yard Butterfly	50–54	Mary Lippold	11
100-Yard IM	50–54	Colette Crabbe	26
200-Yard IM	50–54	Colette Crabbe	10
400-Yard IM	50–54	Colette Crabbe	10
50-Yard Freestyle	55–59	Laura Val	17
100-Yard Freestyle	55–59	Laura Val	15
200-Yard Freestyle	55–59	Laura Val	12
500-Yard Freestyle	55–59	Barb Gundred	13
1000-Yard Freestyle	55–59	Barb Gundred	4
1650-Yard Freestyle	55–59	Linda Shoenberger	9
50-Yard Backstroke	55–59	Laura Val	9
100-Yard Backstroke	55–59	Barb Gundred	6
200-Yard Backstroke	55–59	Barb Gundred	7
50-Yard Breaststroke	55–59	Barbara Hummel	7
100-Yard Breaststroke	55–59	Barbara Hummel	5
200-Yard Breaststroke	55–59	Barbara Hummel	8
50-Yard Butterfly	55–59	Charlotte Davis	11
100-Yard Butterfly	55–59	Laura Val	10
200-Yard Butterfly	55–59	Carolyn Roche	7
100-Yard IM	55–59	Laura Val	16
200-Yard IM	55–59	Charlotte Davis	11
400-Yard IM	55–59	Charlotte Davis	9
50-Yard Freestyle	60–64	Carolyn Boak	15
100-Yard Freestyle	60–64	Carolyn Boak	12
200-Yard Freestyle	60–64	Suzanne Dills	13
500-Yard Freestyle	60–64	Suzanne Dills	12
1000-Yard Freestyle	60–64	Beverly Montrella	4
1650-Yard Freestyle	60–64	Suzanne Dills	9
50-Yard Backstroke	60–64	Joy Ward	10
100-Yard Backstroke	60–64	Joy Ward	10
200-Yard Backstroke	60–64	Constance Sasser	7

Event	Age	Champion	Competitors
50-Yard Breaststroke	60–64	Carolyn Boak	12
100-Yard Breaststroke	60–64	Ginger Pierson	12
200-Yard Breaststroke	60–64	Ginger Pierson	10
50-Yard Butterfly	60–64	Carolyn Boak	8
100-Yard Butterfly	60–64	Carolyn Boak	8
200-Yard Butterfly	60–64	Ginger Pierson	5
100-Yard IM	60–64	Carolyn Boak	13
200-Yard IM	60–64	Suzanne Dills	5
400-Yard IM	60–64	Suzanne Dills	6
50-Yard Freestyle	65–69	Beth Schreiner	9
100-Yard Freestyle	65–69	Beth Schreiner	9
200-Yard Freestyle	65–69	Beth Schreiner	9
500-Yard Freestyle	65–69	Jane Birkhead	5
1000-Yard Freestyle	65–69	Susanne Schumann	3
1650-Yard Freestyle	65–69	Susan Munn	3
50-Yard Backstroke	65–69	Barbara Frid	8
100-Yard Backstroke	65–69	Barbara Frid	7
200-Yard Backstroke	65–69	Ida Hlavacek	6
50-Yard Breaststroke	65–69	Barbara Frid	12
100-Yard Breaststroke	65–69	Margit Jebe	6
200-Yard Breaststroke	65–69	Susan Myers	8
50-Yard Butterfly	65–69	Barbara Frid	7
100-Yard Butterfly	65–69	Margit Jebe	5
200-Yard Butterfly	65–69	Ida Hlavacek	5
100-Yard IM	65–69	Barbara Frid	11
200-Yard IM	65–69	Susan Myers	4
400-Yard IM	65–69	Susan Myers	6
50-Yard Freestyle	70–74	Jeanne Little	7
100-Yard Freestyle	70–74	Jeanne Little	6
200-Yard Freestyle	70–74	Jeanne Little	7
500-Yard Freestyle	70–74	Lavalle Stoinoff	1
1000-Yard Freestyle	70–74	Lavalle Stoinoff	2
1650-Yard Freestyle	70–74	Betsy Jordan	2
50-Yard Backstroke	70–74	Betsy Jordan	6
100-Yard Backstroke	70–74	Betsy Jordan	6
200-Yard Backstroke	70–74	Betsy Jordan	3
50-Yard Breaststroke	70–74	Donna Ryman	5
100-Yard Breaststroke	70–74	Donna Ryman	4
200-Yard Breaststroke	70–74	Donna Ryman	3
50-Yard Butterfly	70–74	Helen Bayly	1
100-Yard Butterfly	70–74	Patricia Tullman	2
200-Yard Butterfly	70–74	Jeanne Little	3
100-Yard IM	70–74	Peggy Buchannan	2
200-Yard IM	70–74	Betsy Jordan	3
400-Yard IM	70–74	Betsy Jordan	2
50-Yard Freestyle	75–79	Nan Bohl	3
100-Yard Freestyle	75–79	Nan Bohl	5
200-Yard Freestyle	75–79	Nan Bohl	3
1650-Yard Freestyle	75–79	Lida Gaschke	2
50-Yard Backstroke	75–79	Lida Gaschke	4
100-Yard Backstroke	75–79	Lida Gaschke	5
200-Yard Backstroke	75–79	Janet Kavadas	1
50-Yard Breaststroke	75–79	Nan Bohl	4
100-Yard Breaststroke	75–79	Nan Bohl	2
200-Yard Breaststroke	75–79	Georgia Goggin	1
100-Yard IM	75–79	Lida Gaschke	2
50-Yard Freestyle	80–84	Florence Carr	2
100-Yard Freestyle	80–84	Margery Myer	2
200-Yard Freestyle	80–84	Margery Myer	2
500-Yard Freestyle	80–84	Margery Myer	1
1650-Yard Freestyle	80–84	Margery Myer	2
50-Yard Backstroke	80–84	Bernice Phillips	3
100-Yard Backstroke	80–84	Margery Myer	2
200-Yard Backstroke	80–84	Bernice Phillips	2
50-Yard Breaststroke	80–84	Florence Carr	1
200-Yard Breaststroke	80–84	Jane Krauser	2

Event	Age	Champion	Competitors
50-Yard Butterfly	80–84	Florence Carr	3
100-Yard Butterfly	80–84	Jane Krauser	2
200-Yard Butterfly	80–84	Gloria Stupfel	1
100-Yard IM	80–84	Florence Carr	1
400-Yard IM	80–84	Gloria Stupfel	1
50-Yard Freestyle	85–89	Billie Anne Burrill	3
100-Yard Freestyle	85–89	Maurine Kornfeld	5
200-Yard Freestyle	85–89	Maurine Kornfeld	5
500-Yard Freestyle	85–89	Rita Simonton	1
1000-Yard Freestyle	85–89	Rita Simonton	1
50-Yard Backstroke	85–89	Betty Christian	4
100-Yard Backstroke	85–89	Betty Christian	3
200-Yard Backstroke	85–89	Maurine Kornfeld	1
50-Yard Breaststroke	85–89	Betty Christian	1
100-Yard Breaststroke	85–89	Betty Christian	1
200-Yard Breaststroke	85–89	Betty Christian	1
200-Yard IM	85–89	Rita Simonton	1

Swimming (MEN). 2007 Short Course National Championships— Federal Way, Washington—May 14–17

Event	Age	Champion	Competitors
50-Yard Freestyle	40–44	Richard Landry	24
100-Yard Freestyle	40–44	Richard Landry	31
200-Yard Freestyle	40–44	Chris Stevenson	26
500-Yard Freestyle	40–44	Mike Shaffer	9
1000-Yard Freestyle	40–44	Jeff Erwin	6
1650-Yard Freestyle	40–44	Mike Shaffer	5
50-Yard Backstroke	40–44	Jay Yarid	10
100-Yard Backstroke	40–44	Chris Stevenson	15
200-Yard Backstroke	40–44	Chris Stevenson	14
50-Yard Breaststroke	40–44	Richard Landry	20
100-Yard Breaststroke	40–44	Richard Landry	15
200-Yard Breaststroke	40–44	Richard Landry	16
50-Yard Butterfly	40–44	Steve Hiltabiddle	23
100-Yard Butterfly	40–44	Chris Stevenson	24
200-Yard Butterfly	40–44	Mike Shaffer	9
100-Yard IM	40–44	Brad Meacham	22
200-Yard IM	40–44	Brad Meacham	13
400-Yard IM	40–44	Brad Meacham	13
50-Yard Freestyle	45–49	Brad Hering	57
100-Yard Freestyle	45–49	Thomas Emison	59
200-Yard Freestyle	45–49	Dennis Baker	42
500-Yard Freestyle	45–49	Dennis Baker	21
1000-Yard Freestyle	45–49	John Morales	10
1650-Yard Freestyle	45–49	Pete Colbeck	10
50-Yard Backstroke	45–49	Brad Hering	25
100-Yard Backstroke	45–49	William Specht	25
200-Yard Backstroke	45–49	Lincoln Djang	18
50-Yard Breaststroke	45–49	Jon Blank	26
100-Yard Breaststroke	45–49	Jon Blank	24
200-Yard Breaststroke	45–49	Jon Blank	15
50-Yard Butterfly	45–49	Brad Hering	43
100-Yard Butterfly	45–49	Dennis Baker	39
200-Yard Butterfly	45–49	Dennis Baker	14
100-Yard IM	45–49	Brad Hering	46
200-Yard IM	45–49	Dennis Baker	18
400-Yard IM	45–49	John Kenny	15
50-Yard Freestyle	50–54	Jack Groselle	42
100-Yard Freestyle	50–54	Jack Groselle	47
200-Yard Freestyle	50–54	Jack Groselle	41
500-Yard Freestyle	50–54	Matthew Kanzler	20
1000-Yard Freestyle	50–54	Tim Buckley	12
1650-Yard Freestyle	50–54	Matthew Kanzler	14
50-Yard Backstroke	50–54	Philip Djang	27

Event	Age	Champion	Competitors
100-Yard Backstroke	50–54	Philip Djang	25
200-Yard Backstroke	50–54	Robert Supple	12
50-Yard Breaststroke	50–54	Jack Groselle	24
100-Yard Breaststroke	50–54	Jack Groselle	20
200-Yard Breaststroke	50–54	Spencer Eldred	20
50-Yard Butterfly	50–54	Maxwell Stinchcombe	26
100-Yard Butterfly	50–54	Kerry O'Brien	21
200-Yard Butterfly	50–54	Kerry O'Brien	17
100-Yard IM	50–54	Jack Groselle	42
200-Yard IM	50–54	Spencer Eldred	18
400-Yard IM	50–54	Matthew Kanzler	14
50-Yard Freestyle	55–59	Ronald Jacobs	23
100-Yard Freestyle	55–59	Glen Gruber	27
200-Yard Freestyle	55–59	Jim McConica	19
500-Yard Freestyle	55–59	Jim McConica	16
1000-Yard Freestyle	55–59	Jim Clemmons	10
1650-Yard Freestyle	55–59	Jim McConica	12
50-Yard Backstroke	55–59	Steve Mann	15
100-Yard Backstroke	55–59	Clifford Johnson	11
200-Yard Backstroke	55–59	Chuck Fischer	12
50-Yard Breaststroke	55–59	Jim Capers	20
100-Yard Breaststroke	55–59	Jim Capers	18
200-Yard Breaststroke	55–59	Lee MacDonald	13
50-Yard Butterfly	55–59	Fred Baird	16
100-Yard Butterfly	55–59	Fred Baird	14
200-Yard Butterfly	55–59	Jim McConica	9
100-Yard IM	55–59	Hubie Kerns	22
200-Yard IM	55–59	Jim McConica	15
400-Yard IM	55–59	Jim Clemmons	11
50-Yard Freestyle	60–64	Richard Abrahams	24
100-Yard Freestyle	60–64	Richard Abrahams	27
200-Yard Freestyle	60–64	Richard Abrahams	20
500-Yard Freestyle	60–64	Paul McCormick	12
1000-Yard Freestyle	60–64	Paul McCormick	6
1650-Yard Freestyle	60–64	James McCleery	12
50-Yard Backstroke	60–64	Richard Burns	8
100-Yard Backstroke	60–64	Richard Burns	9
200-Yard Backstroke	60–64	Richard Burns	7
50-Yard Breaststroke	60–64	Robert Strand	18
100-Yard Breaststroke	60–64	Robert Strand	14
200-Yard Breaststroke	60–64	Robert Strand	10
50-Yard Butterfly	60–64	Richard Abrahams	10
100-Yard Butterfly	60–64	Richard Abrahams	7
200-Yard Butterfly	60–64	Carl Selles	6
100-Yard IM	60–64	Richard Abrahams	18
200-Yard IM	60–64	Robert Strand	10
400-Yard IM	60–64	Michael McColly	10
50-Yard Freestyle	65–69	Tom Landis	8
100-Yard Freestyle	65–69	Tom Landis	8
200-Yard Freestyle	65–69	Tom Landis	8
500-Yard Freestyle	65–69	Tom Landis	11
1000-Yard Freestyle	65–69	Dick Stewart	6
1650-Yard Freestyle	65–69	Tom Landis	5
50-Yard Backstroke	65–69	Hugh Roddin	11
100-Yard Backstroke	65–69	Hugh Roddin	10
200-Yard Backstroke	65–69	Richard Todd	11
50-Yard Breaststroke	65–69	Richard Todd	12
100-Yard Breaststroke	65–69	Richard Todd	13
200-Yard Breaststroke	65–69	Richard Todd	15
50-Yard Butterfly	65–69	Cappy Sheeley	4
100-Yard Butterfly	65–69	Cappy Sheeley	11
200-Yard Butterfly	65–69	Hugh Roddin	6
100-Yard IM	65–69	Richard Todd	9
200-Yard IM	65–69	Mike Freshley	6
400-Yard IM	65–69	Tom Landis	8
50-Yard Freestyle	70–74	Jeff Farrell	8

Event	Age	Champion	Competitors
100-Yard Freestyle	70–74	Jeff Farrell	7
200-Yard Freestyle	70–74	David Radcliff	7
500-Yard Freestyle	70–74	David Radcliff	5
1000-Yard Freestyle	70–74	David Radcliff	2
1650-Yard Freestyle	70–74	Will Rauch	3
50-Yard Backstroke	70–74	Marshall Greer	3
100-Yard Backstroke	70–74	Ron Mugavin	5
200-Yard Backstroke	70–74	Dick Peterson	4
50-Yard Breaststroke	70–74	Jeff Farrell	10
100-Yard Breaststroke	70–74	Bob Johnston	6
200-Yard Breaststroke	70–74	Dick Peterson	7
50-Yard Butterfly	70–74	Jeff Farrell	6
100-Yard Butterfly	70–74	Dennis O'Brien	4
200-Yard Butterfly	70–74	Dennis O'Brien	4
100-Yard IM	70–74	Jeff Farrell	8
200-Yard IM	70–74	Dennis O'Brien	5
400-Yard IM	70–74	Dick Peterson	6
50-Yard Freestyle	75–79	Donald Sonia	9
100-Yard Freestyle	75–79	Graham Johnston	7
200-Yard Freestyle	75–79	Graham Johnston	7
500-Yard Freestyle	75–79	Thomas Taylor	5
1000-Yard Freestyle	75–79	Bob Miller	3
1650-Yard Freestyle	75–79	Graham Johnston	3
50-Yard Backstroke	75–79	Bob Miller	8
100-Yard Backstroke	75–79	Bob Miller	6
200-Yard Backstroke	75–79	Bob Miller	6
50-Yard Breaststroke	75–79	Ashley Jones	8
100-Yard Breaststroke	75–79	Ashley Jones	7
200-Yard Breaststroke	75–79	Ashley Jones	8
50-Yard Butterfly	75–79	Ashley Jones	5
100-Yard Butterfly	75–79	William Bond	1
200-Yard Butterfly	75–79	Gordon Gillin	1
100-Yard IM	75–79	Ashley Jones	5
200-Yard IM	75–79	Graham Johnston	3
400-Yard IM	75–79	Graham Johnston	3
50-Yard Freestyle	80–84	Frank Piemme	7
100-Yard Freestyle	80–84	Frank Piemme	10
200-Yard Freestyle	80–84	Frank Piemme	10
500-Yard Freestyle	80–84	Jurgen Schmidt	6
1000-Yard Freestyle	80–84	James Edwards	2
1650-Yard Freestyle	80–84	Jurgen Schmidt	6
50-Yard Backstroke	80–84	Dale Webster	9
100-Yard Backstroke	80–84	Dale Webster	8
200-Yard Backstroke	80–84	Dale Webster	8
50-Yard Breaststroke	80–84	Paul Lowry	3
100-Yard Breaststroke	80–84	Frank Piemme	4
200-Yard Breaststroke	80–84	Paul Lowry	3
50-Yard Butterfly	80–84	Frank Piemme	3
100-Yard Butterfly	80–84	Warren Foster	1
200-Yard Butterfly	80–84	Lou Silverstein	1
100-Yard IM	80–84	Frank Piemme	5
200-Yard IM	80–84	Warren Foster	2
400-Yard IM	80–84	Lou Silverstein	2
50-Yard Freestyle	85–89	Gilbert Young	4
100-Yard Freestyle	85–89	Gilbert Young	4
200-Yard Freestyle	85–89	Gilbert Young	2
500-Yard Freestyle	85–89	Gilbert Young	3
1650-Yard Freestyle	85–89	Gilbert Young	2
50-Yard Breaststroke	85–89	Gilbert Young	1
50-Yard Butterfly	85–89	Andrew Holden	1
100-Yard Butterfly	85–89	Andrew Holden	1
200-Yard Butterfly	85–89	Andrew Holden	1
100-Yard IM	85–89	William Johnston	1

Swimming (WOMEN) 2007 Long Course National Championships—Woodlands, Texas—August 10–13

Event	Age	Champion	Competitors
50-Yard Freestyle	40–44	Lisa Rapuano	28
100-Yard Freestyle	40–44	Anna Scott	24
200-Yard Freestyle	40–44	Laureen Welting	25
500-Yard Freestyle	40–44	Birgit Lohberg	21
1000-Yard Freestyle	40–44	Laureen Welting	10
1650-Yard Freestyle	40–44	Amy Dantzler	6
50-Yard Backstroke	40–44	Janis Gebhart	16
100-Yard Backstroke	40–44	Janis Gebhart	10
200-Yard Backstroke	40–44	Birgit Lohberg	14
50-Yard Breaststroke	40–44	Susan Von der Lippe	18
100-Yard Breaststroke	40–44	Susan Von der Lippe	21
200-Yard Breaststroke	40–44	Susan Von der Lippe	14
50-Yard Butterfly	40–44	Anna Scott	17
100-Yard Butterfly	40–44	Susan Von der Lippe	8
200-Yard Butterfly	40–44	Susan Von der Lippe	6
100-Yard IM	40–44	Elizabeth Nowak	25
200-Yard IM	40–44	Susan Von der Lippe	17
400-Yard IM	40–44	Laureen Welting	8
50-Yard Freestyle	45–49	Liz Hobbs	28
100-Yard Freestyle	45–49	Karlyn Pipes-Neilsen	30
200-Yard Freestyle	45–49	Karlyn Pipes-Neilsen	32
500-Yard Freestyle	45–49	Susanne Simpson	18
1000-Yard Freestyle	45–49	Susanne Simpson	7
1650-Yard Freestyle	45–49	Denise Brown	9
50-Yard Backstroke	45–49	Karlyn Pipes-Neilsen	20
100-Yard Backstroke	45–49	Karlyn Pipes-Neilsen	19
200-Yard Backstroke	45–49	Zena Courtney	12
50-Yard Breaststroke	45–49	Caroline Krattli	31
100-Yard Breaststroke	45–49	Caroline Krattli	26
200-Yard Breaststroke	45–49	Caroline Krattli	19
50-Yard Butterfly	45–49	Traci Granger	24
100-Yard Butterfly	45–49	Andrea Block	14
200-Yard Butterfly	45–49	Susanne Simpson	12
100-Yard IM	45–49	Karlyn Pipes-Neilsen	40
200-Yard IM	45–49	Kim Crouch	14
400-Yard IM	45–49	Lisa Pace	15
50-Yard Freestyle	50–54	Leianne Critenden	25
100-Yard Freestyle	50–54	Leianne Critenden	17
200-Yard Freestyle	50–54	Charlene O'Brien	17
500-Yard Freestyle	50–54	Charlene O'Brien	16
1000-Yard Freestyle	50–54	Terry Latham	9
1650-Yard Freestyle	50–54	Charlene O'Brien	10
50-Yard Backstroke	50–54	Patty Landers	17
100-Yard Backstroke	50–54	Patty Landers	10
200-Yard Backstroke	50–54	Patty Landers	10
50-Yard Breaststroke	50–54	Leianne Critenden	21
100-Yard Breaststroke	50–54	Karen Melick	16
200-Yard Breaststroke	50–54	Karen Melick	15
50-Yard Butterfly	50–54	Karen Rosner	14
100-Yard Butterfly	50–54	Mary Lippold	11
200-Yard Butterfly	50–54	Mary Lippold	11
100-Yard IM	50–54	Colette Crabbe	26
200-Yard IM	50–54	Colette Crabbe	10
400-Yard IM	50–54	Colette Crabbe	10
50-Yard Freestyle	55–59	Laura Val	17
100-Yard Freestyle	55–59	Laura Val	15
200-Yard Freestyle	55–59	Laura Val	12
500-Yard Freestyle	55–59	Barb Gundred	13
1000-Yard Freestyle	55–59	Barb Gundred	4
1650-Yard Freestyle	55–59	Linda Shoenberger	9
50-Yard Backstroke	55–59	Laura Val	9
100-Yard Backstroke	55–59	Barb Gundred	6
200-Yard Backstroke	55–59	Barb Gundred	7

Event	Age	Champion	Competitors
50-Yard Breaststroke	55–59	Barbara Hummel	7
100-Yard Breaststroke	55–59	Barbara Hummel	5
200-Yard Breaststroke	55–59	Barbara Hummel	8
50-Yard Butterfly	55–59	Charlotte Davis	11
100-Yard Butterfly	55–59	Laura Val	10
200-Yard Butterfly	55–59	Carolyn Roche	7
100-Yard IM	55–59	Laura Val	16
200-Yard IM	55–59	Charlotte Davis	11
400-Yard IM	55–59	Charlotte Davis	9
50-Yard Freestyle	60–64	Carolyn Boak	15
100-Yard Freestyle	60–64	Carolyn Boak	12
200-Yard Freestyle	60–64	Suzanne Dills	13
500-Yard Freestyle	60–64	Suzanne Dills	12
1000-Yard Freestyle	60–64	Beverly Montrella	4
1650-Yard Freestyle	60–64	Suzanne Dills	9
50-Yard Backstroke	60–64	Joy Ward	10
100-Yard Backstroke	60–64	Joy Ward	10
200-Yard Backstroke	60–64	Constance Sasser	7
50-Yard Breaststroke	60–64	Carolyn Boak	12
100-Yard Breaststroke	60–64	Ginger Pierson	12
200-Yard Breaststroke	60–64	Ginger Pierson	10
50-Yard Butterfly	60–64	Carolyn Boak	8
100-Yard Butterfly	60–64	Carolyn Boak	8
200-Yard Butterfly	60–64	Ginger Pierson	5
100-Yard IM	60–64	Carolyn Boak	13
200-Yard IM	60–64	Suzanne Dills	5
400-Yard IM	60–64	Suzanne Dills	6
50-Yard Freestyle	65–69	Beth Schreiner	9
100-Yard Freestyle	65–69	Beth Schreiner	9
200-Yard Freestyle	65–69	Beth Schreiner	9
500-Yard Freestyle	65–69	Jane Birkhead	5
1000-Yard Freestyle	65–69	Susanne Schumann	3
1650-Yard Freestyle	65–69	Susan Munn	3
50-Yard Backstroke	65–69	Barbara Frid	8
100-Yard Backstroke	65–69	Barbara Frid	7
200-Yard Backstroke	65–69	Ida Hlavacek	6
50-Yard Breaststroke	65–69	Barbara Frid	12
100-Yard Breaststroke	65–69	Margit Jebe	6
200-Yard Breaststroke	65–69	Susan Myers	8
50-Yard Butterfly	65–69	Barbara Frid	7
100-Yard Butterfly	65–69	Margit Jebe	5
200-Yard Butterfly	65–69	Ida Hlavacek	5
100-Yard IM	65–69	Barbara Frid	11
200-Yard IM	65–69	Susan Myers	4
400-Yard IM	65–69	Susan Myers	6
50-Yard Freestyle	70–74	Jeanne Little	7
100-Yard Freestyle	70–74	Jeanne Little	6
200-Yard Freestyle	70–74	Jeanne Little	7
500-Yard Freestyle	70–74	Lavalle Stoinoff	1
1000-Yard Freestyle	70–74	Lavalle Stoinoff	2
1650-Yard Freestyle	70–74	Betsy Jordan	2
50-Yard Backstroke	70–74	Betsy Jordan	6
100-Yard Backstroke	70–74	Betsy Jordan	6
200-Yard Backstroke	70–74	Betsy Jordan	3
50-Yard Breaststroke	70–74	Donna Ryman	5
100-Yard Breaststroke	70–74	Donna Ryman	4
200-Yard Breaststroke	70–74	Donna Ryman	3
50-Yard Butterfly	70–74	Helen Bayly	1
100-Yard Butterfly	70–74	Patricia Tullman	2
200-Yard Butterfly	70–74	Jeanne Little	3
100-Yard IM	70–74	Peggy Buchannan	2
200-Yard IM	70–74	Betsy Jordan	3
400-Yard IM	70–74	Betsy Jordan	2
50-Yard Freestyle	75–79	Nan Bohl	3
100-Yard Freestyle	75–79	Nan Bohl	5
200-Yard Freestyle	75–79	Nan Bohl	3

Event	Age	Champion	Competitors
1650-Yard Freestyle	75–79	Lida Gaschke	2
50-Yard Backstroke	75–79	Lida Gaschke	4
100-Yard Backstroke	75–79	Lida Gaschke	5
200-Yard Backstroke	75–79	Janet Kavadas	1
50-Yard Breaststroke	75–79	Nan Bohl	4
100-Yard Breaststroke	75–79	Nan Bohl	2
200-Yard Breaststroke	75–79	Georgia Goggin	1
100-Yard IM	75–79	Lida Gaschke	2
50-Yard Freestyle	80–84	Florence Carr	2
100-Yard Freestyle	80–84	Margery Myer	2
200-Yard Freestyle	80–84	Margery Myer	2
500-Yard Freestyle	80–84	Margery Myer	1
1650-Yard Freestyle	80–84	Margery Myer	2
50-Yard Backstroke	80–84	Bernice Phillips	3
100-Yard Backstroke	80–84	Margery Myer	2
200-Yard Backstroke	80–84	Bernice Phillips	2
50-Yard Breaststroke	80–84	Florence Carr	1
200-Yard Breaststroke	80–84	Jane Krauser	2
50-Yard Butterfly	80–84	Florence Carr	3
100-Yard Butterfly	80–84	Jane Krauser	2
200-Yard Butterfly	80–84	Gloria Stupfel	1
100-Yard IM	80–84	Florence Carr	1
400-Yard IM	80–84	Gloria Stupfel	1
50-Yard Freestyle	85–89	Billie Anne Burrill	3
100-Yard Freestyle	85–89	Maurine Kornfeld	5
200-Yard Freestyle	85–89	Maurine Kornfeld	5
500-Yard Freestyle	85–89	Rita Simonton	1
1000-Yard Freestyle	85–89	Rita Simonton	1
50-Yard Backstroke	85–89	Betty Christian	4
100-Yard Backstroke	85–89	Betty Christian	3
200-Yard Backstroke	85–89	Maurine Kornfeld	1
50-Yard Breaststroke	85–89	Betty Christian	1
100-Yard Breaststroke	85–89	Betty Christian	1
200-Yard Breaststroke	85–89	Betty Christian	1
200-Yard IM	85–89	Rita Simonton	1

Swimming (MEN). 2007 Long Course National Championships— Woodlands, Texas, August 10–13

Event	Age	Champion	Competitors
50-Meter Freestyle	40–44	Ross Davis	24
100-Meter Freestyle	40–44	Ross Davis	26
200-Meter Freestyle	40–44	Ross Davis	20
400-Meter Freestyle	40–44	Henry Clark	10
800-Meter Freestyle	40–44	Kurt Dickson	4
1500-Meter Freestyle	40–44	Jay Yarid	9
50-Meter Backstroke	40–44	Ross Davis	12
100-Meter Backstroke	40–44	Ross Davis	13
200-Meter Backstroke	40–44	Kurt Dickson	11
50-Meter Breaststroke	40–44	Lorenzo Benucci	17
100-Meter Breaststroke	40–44	Brian Summe	15
200-Meter Breaststroke	40–44	Brian Tsuchiya	17
50-Meter Butterfly	40–44	Gregory Sargent	21
100-Meter Butterfly	40–44	Henry Clark	14
200-Meter Butterfly	40–44	Igor Vazhenin	6
200-Meter IM	40–44	Lorenzo Benucci	18
400-Meter IM	40–44	Lorenzo Benucci	9
50-Meter Freestyle	45–49	Steve Wood	44
100-Meter Freestyle	45–49	Steve Wood	42
200-Meter Freestyle	45–49	Steve Wood	21
400-Meter Freestyle	45–49	Gerry Rodrigues	21
800-Meter Freestyle	45–49	Arnaldo Perez	12
1500-Meter Freestyle	45–49	Arnaldo Perez	11
50-Meter Backstroke	45–49	Steve Wood	22
100-Meter Backstroke	45–49	Steve Wood	16
200-Meter Backstroke	45–49	Steve Wood	9

Event	Age	Champion	Competitors
50-Meter Breaststroke	45–49	David Guthrie	16
100-Meter Breaststroke	45–49	David Guthrie	13
200-Meter Breaststroke	45–49	David Guthrie	9
50-Meter Butterfly	45–49	Dirk Marshall	22
100-Meter Butterfly	45–49	Dirk Marshall	14
200-Meter Butterfly	45–49	Michael Schmidt	6
200-Meter IM	45–49	Jerry Dawson	15
400-Meter IM	45–49	Arnaldo Perez	8
50-Meter Freestyle	50–54	Dan Stephenson	29
100-Meter Freestyle	50–54	Dan Stephenson	25
200-Meter Freestyle	50–54	Dan Stephenson	18
400-Meter Freestyle	50–54	Dan Stephenson	13
800-Meter Freestyle	50–54	Dan Stephenson	12
1500-Meter Freestyle	50–54	Wieslaw Musial	4
50-Meter Backstroke	50–54	Jonathan Klein	15
100-Meter Backstroke	50–54	Dan Stephenson	13
200-Meter Backstroke	50–54	Wieslaw Musial	13
50-Meter Breaststroke	50–54	Doug Malcolm	19
100-Meter Breaststroke	50–54	Doug Malcolm	14
200-Meter Breaststroke	50–54	David Gribble	11
50-Meter Butterfly	50–54	John Fields	14
100-Meter Butterfly	50–54	Kerry O'Brien	9
200-Meter Butterfly	50–54	Patrick Murtagh	9
200-Meter IM	50–54	Jack Groselle	16
400-Meter IM	50–54	Jim Callahan	10

Swimming (MEN). 2007 Long Course National Championships— Woodlands, Texas—August 10–13

Event	Age	Champion	Competitors
50-Meter Freestyle	55–59	Joel Stager	19
100-Meter Freestyle	55–59	Joel Stager	18
200-Meter Freestyle	55–59	Jim McConica	10
400-Meter Freestyle	55–59	Jim McConica	12
800-Meter Freestyle	55–59	Steven Van Nort	10
1500-Meter Freestyle	55–59	Marvin Schwartz	5
50-Meter Backstroke	55–59	Mark Pugliese	13
100-Meter Backstroke	55–59	Mark Pugliese	11
200-Meter Backstroke	55–59	Jim McConica	11
50-Meter Breaststroke	55–59	Robert Schmitz	15
100-Meter Breaststroke	55–59	Allen Stark	13
200-Meter Breaststroke	55–59	Allen Stark	10
50-Meter Butterfly	55–59	Mark Pugliese	13
100-Meter Butterfly	55–59	Scott Lautman	9
200-Meter Butterfly	55–59	Scott Lautman	9
200-Meter IM	55–59	Jim McConica	7
400-Meter IM	55–59	Robert Brown	5
50-Meter Freestyle	60–64	Richard Burns	22
100-Meter Freestyle	60–64	Richard Burns	13
200-Meter Freestyle	60–64	Donald Galine	14
400-Meter Freestyle	60–64	Bob Couch	14
800-Meter Freestyle	60–64	Bob Couch	7
1500-Meter Freestyle	60–64	Don Davis	6
50-Meter Backstroke	60–64	Hugh Wilder	12
100-Meter Backstroke	60–64	Hugh Wilder	9
200-Meter Backstroke	60–64	Hugh Wilder	8
50-Meter Breaststroke	60–64	Kenneth Frost	10
100-Meter Breaststroke	60–64	Kenneth Frost	7
200-Meter Breaststroke	60–64	Kenneth Frost	6
50-Meter Butterfly	60–64	Joel Burns	14
100-Meter Butterfly	60–64	Joel Burns	9
200-Meter Butterfly	60–64	Gregory Pash	5
200-Meter IM	60–64	Hugh Wilder	10
400-Meter IM	60–64	Bob Couch	7
50-Meter Freestyle	65–69	Vinus Van Baalen	11

Event	Age	Champion	Competitors
100-Meter Freestyle	65–69	Vinus Van Baalen	9
200-Meter Freestyle	65–69	Don Murff	10
400-Meter Freestyle	65–69	Sandy Galletly	9
800-Meter Freestyle	65–69	Sandy Galletly	8
1500-Meter Freestyle	65–69	Sandy Galletly	4
50-Meter Backstroke	65–69	Vinus Van Baalen	12
100-Meter Backstroke	65–69	Vinus Van Baalen	9
200-Meter Backstroke	65–69	Richard Todd	7
50-Meter Breaststroke	65–69	Richard Todd	4
100-Meter Breaststroke	65–69	Richard Todd	4
200-Meter Breaststroke	65–69	Richard Todd	3
50-Meter Butterfly	65–69	Vinus Van Baalen	8
100-Meter Butterfly	65–69	Mel Goldstein	4
200-Meter Butterfly	65–69	Michael Nordby	4
200-Meter IM	65–69	Don Murff	5
400-Meter IM	65–69	Dan Murphy	4
50-Meter Freestyle	70–74	Bob Bailie	11
100-Meter Freestyle	70–74	Jerry Clark	8
200-Meter Freestyle	70–74	David Harrison	4
400-Meter Freestyle	70–74	David Harrison	5
800-Meter Freestyle	70–74	David Harrison	5
1500-Meter Freestyle	70–74	Marty Mennen	5
50-Meter Backstroke	70–74	Yoshi Oyakawa	6
100-Meter Backstroke	70–74	Yoshi Oyakawa	6
200-Meter Backstroke	70–74	Marty Mennen	5
50-Meter Breaststroke	70–74	Bob Patten	6
100-Meter Breaststroke	70–74	Bob Patten	6
200-Meter Breaststroke	70–74	Bob Patten	6
50-Meter Butterfly	70–74	Bob Bailie	2
100-Meter Butterfly	70–74	Bob Bailie	3
200-Meter Butterfly	70–74	Barry Fasbender	2
200-Meter IM	70–74	Yoshi Oyakawa	3
400-Meter IM	70–74	Barry Fasbender	3
50-Meter Freestyle	75–79	Clark Mitchell	12
100-Meter Freestyle	75–79	Graham Johnston	10
200-Meter Freestyle	75–79	Graham Johnston	7
400-Meter Freestyle	75–79	Graham Johnston	7
800-Meter Freestyle	75–79	Richard Ellis	1
1500-Meter Freestyle	75–79	Graham Johnston	4
50-Meter Backstroke	75–79	Clark Mitchell	7
100-Meter Backstroke	75–79	Clark Mitchell	7
200-Meter Backstroke	75–79	Clark Mitchell	3
50-Meter Breaststroke	75–79	Charles Baldwin	7
100-Meter Breaststroke	75–79	Norman Stupfel	5
200-Meter Breaststroke	75–79	Norman Stupfel	6
50-Meter Butterfly	75–79	Clark Mitchell	2
100-Meter Butterfly	75–79	Clark Mitchell	1
200-Meter Butterfly	75–79	Chris Smith	1
200-Meter IM	75–79	Graham Johnston	3
400-Meter IM	75–79	Graham Johnston	2
50-Meter Freestyle	80–84	Baker Shannon	1
100-Meter Freestyle	80–84	Baker Shannon	2
200-Meter Freestyle	80–84	Glynn Jones	2
400-Meter Freestyle	80–84	Jack Truby	3
800-Meter Freestyle	80–84	Lou Silverstein	2
50-Meter Backstroke	80–84	Jack Truby	2
100-Meter Backstroke	80–84	Paul Lowry	2
200-Meter Backstroke	80–84	Paul Lowry	4
50-Meter Breaststroke	80–84	Paul Lowry	1
100-Meter Breaststroke	80–84	Paul Lowry	2
200-Meter Breaststroke	80–84	Paul Lowry	2
100-Meter Butterfly	80–84	Doug Strong	1
200-Meter Butterfly	80–84	Lou Silverstein	2
400-Meter IM	80–84	Lou Silverstein	1
50-Meter Freestyle	85–89	Herbert Siegel	1
100-Meter Freestyle	85–89	Herbert Siegel	1

Event	Age	Champion	Competitors
200-Meter Freestyle	85–89	James Edwards	1
400-Meter Freestyle	85–89	James Edwards	2
800-Meter Freestyle	85–89	James Edwards	1
50-Meter Backstroke	85–89	James Edwards	1
100-Meter Freestyle	85–89	James Edwards	1
200-Meter Freestyle	85–89	James Edwards	1
50-Meter Freestyle	90–94	Ned Smith	1
100-Meter Freestyle	90–94	Ned Smith	1
50-Meter Backstroke	90–94	Ned Smith	1
50-Meter Breaststroke	90–94	Ned Smith	1

Swimming. 2007 USMS 1-Mile Open Water Championship—Reston, Virginia, May 27

Gender	Age	Champion	Competitors
Women	40–44	Jamie McClellan	12
Women	45–49	Lisa Brooks	10
Women	50–54	Lisa Bennett	3
Women	55–59	Shirley Lostus-Charley	3
Women	60–64	Ann Svenson	2
Women	65–69	Karen Hannam	11
Men	40–44	Rob Jones	9
Men	45–49	John Geyer	18
Men	50–54	John Erb	10
Men	55–59	Terry Laughlin	11
Men	60–64	Willis Braswell	2
Men	65–69	Dan Murphy	3
Men	70–74	George Brunstad	2
Men	75–79	Frank Manheim	1

Swimming. 2007 USMS One Hour Postal Swim Championship—January 1–31

Gender	Age	Champion	Competitors
Women	40–44	Laurie Hug	169
Women	45–49	Vibeke Swanson	200
Women	50–54	Christie Ciraulo	123
Women	55–59	Laura Val	90
Women	60–64	Sally Dillon	46
Women	65–69	Betsy Jordon	33
Women	70–74	Adrienne Pipes	18
Women	75–79	Joan Campbell	18
Women	80–84	Margery Myer	10
Women	85–89	Rita Simonton	3
Women	90–94	Hilda Buel	1
Men	40–44	Mike Shaffer	158
Men	45–49	Roger Von Jouanne	176
Men	50–54	Sandy MacDonald	165
Men	55–59	Jim McConica	108
Men	60–64	James McCleery	70
Men	65–69	Donald Puchalski	36
Men	70–74	David Radcliff	39
Men	75–79	Graham Johnston	19
Men	80–84	Frank Piemme	10
Men	85–89	Charles Bushey	6
Men	90–94	Frank Tilitson	1

Table Tennis. 2007 U.S. Table Tennis Open—Las Vegas, Nevada, July 4–7*

Event	Gender	Age	Champion
Doubles	Men	Over 40	Norby/Seemiller
Doubles	Men	Over 50	Braithwaite/Li
Doubles	Men	Over 60	Sakai/Sweeris
Doubles	Men	Over 70	Fahlstrom/Neely

Event	Gender	Age	Champion
Singles	Men	Over 40	Yinghua Cheng
Singles	Men	Over 50	Yu Xiang Li
Singles	Men	Over 60	Karl-Josef Assemacher
Singles	Men	Over 65	Chong Tay
Singles	Men	Over 70	Ragnar Fahlstrom
Singles	Men	Over 75	Bill Neely
Singles	Men	Over 80	Ivan Slade
Singles	Women	Over 40	Diane Dongye Chen
Singles	Women	Over 50	Min Ming Zhu
Singles	Women	Over 60	Ann Alverez

Number of competitors not available.

Table Tennis. 2007 U.S. Table Tennis Senior Masters Open Las Vegas, Nevada—July 4–7

Event	Gender	Age	Champion
Singles	Women	40–49	Marina Cravens
Singles	Women	50–59	Charlene Xiaoying Liu
Singles	Women	60–69	Judy Pelletier
Singles	Women	70–79	Joyce Apron
Singles	Women	80–89	Heather Fox
Singles	Men	40–49	Pak Yan Yung
Singles	Men	50–59	Lim Ming Chui
Singles	Men	60–69	Michael Cheung
Singles	Men	70–79	Viktor Troppmann
Singles	Men	80–89	William Brin
Doubles	Women	40–49	Cravens/Caples
Doubles	Women	50–59	Hui/Hsiu
Doubles	Women	60–69	Starr/Brin
Doubles	Women	70–79	Apron/Quon
Doubles	Men	40–49	Cheung/Yung
Doubles	Men	50–59	Roberts/Gorsira
Doubles	Men	60–69	Marcotulli/Troconis
Doubles	Men	70–79	Troppmenn/Lam
Doubles	Mixed	40–49	Yung/Ho
Doubles	Mixed	50–59	Chui/Liu
Doubles	Mixed	60–69	Stadelman/Apron
Doubles	Mixed	70–79	Troppmann/Quon

Number of competitors not available

Table Tennis. 2007 U.S. Table Tennis Nationals— Las Vegas, Nevada, December 15–18*

Event	Gender	Age	Champion
Doubles	Men	40+	Norby/Seemiller
Doubles	Men	50+	Sakai/Seemiller
Doubles	Men	60+	Chong Keng/Che-Him
Doubles	Men	70+	Mintsiveris/Grossman
Hardbat Singles	Men	40+	Ngo Loc Bao
Singles	Men	40+	Yinghua Cheng
Singles	Men	50+	Daniel Seemiller
Singles	Men	60+	Richard Hicks
Singles	Men	70+	Richard Hicks
Singles	Men	80+	Byng Forsberg
Singles—Under 1600	Men	40+	Hossein Sharifi
Veteran Singles	Men	40–49	Ge-Liang Liang
Veteran Singles	Men	50–59	Ge-Liang Liang
Veteran Singles	Men	70–74	Bill Neely
Veteran Singles	Men	75–79	Al Miller
Veteran Singles	Men	80–84	Neil Smyth
Veteran Singles	Men	85+	Si Wasserman
Veteran Doubles	Open	40–64	Hawk/Ma
Veteran Doubles	Open	65+	Szulczyk/Forsberg
Singles	Women	40+	Diane Dongye Chen

Event	Gender	Age	Champion
Singles	Women	50+	Charlene Liu
Singles	Women	60+	Ann Alverez
Singles	Women	70+	Jane Magras
Veteran Singles	Women	40–49	Li-Jun Ma
Veteran Singles	Women	50–59	Bella Livshin
Veteran Singles	Women	70–74	Joyce Apron
Veteran Singles	Women	75–79	Harriet Brin
Veteran Singles	Women	80–84	Berta Speisman

Tennis. 2007 Clay Court Singles and Doubles— Multiple Locations and Dates

Event	Gender	Age	Champion	Competitors
Singles	Men	40's	Oren Motevassel	80
Singles	Men	45's	Vallis Wilder	93
Singles	Men	50's	Mark Vines	91
Singles	Men	55's	Larry Turville	73
Singles	Men	60's	Jimmy Parker	80
Singles	Men	65's	Fred Drilling	83
Singles	Men	70's	Robert Duesler	60
Singles	Men	75's	George McCabe	56
Singles	Men	80's	Graydon Nichols	48
Singles	Men	85's	Henry Tiberio	27
Singles	Men	90's	Alex Swetka	12
Singles	Women	40's	Renata Marcinkowska	13
Singles	Women	45's	Francis Chandler	32
Singles	Women	50's	Diane Fishburn	15
Singles	Women	55's	Chieko Holt	33
Singles	Women	60's	Brenda Carter	22
Singles	Women	65's	Heide Orth	39
Singles	Women	70's	Dorothy Matthiessen	22
Singles	Women	75's	Marietta Boswell	27
Singles	Women	80's	Irene Shepard	16
Singles	Women	85's	Lucille Detmer	8
Doubles	Men	40's	Motevassel/Bonner	50
Doubles	Men	45's	Fedderly/Wilder	40
Doubles	Men	50's	Cash/Guerry	64
Doubles	Men	55's	Newman/Turville	38
Doubles	Men	60's	Beautyman/Cheney	56
Doubles	Men	65's	Housman/Stewart	59
Doubles	Men	70's	Duesler/Nelson	58
Doubles	Men	75's	De Voe/Thomas	32
Doubles	Men	80's	Franco/Nichols	32
Doubles	Men	85's	Henderson/Sherman	26
Doubles	Men	90's	MacDonald/Swetka	12
Doubles	Women	40's	Dailey/Fishburne	16
Doubles	Women	45's	Chandler/Vick	41
Doubles	Women	50's	Robertson/Wright	14
Doubles	Women	55's	Bennett/Orth	37
Doubles	Women	60's	Carter/Wachob	36
Doubles	Women	65's	Hillebrand/Steel	46
Doubles	Women	70's	Matthiessen/Von Nostrand	20
Doubles	Women	75's	Boswell/Russ	34
Doubles	Women	80's	Shepard/Skiffington	14
Doubles	Women	85's	Detmer/Stroud	12

Tennis. 2007 Hard Court Singles and Doubles— Multiple Locations and Dates

Event	Gender	Age	Champion	Competitors
Singles	Men	40's	Peter Smith	99
Singles	Men	45's	Polo Cowan	85
Singles	Men	50's	Sal Castillo	63
Singles	Men	55's	Larry Turville	90

Event	Gender	Age	Champion	Competitors
Singles	Men	60's	Brian Cheney	78
Singles	Men	65's	Allan Carter	69
Singles	Men	70's	Robert Duesler	49
Singles	Men	75's	Charles De Voe	40
Singles	Men	80's	Graydon Nichols	22
Singles	Men	85's	Marvin Henderson	19
Singles	Men	90's	Alex Swetka	23
Singles	Women	40's	Manola Colter	23
Singles	Women	45's	Mariana Hollman	22
Singles	Women	50's	Diane Fishburne	50
Singles	Women	55's	Martha Downing	13
Singles	Women	60's	Brenda Carter	38
Singles	Women	65's	Suella Steel	23
Singles	Women	70's	Dori deVries	35
Singles	Women	75's	Marietta Boswell	14
Singles	Women	80's	Betty Eisenstein	15
Singles	Women	85's	Lou Cille Scoggins	3
Singles	Women	90's	Dodo Cheney	4
Doubles	Men	40's	Hernandez/Zanio	74
Doubles	Men	45's	Fedderly/Wilder	54
Doubles	Men	50's	Bligard/Castillo	53
Doubles	Men	55's	Newman/Turville	84
Doubles	Men	60's	Cheney/Hoeveler	74
Doubles	Men	65's	Hernando/Sarantos	52
Doubles	Men	70's	Duesler/Nelson	49
Doubles	Men	75's	Powless/Seymour	30
Doubles	Men	80's	Flater/Nichols	12
Doubles	Men	85's	Druliner/Tyler	14
Doubles	Men	90's	Coker/Swetka	16
Doubles	Women	40's	Magers/May Fritz	28
Doubles	Women	45's	Chandler/Vick	32
Doubles	Women	50's	May Fritz/Wright	74
Doubles	Women	55's	Harris/Vallejo	24
Doubles	Women	60's	Carter/Wachob	57
Doubles	Women	65's	Hillebrand/Steel	28
Doubles	Women	70's	Herrick/Matthiessen	36
Doubles	Women	75's	Boswell/Russ	18
Doubles	Women	80's	Price/Tyrell	18
Doubles	Women	85's	Cheney/Dettmer	4
Doubles	Women	90's	Harris/Yeomans	4
Doubles	Mixed	40's	Kepler/Smith	34

Tennis. 2007 Grass Court Singles and Doubles— Multiple Locations and Dates

Event	Gender	Age	Champion	Competitors
Singles	Men	40's	Richard Schmidt	45
Singles	Men	45's	Glenn Erickson	86
Singles	Men	50's	Mark Vines	107
Singles	Men	55's	Philip Landaur	67
Singles	Men	60's	Brian Cheney	53
Singles	Men	65's	Fred Drilling	84
Singles	Men	70's	Robert Duesler	66
Singles	Men	75's	John Powless	41
Singles	Men	80's	Graydon Nichols	32
Singles	Men	85's	Robert Sherman	18
Singles	Men	90's	Alex Swetka	9
Singles	Women	40's	Yukie Koizumi	8
Singles	Women	45's	Yukie Koizumi	25
Singles	Women	50's	Kathy May Fritz	27
Singles	Women	55's	Mary Ginnard	27
Singles	Women	60's	Betty Wachob	30
Singles	Women	65's	Suella Steel	24
Singles	Women	70's	Dorothy Matthiessen	22
Singles	Women	75's	Marietta Boswell	11

Event	Gender	Age	Champion	Competitors
Singles	Women	80's	Diane Hoffman	12
Singles	Women	85's	Lou Cille Scroggins	4
Doubles	Men	40's	Litsky/Ward	25
Doubles	Men	45's	Fedderly/Wilder	76
Doubles	Men	50's	Jones/Pierce	76
Doubles	Men	55's	Cheney/Litwin	45
Doubles	Men	60's	Bryant/Parker	26
Doubles	Men	65's	Sarantos/Stewart	76
Doubles	Men	70's	Duesler/Nelson	44
Doubles	Men	75's	Powless/Seymour	32
Doubles	Men	80's	Franco/Nichols	24
Doubles	Men	85's	Henderson/Sherman	23
Doubles	Men	90's	Scallet/Stoll	12
Doubles	Women	40's	Judge/Koizumi	12
Doubles	Women	45's	Hollman/Thompson	40
Doubles	Women	50's	May Fritz/Wright	32
Doubles	Women	55's	Ginnard/Karwasky	42
Doubles	Women	60's	Carter/Steel	33
Doubles	Women	65's	Hillebrand/Steel	35
Doubles	Women	70's	King/Reed	18
Doubles	Women	75's	Boswell/Russ	14
Doubles	Women	80's	Hall/Niehaus	10
Doubles	Women	85's	Burr/Cheney	4

Tennis. 2007 Indoor Singles and Doubles—Multiple Locations and Dates

Event	Gender	Age	Champion	Competitors
Singles	Men	40's	Richard Schmidt	37
Singles	Men	45's	Vallis Wilder	41
Singles	Men	50's	Sal Castillo	47
Singles	Men	55's	Leonard Wofford	26
Singles	Men	60's	Brian Cheney	36
Singles	Men	65's	Leland Housman	65
Singles	Men	70's	Herman Ahlers	42
Singles	Men	75's	Thomas Springer	39
Singles	Men	80's	Roald Flater	16
Singles	Men	85's	Marvin Henderson	9
Singles	Men	90's	Alex Swetka	11
Singles	Women	40's	Robin Keener	14
Singles	Women	45's	Susan Love	21
Singles	Women	50's	Diane Fishburne	22
Singles	Women	55's	Tina Kawarsky	21
Singles	Women	60's	Brenda Carter	14
Singles	Women	65's	Suella Steel	32
Singles	Women	70's	Dorothy Matthiessen	29
Singles	Women	75's	Marietta Boswell	14
Singles	Women	80's	Rita Price	13
Singles	Women	90's	Dodo Cheney	3
Doubles	Men	40's	Cory/Kepler	28
Doubles	Men	45's	Fedderly/Wilder	30
Doubles	Men	50's	Persons/Pierce	32
Doubles	Men	55's	Wofford/Wulf	20
Doubles	Men	60's	Bronson/Cheney	36
Doubles	Men	65's	Lindborg/Sarantos	53
Doubles	Men	70's	Landin/Lindborg	43
Doubles	Men	75's	Denison/Russell	22
Doubles	Men	80's	Land/Meyerdierks	10
Doubles	Men	85's	Botman/Henderson	10
Doubles	Men	90's	Mix/Swetka	12
Doubles	Women	40's	Keener/Welsher	21
Doubles	Women	45's	Fahrenholz/Lackey	20
Doubles	Women	50's	Bronson/Wright	26
Doubles	Women	55's	Ginnard/Kawarsky	24
Doubles	Women	60's	Delay/Louie	22
Doubles	Women	65's	Hillebrand/Steel	38
Doubles	Women	70's	Langer/Tietz	30

Event	Gender	Age	Champion	Competitors
Doubles	Women	75's	Boswell/Russ	18
Doubles	Women	80's	Hall/Niehaus	14
Doubles	Women	90's	Cheney/Greene	4
Doubles	Mixed	60's	Bryant/Bucklin	18

Track & Field (MEN). 2008 USA Master Indoor Track & Field Championships—Boston, Massachusetts—March 28–31

Event	Age	Champion	Competitors
1 Mile Run	40–44	Stephen Sergeant	13
1 Mile Run	45–49	John Hinton	14
1 Mile Run	50–54	David Cannon	17
1 Mile Run	55–59	Nolan Shaheed	12
1 Mile Run	60–64	Kevin Solomon	8
1 Mile Run	65–69	Frank Condon	8
1 Mile Run	70–74	Joe Cordero	7
1 Mile Run	75–79	Casey Jones	4
1 Mile Run	80–84	Joe King	1
1 Mile Run	85–89	Roy Englert	1
1 Mile Run	90–94	Orville Rogers	1
200 Meter Dash	40–44	Eric Merriweather	5
200 Meter Dash	45–49	Everad Samuels	14
200 Meter Dash	50–54	John Brooks	6
200 Meter Dash	55–59	Bill Collins	14
200 Meter Dash	60–64	Charles Allie	8
200 Meter Dash	65–69	Richard Jones	9
200 Meter Dash	70–74	Gary Sims	4
200 Meter Dash	75–79	Dennis Melanson	2
200 Meter Dash	80–84	Bill Melville	3
200 Meter Dash	85–89	John Means	2
200 Meter Dash	90–94	Goldy Champion	2
3000 Meter Race Walk	40–44	Joseph Ols	1
3000 Meter Race Walk	45–49	Donald Lawrence	4
3000 Meter Race Walk	50–54	Tony Hackney	2
3000 Meter Race Walk	55–59	Andrew Smith	3
3000 Meter Race Walk	60–64	Robert Keating	6
3000 Meter Race Walk	65–69	Joel Dubow	3
3000 Meter Race Walk	70–74	Paul Johnson	4
3000 Meter Race Walk	75–79	Jack Bray	3
3000 Meter Race Walk	80–84	Marvin Goldenberg	1
3000 Meter Run	40–44	Dan Franek	13
3000 Meter Run	45–49	Chris Chisholm	8
3000 Meter Run	50–54	David Cannon	18
3000 Meter Run	55–59	Sam Torres	6
3000 Meter Run	60–64	Gary Patton	6
3000 Meter Run	65–69	Doug Goodhue	6
3000 Meter Run	70–74	Joe Cordero	5
3000 Meter Run	75–79	Dennis Branham	1
3000 Meter Run	85–89	Roy Englert	1
400 Meter Dash	40–44	Gladstone Jones	6
400 Meter Dash	45–49	Darnell Gatling	12
400 Meter Dash	50–54	James Morton	8
400 Meter Dash	55–59	Bill Collins	7
400 Meter Dash	60–64	Charles Allie	5
400 Meter Dash	65–69	Mel Brooks	6
400 Meter Dash	70–74	Mack Stewart	5
400 Meter Dash	75–79	Donald Leis	2
400 Meter Dash	85–89	John Means	2
400 Meter Dash	90–94	Bob Matteson	1
4X400 Meter Relay	40–49	Mass Velocity TC 'A'	8
4X400 Meter Relay	50–59	Mass Velocity TC 'A'	12
4X400 Meter Relay	60–69	Non Club 'C'	12
4X400 Meter Relay	70–79	Non Club 'A'	4
4X800 Meter Relay	40–49	Mass Velocity TC 'A'	16
4X800 Meter Relay	50–59	Colonial Road Runners 'A'	16

Event	Age	Champion	Competitors
4X800 Meter Relay	70–79	Non Club 'A'	4
60 Meter Dash	40–44	Eric Merriweather	10
60 Meter Dash	45–49	Everad Samuels	20
60 Meter Dash	50–54	Marty Krulee	7
60 Meter Dash	55–59	Bill Collins	7
60 Meter Dash	60–64	Charles Allie	7
60 Meter Dash	65–69	Richard Jones	8
60 Meter Dash	70–74	Gary Sims	6
60 Meter Dash	75–79	Dennis Melanson	3
60 Meter Dash	80–84	Melvin Larsen	8
60 Meter Dash	85–89	John Means	3
60 Meter Dash	90–94	Goldy Champion	2
60 Meter Hurdles	40–44	Rod Jett	3
60 Meter Hurdles	45–49	Dexter McCloud	3
60 Meter Hurdles	50–54	Stacey Price	10
60 Meter Hurdles	55–59	Thaddeus Wilson	4
60 Meter Hurdles	60–64	Ty Brown	4
60 Meter Hurdles	65–69	Emil Pawlik	2
60 Meter Hurdles	70–74	Richard Rizzo	2
60 Meter Hurdles	80–84	Frank Brako	1
60 Meter Hurdles	85–89	Edwin Lukens	1
800 Meter Run	40–44	Stephen Sergeant	12
800 Meter Run	45–49	John Hinton	9
800 Meter Run	50–54	James Morton	13
800 Meter Run	55–59	Nolan Shaheed	9
800 Meter Run	60–64	Kevin Solomon	11
800 Meter Run	65–69	Frank Condon	8
800 Meter Run	70–74	Mack Stewart	10
800 Meter Run	75–79	Casey Jones	3
800 Meter Run	80–84	Joe King	1
800 Meter Run	90–94	Orville Rogers	1
High Jump	40–44	Karl Hawke	7
High Jump	45–49	Theodore Robinson	2
High Jump	50–54	Bruce McBarnette	9
High Jump	55–59	Milan Jamrich	6
High Jump	60–64	David Montieth	3
High Jump	65–69	James Cawley	7
High Jump	70–74	Tom Langenfeld	3
High Jump	75–79	Donald Leis	1
High Jump	80–84	Thomas Rice	1
High Jump	90–94	Leland McPhie	1
Long Jump	40–44	Andrew Boyce	4
Long Jump	45–49	Aaron Sampson	5
Long Jump	50–54	Gregory Turner	9
Long Jump	55–59	David Ortman	8
Long Jump	60–64	Edward Jones	8
Long Jump	65–69	John Clifford	6
Long Jump	70–74	Robert Hewitt	4
Long Jump	75–79	Donald Leis	1
Long Jump	80–84	Thomas Rice	3
Long Jump	85–89	Edwin Lukens	3
Long Jump	90–94	Leland McPhie	1
Pentathlon	50–54	Jim Russ	6
Pentathlon	55–59	Sam McClellan	5
Pentathlon	60–64	Randall Olsen	1
Pentathlon	65–69	Emil Pawlik	3
Pentathlon	70–74	Robert Hewitt	3
Pentathlon	80–84	Frank Brako	1
Pentathlon	85–89	Ralph Maxwell	1
Pole Vault	40–44	Kris Whitfield	2
Pole Vault	45–49	James Tylock	4
Pole Vault	50–54	Gary Hunter	5
Pole Vault	55–59	John Hawkins	5
Pole Vault	60–64	Tomlinson Rauscher	5
Pole Vault	65–69	Ron Colliver	3
Pole Vault	75–79	Jerry Donley	1

Event	Age	Champion	Competitors
Pole Vault	80–84	Thomas Rice	1
Shot Put	40–44	Todd Adelgren	6
Shot Put	45–49	Robert Arello	6
Shot Put	50–54	Joseph Kessell	8
Shot Put	55–59	Michael Shiaras	5
Shot Put	60–64	Charles Roll	6
Shot Put	65–69	Ron Colliver	5
Shot Put	70–74	Gerald Vaughn	4
Shot Put	75–79	Ray Feick	2
Shot Put	80–84	Phillip Brusca	4
Shot Put	85–89	William Nettles	3
Shot Put	90–94	Goldy Champion	3
Super Weight	40–44	John Katalinas	3
Super Weight	45–49	Robert Arello	2
Super Weight	50–54	James Wetenhall	6
Super Weight	55–59	Dennis Cameron	3
Super Weight	60–64	George Matthews	5
Super Weight	65–69	Robert Cahners	3
Super Weight	70–74	William Gramley	3
Super Weight	75–79	Ray Feick	3
Super Weight	80–84	Val McGann	5
Super Weight	85–89	William Nettles	1
Super Weight	90–94	David Schlothauer	2
Triple Jump	40–44	Adarian Barr	3
Triple Jump	45–49	David McFadgen	2
Triple Jump	50–54	David Quick	9
Triple Jump	55–59	John Hawkins	5
Triple Jump	60–64	Roger Crockett	5
Triple Jump	65–69	James Cawley	4
Triple Jump	70–74	Jerry LeVasseur	3
Triple Jump	75–79	Donald Leis	1
Triple Jump	80–84	Thomas Rice	1
Triple Jump	85–89	Edwin Lukens	2
Triple Jump	90–94	Leland McPhie	1
Weight Throw	40–44	William Cotter	5
Weight Throw	45–49	Robert Arello	3
Weight Throw	50–54	Ken Jansson	11
Weight Throw	55–59	Ronald Summers	7
Weight Throw	60–64	George Matthews	8
Weight Throw	65–69	Robert Cahners	4
Weight Throw	70–74	William Gramley	4
Weight Throw	75–79	Roy Carstensen	3
Weight Throw	80–84	Val McGann	4
Weight Throw	85–89	William Nettles	1
Weight Throw	90–94	David Schlothauer	2

Track & Field. (WOMEN) 2008 USA Master Indoor Track & Field Championships—Boston, Massachusetts, March 28–31

Event	Age	Champion	Competitors
1 Mile Run	40–44	Bernadin Pritchett	7
1 Mile Run	45–49	Charlotte Rizzo	6
1 Mile Run	50–54	Mary Richards	4
1 Mile Run	55–59	Kathryn Martin	1
1 Mile Run	60–64	Barbara Spannaus	1
1 Mile Run	65–69	Jane VanEeuwen	1
200 Meter Dash	40–44	Rebecca Connolly	3
200 Meter Dash	45–49	Kathleen Shook	6
200 Meter Dash	50–54	Rita Hanscom	7
200 Meter Dash	55–59	Sharon Warren	3
200 Meter Dash	60–64	Phil Raschker	3
200 Meter Dash	65–69	Jane VanEeuwen	1
200 Meter Dash	70–74	Barbara Jordon	3
200 Meter Dash	75–79	Edythe Leek	2
3000 Meter Race Walk	40–44	Rebecca Garson	1

Event	Age	Champion	Competitors
3000 Meter Race Walk	45–49	Rutledge Gutsche	2
3000 Meter Race Walk	50–54	Nancy Sweazey	1
3000 Meter Race Walk	55–59	Dolores Wilkes	1
3000 Meter Race Walk	60–64	Panseluta Geer	2
3000 Meter Race Walk	65–69	Joanne Harriman	2
3000 Meter Race Walk	80–84	Miriam Gordon	1
3000 Meter Run	40–44	Bernadin Pritchett	7
3000 Meter Run	45–49	Margot Sheehan	4
3000 Meter Run	50–54	Marge Bellisle	4
3000 Meter Run	55–59	Kathryn Martin	2
3000 Meter Run	70–74	Mary Harada	1
400 Meter Dash	40–44	Charmaine Roberts	4
400 Meter Dash	45–49	Kathleen Shook	4
400 Meter Dash	50–54	Lesle Chaplin-Swann	6
400 Meter Dash	55–59	Coreen Steinbach	3
400 Meter Dash	60–64	Phil Raschker	2
400 Meter Dash	65–69	Jane VanEeuwen	1
400 Meter Dash	75–79	Janet Sweet	1
400 Meter Dash	80–84	Helen Schley	1
4X400 Meter Relay	40–49	Athena Track 'A'	12
4X400 Meter Relay	60–69	Liberty Athletic Club 'B'	4
4X400 Meter Relay	80–89	Atlanta Track Club 'A'	8
4X800 Meter Relay	40–49	Athena Track 'A'	8
4X800 Meter Relay	50–59	Liberty Athletic Club 'A'	4
4X800 Meter Relay	60–69	Liberty Athletic Club 'A'	4
60 Meter Dash	40–44	Tracey Berryman	1
60 Meter Dash	45–49	Liz Palmer	6
60 Meter Dash	50–54	Rita Hanscom	6
60 Meter Dash	55–59	Sharon Warren	5
60 Meter Dash	60–64	Kathy Jager	2
60 Meter Dash	65–69	Kathy Bergen	2
60 Meter Dash	70–74	Barbara Jordon	3
60 Meter Dash	75–79	Edythe Leek	1
60 Meter Dash	80–84	Ann McGowan	1

Track & Field 2008 USA Master Indoor
Track & Field Championships (WOMEN)
Boston, Massachusetts—March 28–31

Event	Age	Champion	Competitors
60 Meter Hurdles	45–49	Liz Palmer	4
60 Meter Hurdles	50–54	Rita Hanscom	4
60 Meter Hurdles	55–59	Phil Raschker	2
60 Meter Hurdles	70–74	Barbara Jordon	2
60 Meter Hurdles	80–84	Johnnye Valien	1
800 Meter Run	40–44	Bernadin Pritchett	9
800 Meter Run	45–49	Terri Cassel	5
800 Meter Run	50–54	Lesle Chaplin-Swann	7
800 Meter Run	55–59	Kathryn Martin	2
800 Meter Run	60–64	Lenore Webber	2
800 Meter Run	65–69	Marie-Jo Michelsohn	1
800 Meter Run	70–74	Mary Harada	1
800 Meter Run	80–84	Helen Schley	1
High Jump	40–44	Rebecca Connolly	1
High Jump	45–49	Cary Senn-Griffths	5
High Jump	50–54	Rita Hanscom	3
High Jump	55–59	Kay Glynn	2
High Jump	60–64	Phil Raschker	3
High Jump	65–69	Kathy Bergen	2
High Jump	70–74	Christel Donley	1
High Jump	75–79	Edythe Leek	1
Long Jump	40–44	Tracey Berryman	1
Long Jump	45–49	Elaine Iba	4
Long Jump	50–54	Kimberly Williams	2
Long Jump	55–59	Kay Glynn	2

Appendix A

Event	Age	Champion	Competitors
Long Jump	60–64	Phil Raschker	3
Long Jump	65–69	Jane Van Euwen	1
Long Jump	70–74	Audrey Lary	1
Long Jump	75–79	Edythe Leek	1
Long Jump	80–84	Johnnye Valien	2
Pentathlon	45–49	Cary Senn-Griffths	3
Pentathlon	50–54	Claudia Simpson	3
Pentathlon	55–59	Kay Glynn	1
Pentathlon	65–69	Jane Van Euwen	1
Pentathlon	70–74	Christel Donley	1
Pole Vault	40–44	Karen Rieger	1
Pole Vault	50–54	Rita Hanscom	1
Pole Vault	55–59	Kay Glynn	2
Pole Vault	60–64	Kathy Jager	2
Shot Put	40–44	Susan Wiemer	1
Shot Put	45–49	Oneithea Lewis	5
Shot Put	50–54	Ruth Welding	6
Shot Put	55–59	Myrle Mensey	4
Shot Put	60–64	Kathy Jager	3
Shot Put	65–69	Karen Huff-Pawlik	3
Shot Put	70–74	Mary Roman	3
Shot Put	75–79	Gloria Krug	5
Shot Put	80–84	Johnnye Valien	2
Shot Put	85–89	Doris Berlepsch	1
Shot Put	90–94	Betty Jarvis	1
Super Weight	45–49	Oneithea Lewis	4
Super Weight	50–54	Ruth Welding	4
Super Weight	55–59	Myrle Mensey	3
Super Weight	60–64	Patricia Fogg	1
Super Weight	65–69	Carol Young	2
Super Weight	70–74	Mary Roman	3
Super Weight	75–79	Lillian Snaden	3
Super Weight	90–94	Betty Jarvis	1
Triple Jump	40–44	Tracey Berryman	1
Triple Jump	45–49	Caren Ware	4
Triple Jump	50–54	Irene Thompson	2
Triple Jump	55–59	Linda Lowery	2
Triple Jump	60–64	Phil Raschker	1
Triple Jump	65–69	Jane Van Euwen	1
Triple Jump	70–74	Audrey Lary	2
Triple Jump	75–79	Edythe Leek	1
Triple Jump	80–84	Johnnye Valien	1
Weight Throw	45–49	Oneithea Lewis	4
Weight Throw	50–54	Ruth Welding	4
Weight Throw	55–59	Myrle Mensey	4
Weight Throw	60–64	Patricia Fogg	1
Weight Throw	65–69	Carol Young	3
Weight Throw	70–74	Mary Roman	1
Weight Throw	75–79	Gloria Krug	4
Weight Throw	85–89	Doris Berlepsch	1
Weight Throw	90–94	Betty Jarvis	1
100 Meter Dash	40–44	Renee Henderson	9
100 Meter Dash	45–49	Jai Black	9
100 Meter Dash	50–54	Karla Del Grande	7
100 Meter Dash	55–59	Deborah Carter	3
100 Meter Dash	60–64	Phil Raschker	4
100 Meter Dash	65–69	Nadine O'Conner	9
100 Meter Dash	70–74	Barbara Jordon	4
100 Meter Dash	75–79	Edythe Leek	1
100 Meter Dash	80–84	Patricia Peterson	2
1500 Meter Run	40–44	Alisa Harvey	8
1500 Meter Run	45–49	Patty Blanchard	7
1500 Meter Run	50–54	Debbie Lee	7
1500 Meter Run	55–59	Kathryn Martin	4
1500 Meter Run	60–64	Mary Trotto	1
1500 Meter Run	65–69	Yvonne Tasker-Rothenberg	3

Event	Age	Champion	Competitors
1500 Meter Run	70–74	Jeanne Daprano	3
1500 Meter Run	75–79	Thelma Wilson	2
200 Meter Dash	40–44	Renee Henderson	9
200 Meter Dash	45–49	Jai Black	9
200 Meter Dash	50–54	Karla Del Grande	7
200 Meter Dash	55–59	Rhona Trott	2
200 Meter Dash	60–64	Phil Raschker	5
200 Meter Dash	65–69	Nadine O'Conner	5
200 Meter Dash	70–74	Barbara Jordon	4
200 Meter Dash	75–79	Edythe Leek	1
200 Meter Dash	80–84	Patricia Peterson	1
400 Meter Dash	40–44	Charmaine Roberts	9
400 Meter Dash	45–49	Jai Black	9
400 Meter Dash	50–54	Karla Del Grande	6
400 Meter Dash	55–59	Catherine Nicoletti	4
400 Meter Dash	60–64	Phil Raschker	3
400 Meter Dash	65–69	Marg Radcliffe	3
400 Meter Dash	70–74	Joyce Hodges-Hite	1
400 Meter Dash	80–84	Patricia Peterson	1
5000 Meter Run	40–44	Sanya Syrstad	5
5000 Meter Run	45–49	Patty Blanchard	5
5000 Meter Run	50–54	Jan Merrill-Morin	7
5000 Meter Run	55–59	Kathryn Martin	2
5000 Meter Run	65–69	Yvonne Tasker-Rothenberg	1
5000 Meter Run	70–74	Mary Harada	2
5000 Meter Run	75–79	Thelma Wilson	2
5000 Meter Run	80–84	Helen Lachman	1
800 Meter Dash	40–44	Alisa Harvey	9
800 Meter Dash	45–49	Lorraine Jasper	6
800 Meter Dash	50–54	Debbie Lee	5
800 Meter Dash	55–59	Kathryn Martin	4
800 Meter Dash	60–64	Jolene Steigerwalt	2
800 Meter Dash	65–69	Marie-Louise Michaelsohn	3
800 Meter Dash	70–74	Jeanne Daprano	2
800 Meter Dash	75–79	Thelma Wilson	1

Track & Field. (WOMEN) 2007 USA Master Outdoor Track & Field Championships—Orono, Maine, August 2–5

Event	Age	Champion	Competitors
10000 Meter Run	40–44	Emily Bryans	5
10000 Meter Run	50–54	Debbie Lee	3
10000 Meter Run	55–59	Kathryn Martin	1
10000 Meter Run	60–64	Joanne Harriman	1
10000 Meter Run	70–74	Joyce Hodges-Hite	1
10000 Meter Run	75–79	Lois Gilmore	1
2000 Meter Steeplechase	40–44	Marisa Hanson	3
2000 Meter Steeplechase	45–49	Caren Ware	2
2000 Meter Steeplechase	50–54	Denise Janneck	2
2000 Meter Steeplechase	55–59	Ashley Childs	1
2000 Meter Steeplechase	60–64	Mart Trotto	1
2000 Meter Steeplechase	65–69	Marie-Louise Michaelsohn	2
High Jump	45–49	Caryl Senn-Griffiths	4
High Jump	50–54	Kay Glynn	3
High Jump	55–59	Eleanor Gipson	1
High Jump	60–64	Phil Raschker	5
High Jump	65–69	Marg Radcliffe	3
High Jump	70–74	Christel Donley	1
Long Hurdles 30"	40–44	Susan Wiemer	3
Long Hurdles 30"	45–49	Caryl Senn-Griffiths	4
Long Hurdles 30"	50–54	Kay Glynn	4
Long Hurdles 30"	55–59	Rhona Trott	2
Long Hurdles 30"	60–64	Phil Raschker	1
Long Jump	40–44	Tracey Singleton	3
Long Jump	45–49	Veronica Amarasekara	9

Event	Age	Champion	Competitors
Long Jump	50–54	Kay Glynn	7
Long Jump	55–59	Linda Lowery	2
Long Jump	60–64	Phil Raschker	7
Long Jump	65–69	Carol LaFayette-Boyd	3
Long Jump	70–74	Barbara Jordon	2
Long Jump	75–79	Gloria Krug	2
Long Jump	80–84	Ann McGowan	1
Short Hurdles 30"	40–44	Susan Wiemer	3
Short Hurdles 30"	45–49	Liz Palmer	4
Short Hurdles 30"	50–54	Irene Thompson	4
Short Hurdles 30"	55–59	Rhona Trott	2
Short Hurdles 30"	60–64	Phil Raschker	1
Short Hurdles 30"	65–69	Becky Sisley	2
Short Hurdles 30"	70–74	Barbara Jordon	2
Triple Jump	40–44	Tracey Singleton	3
Triple Jump	40–44	Patricia Porter	3
Triple Jump	45–49	Caren Ware	4
Triple Jump	50–54	Linda Cohn	4
Triple Jump	55–59	Linda Lowery	2
Triple Jump	60–64	Phil Raschker	4
Triple Jump	65–69	Carol LaFayette-Boyd	3
Triple Jump	70–74	Barbara Jordon	2
Triple Jump	75–79	Gloria Krug	2
5000 Meter Race Walk	40–44	Rebecca Garson	3
5000 Meter Race Walk	45–49	Maryanne Daniel	1
5000 Meter Race Walk	50–54	Debbie Topham	3
5000 Meter Race Walk	55–59	Lynn Tracy	3
5000 Meter Race Walk	60–64	Panseluta Geer	4
5000 Meter Race Walk	65–69	Louise Walters	2
5000 Meter Race Walk	70–74	Essie Faria	1
5000 Meter Race Walk	80–84	Miriam Gordon	1
Discus Throw	40–44	Lesley Duncan	5
Discus Throw	45–49	Lisa Hampton	5
Discus Throw	50–54	Carol Finsrud	9
Discus Throw	55–59	Mary Hartzler	3
Discus Throw	60–64	Lorraine Tucker	9
Discus Throw	65–69	Carol Young	5
Discus Throw	70–74	Joan Berman	7
Discus Throw	75–79	Gloria Krug	1
Discus Throw	80–84	Bernice Holland	2
Discus Throw	85–89	Olga Kotelko	1
Hammer Throw	40–44	Kelly Thompson	2
Hammer Throw	45–49	Lisa Hampton	3
Hammer Throw	50–54	Carol Finsrud	6
Hammer Throw	55–59	Mary Hartzler	3
Hammer Throw	60–64	Georgia Cutler	5
Hammer Throw	65–69	Carol Young	3
Hammer Throw	70–74	Mary Roman	6
Hammer Throw	75–79	Gloria Krug	1
Hammer Throw	80–84	Ann McGowan	1
Hammer Throw	90–94	Betty Jarvis	1
Javelin Throw	40–44	Lesley Duncan	5
Javelin Throw	45–49	Caryl Senn-Griffiths	7
Javelin Throw	50–54	Linda Cohn	11
Javelin Throw	55–59	Linda Rowe	4
Javelin Throw	60–64	Barbara LoPiccolo	11
Javelin Throw	65–69	Marg Radcliffe	7
Javelin Throw	70–74	Christel Donley	7
Javelin Throw	75–79	Gloria Krug	2
Javelin Throw	80–84	Bernice Holland	3
Javelin Throw	90–94	Betty Jarvis	1
Pole Vault	40–44	Pamela Swan	2
Pole Vault	50–54	Kay Glynn	2
Pole Vault	55–59	Hillen von Maltzahn	2
Pole Vault	60–64	Phil Raschker	4
Pole Vault	65–69	Florence Meiler	1

Event	Age	Champion	Competitors
Shot Put	40–44	Susan Wiemer	4
Shot Put	45–49	Oneithea Lewis	6
Shot Put	50–54	Carol Finsrud	8
Shot Put	55–59	Mary Hartzler	3
Shot Put	60–64	Barbara LoPiccolo	9
Shot Put	65–69	Mary Robinson	3
Shot Put	70–74	Mary Roman	7
Shot Put	75–79	Gloria Krug	2
Shot Put	80–84	Bernice Holland	3
Shot Put	85–89	Olga Kotelko	1
Shot Put	90–94	Betty Jarvis	1
10000 Meter Race Walk	40–44	Rebecca Garson	2
10000 Meter Race Walk	45–49	Marcia Gutsche-Rutledge	1
10000 Meter Race Walk	50–54	Debbie Topham	2
10000 Meter Race Walk	55–59	Lynn Tracy	3
10000 Meter Race Walk	60–64	Panseluta Geer	5
10000 Meter Race Walk	65–69	Louise Walters	3
10000 Meter Race Walk	70–74	Essie Faria	1
10000 Meter Race Walk	80–84	Miriam Gordon	1
4X100 Relay CLUB	40–49	Golden West Athletic Club	8
4X100 Relay Non-Club	40–49	Non Club 'D'	4
4X100 Relay Non-Club	50–59	Non Club Female 'C'	4
4X100 Relay Non-Club	60–69	Non Club Female 'E'	8
4X400 Relay CLUB	40–49	Athena Track	12
4X800 Relay CLUB	40–49	Athena Track	16
Pentathlon	40–44	Susan Wiemer	3
Pentathlon	45–49	BJ Freeman	4
Pentathlon	50–54	Kay Glynn	4
Pentathlon	55–59	Rhona Trott	2
Pentathlon	60–64	Phil Raschker	2
Pentathlon	65–69	Ann Carter	2
Pentathlon	70–74	Christel Donley	2
Pentathlon	75–79	Edythe Leek	1
Weight Throw	40–44	Kelly Thompson	2
Weight Throw	45–49	Oneithea Lewis	3
Weight Throw	50–54	Carol Finsrud	6
Weight Throw	55–59	Mary Hartzler	1
Weight Throw	60–64	Barbara LoPiccolo	4
Weight Throw	65–69	Carol Young	2
Weight Throw	70–74	Mary Roman	2
Weight Throw	75–79	Gloria Krug	1
Weight Throw	90–94	Betty Jarvis	1

Track & Field (MEN). 2007 USA Master Outdoor Track & Field Championships—Orono, Maine, August 2–5

Event	Age	Champion	Competitors
100 Meter Dash	40–44	Louis Merricks	15
100 Meter Dash	45–49	Val Barnwell	12
100 Meter Dash	50–54	Oscar Peyton	8
100 Meter Dash	55–59	Bill Collins	14
100 Meter Dash	60–64	Stephen Robbins	12
100 Meter Dash	65–69	Albert Williams	6
100 Meter Dash	70–74	Wayne Bennett	7
100 Meter Dash	75–79	James Stookey	5
100 Meter Dash	80–84	Bill Melville	6
100 Meter Dash	85–89	John Means	5
100 Meter Dash	90–94	Champion Goldy	2
1500 Meter Run	40–44	Brian Pope	16
1500 Meter Run	45–49	Kevin Pawlik	11
1500 Meter Run	50–54	Jorge Ortiz Rivera	22
1500 Meter Run	55–59	Nolan Shaheed	16
1500 Meter Run	60–64	Harold Nolan	9
1500 Meter Run	65–69	Frank Condon	11
1500 Meter Run	70–74	Bill Spencer	6

Event	Age	Champion	Competitors
1500 Meter Run	75–79	James Sutton	4
1500 Meter Run	80–84	Craig McMicken	1
1500 Meter Run	85–89	Bill Tribou	2
1500 Meter Run	90–94	Bob Matteson	1
200 Meter Dash	40–44	Robert Thomas	11
200 Meter Dash	45–49	Michael Sullivan	11
200 Meter Dash	50–54	Oscar Peyton	13
200 Meter Dash	55–59	Bill Collins	14
200 Meter Dash	60–64	Stephen Robbins	15
200 Meter Dash	65–69	Albert Williams	9
200 Meter Dash	70–74	Robert Lida	8
200 Meter Dash	75–79	Joe Summerlin	4
200 Meter Dash	80–84	Bill Melville	4
200 Meter Dash	85–89	John Means	2
200 Meter Dash	90–94	Champion Goldy	3
400 Meter Dash	40–44	Khalid Mulazim	12
400 Meter Dash	45–49	Saladin Allah	14
400 Meter Dash	50–54	Ben James	15
400 Meter Dash	55–59	Bill Collins	10
400 Meter Dash	60–64	Roger Pierce	11
400 Meter Dash	65–69	Mack Stewart	6
400 Meter Dash	70–74	Robert Lida	4
400 Meter Dash	75–79	Earl Fee	3
400 Meter Dash	80–84	Raoul Rodreques	1
400 Meter Dash	85–89	John Means	2
400 Meter Dash	90–94	Bob Matteson	2
800 Meter Run	40–44	Kevin Forde	9
800 Meter Run	45–49	Saladin Allah	13
800 Meter Run	50–54	Jorge Ortiz Rivera	18
800 Meter Run	55–59	Nolan Shaheed	10
800 Meter Run	60–64	Larry Barnum	9
800 Meter Run	65–69	Frank Condon	10
800 Meter Run	70–74	C. Christopher Rush	4
800 Meter Run	75–79	Earl Fee	5
800 Meter Run	85–89	Bill Tribou	2
800 Meter Run	90–94	Bob Matteson	2
10000 Meter Run	40–44	Brian Pope	7
10000 Meter Run	45–49	Mark Stickley	6
10000 Meter Run	50–54	David Cannon	9
10000 Meter Run	55–59	Tom Bernhard	6
10000 Meter Run	60–64	Patrick Glover	6
10000 Meter Run	65–69	Doug Goodhue	6
10000 Meter Run	70–74	Bill Iffrig	2
10000 Meter Run	75–79	Ed Whitlock	2
10000 Meter Run	80–84	Craig McMicken	1
2000 Meter Steeplechase	60–64	Robert Barber	4
2000 Meter Steeplechase	65–69	Joe Cordero	6
2000 Meter Steeplechase	70–74	Thomas Butterfield	5
2000 Meter Steeplechase	75–79	George Freeman	1
3000 Meter Steeplechase	40–44	Christopher Yorges	3
3000 Meter Steeplechase	45–49	Michael Fussell	8
3000 Meter Steeplechase	50–54	Daniel Dillon	6
3000 Meter Steeplechase	55–59	Mark Weeks	3
5000 Meter Run	40–44	Brian Pope	7
5000 Meter Run	45–49	Daniel Verrington	10
5000 Meter Run	50–54	Stephen Chantry	12
5000 Meter Run	55–59	Tom Bernhard	10
5000 Meter Run	60–64	Harold Nolan	7
5000 Meter Run	65–69	Gerard Malaczynski	11
5000 Meter Run	70–74	Bill Spencer	6
5000 Meter Run	75–79	Ed Whitlock	4
Long Hurdles	40–44	Getulio Echeandia	4
Long Hurdles	45–49	Darnell Gatling	5
Long Hurdles	50–54	Ricky Easley	6
Long Hurdles	55–59	Rick Lapp	7
Long Hurdles	60–64	Lester Mount	4

Event	Age	Champion	Competitors
Long Hurdles	65–69	Emil Pawlik	1
Long Hurdles	70–74	Robert Paulen	5
Long Hurdles	75–79	Earl Fee	2
Long Jump	40–44	Todd Crawford	9
Long Jump	45–49	Adrian Sampson	13
Long Jump	50–54	Robert Clark	9
Long Jump	55–59	Thaddeus Wilson	5
Long Jump	60–64	Ty Brown	8
Long Jump	65–69	Alan Slater	5
Long Jump	70–74	Robert Paulen	5
Long Jump	75–79	James Stookey	5
Long Jump	80–84	William Daprano	3
Long Jump	85–89	Edwin Lukens	3
Long Jump	90–94	Max Springer	1
Short Hurdles	40–44	David Ashford	4
Short Hurdles	45–49	Robert Stanley	6
Short Hurdles	50–54	Philip Bujalski	9
Short Hurdles	55–59	Thaddeus Wilson	8
Short Hurdles	60–64	Joe Johnston	6
Short Hurdles	65–69	Bob Osterhoudt	2
Short Hurdles	70–74	Robert Paulen	6
Short Hurdles	75–79	James Stookey	3
Short Hurdles	80–84	Denver Smith	1
Short Hurdles	85–89	Ralph Maxwell	1
5000 Meter Race Walk	40–44	Edgardo Rodriguez	2
5000 Meter Race Walk	45–49	Donald Lawrence	3
5000 Meter Race Walk	50–54	Klaus Thiedman	4
5000 Meter Race Walk	55–59	Michael Wiggins	3
5000 Meter Race Walk	60–64	Leon Jasionowski	6
5000 Meter Race Walk	65–69	Paul Johnson	7
5000 Meter Race Walk	70–74	Jack Bray	3
5000 Meter Race Walk	75–79	John Starr	4
5000 Meter Race Walk	80–84	Marvin Goldberg	2
5000 Meter Race Walk	85–89	John Levinson	1
High Jump	40–44	Igor Agaev	3
High Jump	45–49	Bruce McBarnette	4
High Jump	50–54	James Barrineau	8
High Jump	55–59	Milan Jamrich	7
High Jump	60–64	David Montieth	6
High Jump	65–69	Emil Paulik	5
High Jump	70–74	Tom Langenfeld	5
High Jump	75–79	Richarad Lowery	5
High Jump	80–84	Denver Smith	5
High Jump	85–89	Ralph Maxwell	1
Pole Vault	40–44	Trevor Richards	3
Pole Vault	45–49	Thad Brady	3
Pole Vault	50–54	Gary Hunter	5
Pole Vault	55–59	Steve Hardison	4
Pole Vault	60–64	Matti Kipelainen	5
Pole Vault	65–69	Terry Cannon	5
Pole Vault	70–74	Bob Land	2
Pole Vault	75–79	David Rider	1
Pole Vault	80–84	Denver Smith	1
Shot Put	40–44	Glenn Thompson	6
Shot Put	45–49	Warren Taylor	9
Shot Put	50–54	John Nespoli	10
Shot Put	55–59	Tim Muller	7
Shot Put	60–64	Charles Roll	6
Shot Put	65–69	Carl Wallin	5
Shot Put	70–74	Gerald Vaughn	9
Shot Put	75–79	Larry Horine	3
Shot Put	80–84	Phillip Brusca	6
Shot Put	85–89	David Schlothauer	2
Shot Put	90–94	Champion Goldy	1
Triple Jump	40–44	Brian Rowles	8
Triple Jump	45–49	Marcus Battle	4

Event	Age	Champion	Competitors
Triple Jump	50–54	Mike Lariza	7
Triple Jump	55–59	Robert Rockwell	7
Triple Jump	60–64	William Angus	4
Triple Jump	65–69	Alan Slater	4
Triple Jump	70–74	Robert Paulen	3
Triple Jump	75–79	James Stookey	1
Triple Jump	80–84	Denver Smith	4
Triple Jump	85–89	Edwin Lukens	3
Triple Jump	90–94	Max Springer	1
Discus Throw	40–44	Glenn Thompson	11
Discus Throw	45–49	Warren Taylor	8
Discus Throw	50–54	Jay McKeen	12
Discus Throw	55–59	Thomas Fahey	6
Discus Throw	60–64	Bill Hiney	6
Discus Throw	65–69	Larry Pratt	7
Discus Throw	70–74	Stephen Holmes	7
Discus Throw	75–79	Doug Tomlinson	6
Discus Throw	80–84	Phillip Brusca	6
Discus Throw	85–89	David Schlothauer	1
Discus Throw	90–94	Champion Goldy	1
Hammer Throw	40–44	Michael Ostrom	6
Hammer Throw	45–49	Michael Venning	5
Hammer Throw	50–54	Ronald Summers	8
Hammer Throw	55–59	Roger Conboy	3
Hammer Throw	60–64	George Mathews	3
Hammer Throw	65–69	Robert Cahners	5
Hammer Throw	70–74	Edgar Holmes	6
Hammer Throw	75–79	Doug Tomlinson	5
Hammer Throw	80–84	Richard Mulkern	4
Hammer Throw	85–89	David Schlothauer	2
Javelin Throw	40–44	John Tullo	7
Javelin Throw	45–49	Ron McConnell	11
Javelin Throw	50–54	Kent Womack	10
Javelin Throw	55–59	Robert Kouvolo	5
Javelin Throw	60–64	Buzz Gagne	6
Javelin Throw	65–69	James Kenney	3
Javelin Throw	70–74	Stephen Holmes	4
Javelin Throw	75–79	James Duncan	6
Javelin Throw	80–84	Denver Smith	5
Javelin Throw	90–94	Champion Goldy	1
Pentathlon	40–44	Todd Crawford	6
Pentathlon	45–49	Stephen Winkel	9
Pentathlon	50–54	Liviene Solomon	7
Pentathlon	55–59	David Salazar	8
Pentathlon	60–64	Robert Baker	6
Pentathlon	65–69	Jack Karbens	3
Pentathlon	70–74	William Jankovich	1
Pentathlon	75–79	James Duncan	2
Pentathlon	80–84	William Daprano	2
10000 Meter Race Walk	40–44	John Soucheck	2
10000 Meter Race Walk	45–49	Tommy Aunan	3
10000 Meter Race Walk	50–54	Klaus Thiedman	2
10000 Meter Race Walk	55–59	Michael Wiggins	5
10000 Meter Race Walk	60–64	Norman Frable	6
10000 Meter Race Walk	65–69	Paul Johnson	4
10000 Meter Race Walk	70–74	Jack Bray	3
10000 Meter Race Walk	75–79	Alfred Dubois	3
4X100 Meter Relay CLUB	40–49	So Cal Track Fleet Feet 'B'	4
4X100 Meter Relay CLUB	50–59	Houston Elite	12
4X100 Meter Relay CLUB	60–69	Florida Athletic 'B'	12
4X100 Meter Relay CLUB	70–79	Florida Athletic 'C'	4
4X100 Meter Relay Non-Club	40–49	Non-Club Male 'B'	4
4X100 Meter Relay Non-Club	50–59	Non-Club Male	8
4X100 Meter Relay Non-Club	60–69	Non-Club Male 'F'	4
4X100 Meter Relay Non-Club	70–79	Non-Club Male 'E'	4
4X400 Meter Relay CLUB	40–49	Southwest Sprinters Track	8

Event	Age	Champion	Competitors
4X400 Meter Relay CLUB	50–59	Houston Elite	12
4X400 Meter Relay CLUB	60–69	Golden West Athletic 'B'	4
4X400 Meter Relay CLUB	70–79	Florida Athletic 'C'	4
4X400 Meter Relay Non-Club	40–49	Non-Club Male 'B'	4
4X400 Meter Relay Non-Club	60–69	Non-Club Male 'D'	8
4X800 Meter Relay CLUB	40–49	Philadelphia Athletic Charitie	4
4X800 Meter Relay CLUB	60–69	Golden West Athletic 'B'	4
4X800 Meter Relay CLUB	70–79	Florida Athletic 'C'	4
4X800 Meter Relay Non-Club	40–49	Non-Club Male	12
4X800 Meter Relay Non-Club	50–59	Non-Club Male 'D'	4
4X800 Meter Relay Non-Club	60–69	Non-Club Male 'E'	4
Meter Shuttle Hurdle	40–44	Non-Club Male 'B'	2
Meter Shuttle Hurdle	50–54	Non-Club Male	3
Weight Throw	40–44	Glenn Thompson	5
Weight Throw	45–49	Robert Arello	3
Weight Throw	50–54	Lawrence Schrader	4
Weight Throw	55–59	Roger Conboy	2
Weight Throw	60–64	Jerry Bookin-Weiner	1
Weight Throw	65–69	Carl Wallin	4
Weight Throw	70–74	Edgar Holmes	3
Weight Throw	75–79	Doug Tomlinson	1
Weight Throw	80–84	Richard Mulkern	2

Triathlon. 2006 Age Group National Championship —Kansas City, Missouri, July 11

Gender	Age	Champion	Competitors
Men	40–44	Brian Bich	54
Men	45–49	Kyle Welch	36
Men	50–54	Curt Eggers	34
Men	55–59	Steven Smith	28
Men	60–64	David Roadhouse	24
Men	65–69	George Toberman	26
Men	70–74	Craig Kuglen	5
Men	75–79	Ken Nash	2
Men	85–89	Charles Futrell	1
Women	40–44	Holly Nybo	40
Women	45–49	Elizabeth Bulman	33
Women	50–54	Laura Sophiea	23
Women	55–59	Diane Proud	16
Women	60–64	Trish Kimper	9
Women	65–69	Susan Bradley-Cox	8
Women	70–74	Pat Fossum	2
Women	75–79	Peggy Gudbrandsen	1

Volleyball. USA Volleyball Adult Open Championship— Austin, Texas, May 26–June 2

Gender	Age	Champion (Region)	Competitors*
Women	40 & Over	Kashi (Southern California)	96
Women	45 & Over	B.A.D. (Northern California)	56
Women	50 & Over	BLT (Southern California)	88
Women	55 & Over	Brazil Mix 55 (Brazil)	56
Women	60 & Over	Shinkara Floor Play 60 (Rocky Mountain)	64
Women	65 & Over	California Golden Girls (Southern California)	40
Women	70 & Over	Texas Kickers 70 (Lone Star)	32
Men	40 & Over	Decker's/Roof 40 (Southern California)	64
Men	45 & Over	Fog Canada 45 (Canada)	64
Men	50 & Over	RobertBruceRealtor.com (Southern California)	160
Men	55 & Over	King's Mountain Fog 55 (Northern California)	176
Men	60 & Over	Quicksilver Legends 60's (Southern California)	120
Men	65 & Over	Molten USA 65 (Puget Sound)	96
Men	70 & Over	Molten USA 70 (Puget Sound)	72
Men	75 & Over	Cool (Rocky Mountain)	40

*Assumes an average of 8 players (competitors) per team

Weightlifting. 2007 National Masters— Savannah, GA, March 30–April 1

Event	Gender	Age	Champion	Competitors
105+ kg	Men	40–44	Rick Bucinell	2
105 kg	Men	40–44	Jerry Morales	3
94 kg	Men	40–44	Tim Guarino	4
85 kg	Men	40–44	Michael Mullins	2
77 kg	Men	40–44	Osman Manzanares	1
69 kg	Men	40–44	Philip Friedman	2
105+ kg	Men	45–49	Eric Nofsinger	1
105 kg	Men	45–49	Stephen Clark	4
94 kg	Men	45–49	Michael Cohen	4
85 kg	Men	45–49	Clay Reed	2
77 kg	Men	45–49	George Yearwood	3
56 kg	Men	45–49	Glenn Murphy Jr.	1
105+ kg	Men	50–54	Leonard Bacino	3
105 kg	Men	50–54	Perry Hopper	2
94 kg	Men	50–54	Douglas Briggs	3
85 kg	Men	50–54	John Floyd	3
77 kg	Men	50–54	Joe Delgado	3
69 kg	Men	50–54	Gerald Huth	3
105+ kg	Men	55–59	Ronald Summers	5
105 kg	Men	55–59	David Meltzer	3
94 kg	Men	55–59	Juan Sepulveda	5
85 kg	Men	55–59	Robert Hansen	3
77 kg	Men	55–59	Gary Glass	2
69 kg	Men	55–59	John Cramer	4
56kg	Men	55–59	Dane Hussey	1
105+ kg	Men	60–64	Savas Kappatos	2
105 kg	Men	60–64	Paul Travis	2
94 kg	Men	60–64	Wayne Bailey	2
85 kg	Men	60–64	James Krueger	6
77 kg	Men	60–64	Frederick Lowe	3
69 kg	Men	60–64	William Ourada	2
56kg	Men	60–64	Paul Chen	1
105+ kg	Men	65–69	Gordon Varnedoe	1
105 kg	Men	65–69	Robert Loofboro	3
94 kg	Men	65–69	Simon Rudle	4
85 kg	Men	65–69	Les Cramer	3
77 kg	Men	65–69	John Lombardo	1
69 kg	Men	65–69	Glenn Harris	1
62 kg	Men	65–69	David Gellner	1
56kg	Men	65–69	Monroe Ben Nowotny	1
105 kg	Men	70–74	Robert Strange	3
94 kg	Men	70–74	Dom Ramos	3
85 kg	Men	70–74	Kenneth Moore	3
77 kg	Men	70–74	John Mormol	1
69 kg	Men	70–74	Lev Epshteyn	1
62 kg	Men	70–74	Rudolf Kotlikov	1
85 kg	Men	75–79	Gonzalo Gonzalez	2
77 kg	Men	75–79	Bill Nicholson	3
69 kg	Men	75–79	Howard Cohen	1
62 kg	Men	75–79	Arnold Khalfin	2
105+ kg	Men	80–84	Robert Fusillo	1
105 kg	Men	80–84	Edwin Bengtson	1
85 kg	Men	80–84	Jack Erlandson	1
77 kg	Men	80–84	William Nelson	1
69 kg	Men	80–84	Eddie Bradley	1
56kg	Men	80–84	Eddie Owada	1
105 kg	Men	85–89	C. Jack Lano	1
75 kg	Women	40–44	Linda Tetrault	1
69 kg	Women	40–44	Sarah Atanasoff	2
63 kg	Women	40–44	Eva Twardokens	3
53 kg	Women	40–44	Debbie Millet	1
75 kg	Women	45–49	Mary Leah Hyder	1
63 kg	Women	45–49	Christine Galvin	2

Event	Gender	Age	Champion	Competitors
58 kg	Women	45–49	Theresa Maldonado	1
53 kg	Women	45–49	Anne Lehman	2
75 kg	Women	50–54	Linda Jo Belsito	1
69 kg	Women	50–54	Terri Panzitta Wheeler	1
58 kg	Women	50–54	Christine Catalano	1
53 kg	Women	50–54	Cynthia Catalano	1
75+ kg	Women	55–59	Rebecca Chaplin	1
75 kg	Women	55–59	Madeline Chen	1
69 kg	Women	55–59	Nadine Powell	1
63 kg	Women	55–59	Lorrie Whorton	2
58 kg	Women	55–59	Molly Mehaffy	1
75+ kg	Women	60–64	Elizabeth Henshaw	1
69 kg	Women	60–64	Barbara Boyer	1
75+ kg	Women	65–69	Marilyn Munkres	1
69 kg	Women	65–69	Dorothy Gardner	1
63 kg	Women	65–69	Jan Schlegel	1
58 kg	Women	65–69	Janice Talluto	1

Powerlifting. 2007 USAPL Men Master's Nationals— Milwaukee, WI, May 2–4

Event	Gender	Age	Champion	Competitors
56 kg	Men	40–44	Ervin Gainer Sr.	1
56 kg	Men	45–49	Ralph Caputo	1
56 kg	Men	60–64	Alex Galant	1
60 kg	Men	40–44	Eric Kupperstein	2
60 kg	Men	60–64	Robert Trujillo	1
67.5 kg	Men	40–44	Darren Matsumoto	1
67.5 kg	Men	50–54	Miquel Castro Sr.	3
67.5 kg	Men	55–59	Robert Coleman	1
67.5 kg	Men	60–64	James Yeats	1
75 kg	Men	40–44	Donovan Thompson	3
75 kg	Men	45–49	Carlos Lewis	3
75 kg	Men	50–54	Dave Porter	1
75 kg	Men	55–59	Gregory Kleyn	4
75 kg	Men	60–64	Sam Alduenda	2
75 kg	Men	70–74	Jerry Ochs	1
75 kg	Men	75–79	Dan Goodwin Sr.	1
75 kg	Men	80+	Fred Archambault	1
82.5 kg	Men	40–44	Laddie Gibson	5
82.5 kg	Men	45–49	David Ricks	5
82.5 kg	Men	50–54	Bill Clayton	2
82.5 kg	Men	55–59	Bruce Sullivan	2
82.5 kg	Men	60–64	Roberto Contreras	2
82.5 kg	Men	65–69	Jim Lyons	2
82.5 kg	Men	70–74	Ronald Ringwold	1
90 kg	Men	40–44	Craig Terry	7
90 kg	Men	45–49	Gregory Jones	10
90 kg	Men	50–54	Michael Bridges	7
90 kg	Men	55–59	Mick Stevens	3
90 kg	Men	60–64	W. Fred Price	1
90 kg	Men	70–74	Raymond Curtis	1
100 kg	Men	40–44	Henry Gerard	8
100 kg	Men	45–49	Doug Currence	8
100 kg	Men	50–54	Gary Edwards	5
100 kg	Men	55–59	Larry Wallen	2
100 kg	Men	60–64	Brian Briggs	1
110 kg	Men	40–44	Anthony Harris	4
110 kg	Men	45–49	Gary Pamplin	5
110 kg	Men	50–54	Phil Andrews	5
110 kg	Men	55–59	Frank Panaro	4
110 kg	Men	60–64	Crayton Taylor	2
110 kg	Men	65–69	Bill Helmich	1
125 kg	Men	40–44	Kevin Stewart	6
125 kg	Men	45–49	Dave Gonzales	7

Event	Gender	Age	Champion	Competitors
125 kg	Men	50–54	Roger Hendrix Sr.	2
125 kg	Men	55–59	Al Wood	2
125 kg	Men	60–64	Will Morris	1
125+ kg	Men	40–44	Joe Kunzman	3
125+ kg	Men	45–49	Daniel Gaudreau	5
125+ kg	Men	55–59	Steve Green	1
125+ kg	Men	60–64	Harry Heyman	1

Powerlifting. 2007 USAPL Women's Nationals— Baton Rouge, LA, WI, Feb 16–18

Event	Gender	Age	Champion	Competitors
48 kg	Women	45–49	Catherine Solan	1
48 kg	Women	50–54	Ann Leverett	1
52 kg	Women	40–44	Joni Mach	2
52 kg	Women	45–49	Vera Nelson	1
56 kg	Women	40–44	Patricia Tidmarsh	1
56 kg	Women	45–49	Kate Dingle-Craig	1
56 kg	Women	50–54	Barb Zintsmaster	1
60 kg	Women	45–49	Angela Simons	3
60 kg	Women	50–54	Rita Carlsson	1
60 kg	Women	60–64	Faith Ireland	1
67.5 kg	Women	40–44	Sherry Franks	2
67.5 kg	Women	45–49	Paula Houston	4
67.5 kg	Women	50–54	Ruth Welding	1
67.5 kg	Women	55–59	Gail Moore	1
75 kg	Women	40–44	Laura Stylund	1
75 kg	Women	45–49	Donna Bryant	2
75 kg	Women	50–54	Terry Lee	1
75 kg	Women	60–64	Marsha Serre	1
82.5 kg	Women	40–44	Malinda Baum	2
82.5 kg	Women	65–69	Regina Hackney	1
90 kg	Women	45–49	Jill Arnow	2
90+ kg	Women	40–44	Andrea Anderson	1
90+ kg	Women	50–54	Sue Hallen	1
90+ kg	Women	55–59	Harriet Hall	1

Appendix B

Websites of Sponsoring Organizations

This table lists the sponsoring organization and website of those sports discussed or cited in this book. Please note that organizations occasionally change their web addresses, so, if the organization cannot be found at the address below, it may be necessary to use a search engine to locate it.

Sport	Sponsoring Organization	Website Address
Alpine Skiing	United States Ski and Snow Board Association	*http://www.ussa.org/*
Badminton	USA Badminton	*http://www.usabadminton.org/*
Baseball	Men's Senior Baseball League	*http://www.msblnational.com/*
Baseball	National Adult Baseball Association	*http://www.dugout.org/*
Baseball	Roy Hobbs Baseball	*http://www.royhobbs.com/*
Basketball	The Men's Masters Basketball National Championship	*http://www.mastersbasketball.org/*

Sport	Sponsoring Organization	Website Address
Biathlon	USA Biathlon	*http://www.usbiathlon.com/*
Canoeing	United States Canoe and Kayak Team	*http://www.usacanoekayak.org/*
Canoeing	Unites States Canoe Association	*http://www.uscanoe.com/*
Canoeing	American Canoe Association	*http://www.americancanoe.org/*
Cross-Country Skiing	American Cross-Country Skiers	*http://www.xcskiworld.com/*
Cycling	USA Cycling	*http://www.usacycling.org*
Diving	USA Diving	*www.usadiving.org*
Diving	U.S. Masters Diving	*www.mastersdiving.com*
Fencing	United States Fencing Association	*http://www.usfencing.org/usfa/*
Four-Wall Paddleball	National Paddleball Association	*http://paddleball.org/*
Handball	United States Handball Association	*http://ushandball.org/*
Ice Hockey	Hockey North America	*www.hna.com*
Ice Hockey	USA Hockey	*www.usahockey.com/*
Modern Pentathlon	U.S. Olympic Committee	*http://www.usolympicteam.com/*
One-Wall Paddleball	United States Paddleball Association	*http://uspaddleballassociation.org/*
Orienteering	US Orienteering Federation	*http://www.us.orienteering.org/*
Paddle Tennis	Paddletennis.biz	*http://www.paddletennis.biz/*
Pickleball	USA Pickleball Association	*http://www.usapa.org/*
Platform Tennis	American Platform Tennis Association	*http://www.platformtennis.org/*
Quadrathlon	World Quadrathlon Federation	*http://www.quadrathlon.com/*
Racquetball	USA Racquetball	*http://usra.org/Home.aspx*
Racquetball	National Masters Racquetball Association	*http://www.nmra.info/*
Road Racing	USA Track & Field	*http://www.usatf.org/*
Road Racing	Road Runner Club of America	*http://www.rrca.org/*
Road Racing	All American Trail Running Association	*www.trailrunner.com*
Rowing	USRowing	*http://www.usrowing.org/*
Rowing	Masters Rowing Association	*http://mastersrowing.org/*
Soccer	United States Adult Soccer Association	*www.usasa.com*
Softball	Amateur Softball Association of America	*www.asasoftball.com*
Softball	National Softball Association	*www.playnsa.com*
Softball	Senior Softball—USA	*http://www.seniorsoftball.com*
Softball	Independent Softball Association	*www.isasoftball.com*
Softball	Softball Players Association	*www.spasoftball.com*
Softball	International Senior Softball Association	*http://www.seniorsoftball.org/*
Softball	Las Vegas Senior Softball Association	*http://www.lvssa.com/*
Softball	North American Senior Softball Circuit	*www.nascs.org*
Softball	Women's Senior Softball	*http://www.womenssenior softball.com/*
Speedskating	U.S. Speedskating	*http://www.usspeedskating.org/*
Squash	US Squash	*www.us-squash,org*
Swimming	United States Masters Swimming	*www.usms.org*
Table Tennis	USA Table Tennis	*http://www.usatt.org/*
Tennis	United States Tennis Association	*http://www.usta.com/*
Track & Field	USA Track & Field	*http://www.usatf.org/*
Triathlon	USA Triathlon	*www.usatriathlon.org*
Volleyball	USA Volleyball	*http://www.usavolleyball.org/*
Weightlifting	USA Weightlifting	*www.usaweightlifting.org*
Powerlifting	USA Powerlifting	*http://www.usapowerlifting.com/*
National Senior Olympics	National Senior Games Association	*http://www.nsga.com/*
Huntsman World Senior Games	Huntsman World Senior Games	*http://www.hwsg.com/*
World Masters Games	International Masters Games Association	*http://www.imga.ch/*

Appendix C
Selected Comparisons

The summary in the table below indicates the total number of competitors and the percentage of women, men, and competitors over the ages of 60, 70, and 80. The table is based on the data assembled in Appendix A. However, the table includes only those competitors over 40 years of age who participated in age-group classes. Please note that this summary does *not* indicate the percentage of *all* women, men, or competitors of a given age for the following reasons:

1. All the national championships include competitive classes that are not based on age. For example, many competitors over sixty, seventy, or eighty may have competed in skill-level or open divisions and, therefore, are not included in the table.

2. Many sports define Masters as including athletes who are younger than 40 years of age. For example, U.S. Masters Swimming includes swimmers as young as 18 in their national championships, and US Rowing's Master classes begin at age 27. Therefore, the total number of competitors in the sport's national championships may be significantly larger than the number shown in the table.

3. In certain sports, such as badminton, baseball, and softball, it was not possible to determine the total number of competitors and these cases have been noted as having insufficient data.

Summary of Over-40 Competitors in
Age-Group Classes for National Championships

Sport	# Competitors	% Wmn	% Men	% 60+	% 70+	% 80+
Alpine Skiing	608	25	75	43	17	3
Badminton		insufficient data				
Baseball		insufficient data				
Basketball	405	0	100	38	9	—
Canoe Marathon	266	17	83	32	7	—
Cross-Country Skiing	406	25	75	29	10	2
Cycling-Road Racing	1095	16	84	21	8	5
Cycling-Track Racing	636	19	81	19	2	—
Cycling-Cyclo-Cross	605	10	90	4	0.3	—
Cycling-Mountain Biking	301	13	87	6	—	—
Diving	118	47	53	38	18	3
Fencing	461	34	66	18	—	—
Handball (3 Events)	740	0	100	45	17	1
Ice Hockey		insufficient data				
Orienteering	588	26	74	34	8	1
Platform Tennis	100					
Racquetball (3 Events)	1370	21	79	27	8	2
Road Racing (3 Events)	490	54	46	16	7	2
Rowing	3175	48	52	14	2	0.0
Soccer		insufficient data				
Softball		insufficient data				
Speedskating (2 Events)	233	29	71	27	6	0
Squash	120	14	86	28	13	1
Squash Rankings	518	3	97	20	4	—
Swimming (2 Events)	6322	41	59	31	13	4
Table Tennis		insufficient data				
Tennis (4 Playing Surfaces)	5993	32	68	53	28	10
Track & Field (2 Events)	3267	33	67	52	19	6
Triathlon	342	39	61	23	3	0.3
Volleyball	1224	35	65	38	12	—
Weightlifting	158	18	82	42	15	4
Powerlifting (2 Events)	183	16	84	13	3	1

Appendix D

Outstanding Masters Performances

This table shows some of the outstanding performances by Masters Athletes in a variety of sports and disciplines.

Men	40–44	45–49	50–54	55–59	60–64	65–69	
Run one mile[a]	4:04.98	4:18.33	4:25.04	4:27.70	4:58.20	5:12.21	
Throw a javelin (mtrs)[b]	76.91	71.75	70.71	57.42	58.25	57.67	
Swim 200 yds freestyle[c]	1.43.05	1.44.39	1.47.59	1.50.85	1.56.69	2.01.22	
Bike 20 kilometers—							
Time Trial[d]	30:24.96*	30:28.42*	30:52.80*	26:27.39	28:00.17	28:40.53	
Cross-country ski							
10K classic[e]	41:52.20**	49:48.00**	50:40.20**	48:20.80**	37:54.40	44:01.10	
Paddle a canoe 14 miles[f]	1:52.29.52	1:53.34.87	1:51.54.91	1:53.44.07	1:54.35.36	1:59.44.47	
Row a single scull							
1000 meters[g]	3:33.17	3:25.76	3:41.45	3:45.49	3:27.72	4:01.10	
Bench press (lbs)[h]	501.5	611.8	501.5	534.6	407.9	385.8	

	70–74	75–79	80–84	85–89	90–94	95–99	100–104
Run one mile[a]	5:37.80	5:57.20	7:36.55	9:18.43	10:54.62	14:48.20	—
Throw a javelin (mtrs)[b]	42.53	40.70	30.87	26.16	22.71	20.80	5.98
Swim 200 yds freestyle[c]	2.09.57	2.21.40	2.38.33	2.55.96	3.40.64	4.35.70	6.56.32
Bike 20 kilometers—							
Time Trial[d]	28:34.95	31:48.94	38:07.87	—	—	—	—
Cross-country ski							
10K classic[e]	50:17.40	1:01:28.60	52:39.10	1:13:14.90	—	—	—
Paddle a canoe 14 miles[f]	2:06.53.56	2:16.35.87	—	2:18.31.41	—	—	—
Row a single scull							
1000 meters[g]	3:53.56	4:17.31	4:37.90	—	—	—	—
Bench press (lbs)[h]	198.4	176.4	220.5	—	—	—	—

Women	40–44	45–49	50–54	55–59	60–64	65–69	
Run one mile[a]	4:46.29	5:07.76	5:15.55	5:46.80	5:57.39	6:16.28	
Throw a javelin (mtrs)[b]	42.05	41.57	43.72	28.08	32.45	31.48	
Swim 200 yards[c]	1.51.06	1.54.48	1.59.55	2.00.50	2.25.02	2.32.93	
Bike 20 kilometers—							
Time Trial[d]	34:36.88*	28:15.70	30:03.48	30:27.43	34:17.75	34:18.60	
Cross-country ski							
10K classic[e]	35:46.30	40:40.80	47:36.10	45:57.40	47:56.70	50:21.60	
Paddle a canoe 14 miles[f]	1:54.24.49	1:58.59.36	1:53.16.30	—	—	2:02.34.38	
Row a single scull							
1000 meters[g]	3:41.05	3:58.34	4:00.89	4:02.37	4:32.09	4:52.15	
Bench press (lbs)[h]	242.0	258.5	286.0	302.5	104.5	165.0	

	70–74	75–79	80–84	85–89	90–94	95–99	100–104
Run one mile[a]	6:47.91	—	9:00.52	11:03.11	—	—	—
Throw a javelin (mtrs)[b]	25.58	20.91	17.89	12.26	10.87	—	—
Swim 200 yards[c]	2.35.85	2.53.25	3.10.14	3.39.73	4.42.10	7.04.75	—
Bike 20 kilometers—							
Time Trial[d]	38:17.98	—	—	—	—	—	—

	70–74	75–79	80–84	85–89	90–94	95–99	100–104
Cross-country ski							
10K classic[e]	1.70:34.60	—	—	—	—	—	—
Paddle a canoe 14 miles[f]	—	—	—	—	—	—	—
Row a single scull							
1000 meters[g]	—	—	—	—	—	—	—
Bench press (lbs)[h]	—	—	—	—	—	—	—

a*(USATF) Current American Masters Record)*   e*2007 AXCS Masters Nationals*
b*(USATF) Current American Masters Record)*   f*2007 USCA Marathon Nationals*
c*USMS National Record*   g*2007 US Rowing Masters Nationals*
d*USA Cycling 2007 National Championship*   h*2007 US Power lifters Masters Nationals*

Appendix E

Studies on Exercise and Longevity

"Exercise Intensity and Longevity in Men."
Paffenbarger, Lee, and Hsieh.
***Journal of the American Medical Association*, April 1995**
   Begun in 1962, this study followed 17,321 Harvard alumni as they aged. The subjects were examined and interviewed annually to monitor their lifestyles, including their level of physical activity, as well as their medical condition. The results of the study confirmed the results of previous studies by Dr. Paffenbarger that exercise is associated with a lower death rate. Furthermore, the more you exercise, the greater the benefit.

"Physical Activity Levels and Changes in Relation to Longevity."
Lissener, Bengtsson, Bjorkelund, and Wedel.
***American Journal of Epidemiology*, January 1996.**
   A study of 1,065 Swedish women, ages 38 to 60, over 6 years concluded that decreases in physical activity, as well as low initial levels, are strong risk factors for mortality in women and that their predictive value persists for many years.

"Health Benefits of Physical Activity: The Evidence."
Warburton, Nicol, and Bredin.
***Canadian Medical Association Journal*, March 2006.**
   An evaluation of current literature to provide further insight into the role that physical inactivity plays in the development of chronic disease and premature death. The study concludes, "There appears to be a linear relation between physical activity and health status, such that a further increase in physical activity and fitness will lead to additional improvements in health status."

"Adiposity as Compared with Physical Activity in Predicting Mortality among Women."
Hu, Willett, Li, Stampfer, Colditz, and Manson.
***New England Journal of Medicine*, December 2004.**
   More than 115,000 women between the ages of 30 and 55 filled out biennial health and lifestyle questionnaires between 1976 and 2000. Researchers found that both obesity and physical activity significantly and independently affected mortality. Lead author Frank Hu said, "There is no question that one should be as active as possible no matter what your weight is, but it is equally important to maintain a healthy weight and prevent weight gain through diet and lifestyle."

"Low Physical Activity as a Predictor for Total and Cardiovascular Disease Mortality
 in Middle-Aged Men and Women in Finland."
Barengo, Hu, Lakka, Pekkarinen, Nissinen, and Tuomilehto.
European Heart Journal, October 2004.

A prospective study of 15,853 Finnish men and 16,824 Finnish women between the ages of 30 and 59 over 20 years to investigate whether moderate or high leisure time activity was associated with reduced cardiovascular disease and all-cause mortality. The study concluded that moderate and high levels of physical activity are associated with reduced cardiovascular disease and all-cause mortality among both sexes.

"What Level of Physical Activity Protects against Premature Cardiovascular Death?
 The Caerphilly Study."
Yu, Yarneil, Sweetnam, and Murray.
Heart, 2003.

A study of 1,975 men, ages 49 to 64, from South Wales with an 11-year follow-up to determine the optimal intensity of leisure time physical activity to decrease the risk of all-cause, cardiovascular disease, and coronary heart disease in middle-aged British men. The data from the study concluded that "only leisure exercise classified as heavy or vigorous was independently associated with a reduced risk of premature death from cardiovascular disease."

Index

AAU Basketball 23
adventure racing 133
age-graded tables 80, 132
alpine skiing 9
Amateur Softball Association/USA Softball 91
American Birkebeiner 34
American Canoe Association 27
American Cross Country Skiers 32
American Fencing Magazine 47
American Platform Tennis Association 66
American Ski Marathon Series 32
American Trail Running Association 78
Ausable Canoe Marathon 29

badminton 13
baseball 17
Baseball Today 18
basketball 22
battledore 13
beach volleyball 140
biathlon 133
BMX Association 36
Boston Marathon 8
Buffalo Masters North American Basketball Championship 24

canoe sailing 31
canoeing 26
Christiana (Christy) turns 9
clap skate 101
La Classique International de Canots de la Maurice 29
Corbin, Serge 29
crash-b sprints 83
cross-country skiing 32; classic 33
CrossCourt 14
cycling 26
cyclo-cross 38, 41

decathlon 133
diamond ball 90
diving 43
downhill skiing 10
downriver (wildwater) racing 31
dragon boat racing 31
duathlon 132

epee 48
erg 83

Fast Forward 77, 128
fencing 46
foil 48
freestyle cross-country skiing 33
freestyle (rodeo) kayaking 31

General Clinton Canoe Regatta 29
giant slalom skiing 10

handball 50
Hardball 17
heptathlon 133
Hockey North America 55
Huntsman World Senior Games 97, 155

iBlade 102
ice chips 102
ice hockey 55
Independent Softball Association 96
Inside Diving 44
International Softball Association 97
ironman 135

kayak polo 31
kitten ball 90

Las Vegas Senior Softball Association 97
Libero 142
Local Masters Swim Committees 110

Men's Adult Baseball League 17
Men's Masters Basketball National Championship 23
Men's Senior Baseball League 17
Milo of Crotona 144
mountain biking 41; cross country 38; downhill 38; dual slalom 38; marathon 38; Super D 38
mush ball 90

National Adult Baseball Association 17

national champions 159
National Collegiate Cycling Association 36
National Masters News 128, 132
National Masters Racquetball Association 71
National Off-Road Bicycle Association 36
National Plunging Championships 41
National Senior Games 5, 152
National Senior Games Association 152
National Softball Association 93
National Softball Summit 91, 101
National Tennis Rating Program 122
North American Senior Circuit Softball 98

open water swimming 112
orienteering 60; canoe 31, 61; horseback 61; mountain bike 61; ski 61; trail 61
Orienteering North America 61
outrigger canoe 31

paddle tennis 66
paddleball (one-wall, four-wall) 66
pentathlon, modern 133
pickleball 66
platform tennis 65
pond hockey 58
poona 13
postal swim meets 112
powerlifting 144; bench press 149; deadlift 149; squat 149
pumpkin ball 90

quadrathlon 133

racquetball 69
road cycling: criterium 38; time trials 38
road racing 76
Road Runners Club of America 78
Rogaine 62
rowing 82; coded four 84; coxed four scull 84; coxed pair 84; coxless four 84; coxless four

scull 84; coxless pair 84; double scull 83; eight 84; lightweight crew 85; single scull 83
Roy Hobbs Baseball 18
Running Times 79

saber 48
Senior Masters Table Tennis Program 118
Senior Softball-USA 95
Shakespeare, William 120
slalom skiing 10
soccer 87; Veterans Cup 88
softball 90; fast pitch 98; modified slow pitch 98; slow pitch 98
Softball Players Association 97
speedskating 101; long track 103; marathon 103
squash 104; hardball 105; ratings 106, 107; softball 105
Squash Magazine 106
Studies on Exercise and Longevity 214
super-G skiing 10
Swedish Swallow 41
swimming 109; long course 111; short course 111
synchronized diving 44–45

table tennis 116; hardbat 118; ratings 118
Telemark region 9

tennis 120; ratings 124; Super Seniors 122
Title IX 7, 130
track and field 126
track cycling: Madison 38; points racing 38; sprint 38; time trials 38
TrailRunner 79
triathlon 132; Athena 135; Clydesdale 135

U.S. Canoe and Kayak Team 27
United States Adult Soccer Association 87
United States Canoe Association 26
United States Cycling Federation 36
United States Fencing Association 47
United States Handball Association 51
United States Masters Swimming 110
US Orienteering Federation 60
United States Professional Racing Organization 36
US Rowing 82
United States Ski and Snowboard Association 9
U.S. Speedskating 102
US Squash 105
United States Tennis Association 121

USA Badminton 13
USA Cycling 36
USA Diving 43
USA Hockey 55
USA Powerlifting 146
USA Racquetball 69
USA Table Tennis 116
USA Table Tennis Magazine 116
USA Track & Field 76, 127
USA Triathlon 133
USA Triathlon Times 134
USA Veterans Fencing 48
USA Volleyball 138
USA Weightlifting 145
USMS Swimmer Magazine 110
USSA Masters Regions 10
USTA Tennis League 122

velodromes 40
volleyball 128; co-ed 141; reverse co-ed 141; rules 140; u-volley 141
Volleyball USA 143

weightlifting 144; clean and jerk 146; snatch 146
Weightlifting Magazine 145
whitewater slalom 31
women's baseball 21
women's ice hockey 56
women's senior softball 98
World Masters Games 5, 155

Zug, James 105